Regulating homosexuality in Soviet Russia, 1956–91

MANCHESTER 1824
Manchester University Press

Regulating homosexuality in Soviet Russia, 1956–91

A different history

Rustam Alexander

Manchester University Press

Published by Manchester University Press
Altrincham Street, Manchester M1 7JA

www.manchesteruniversitypress.co.uk

British Library Cataloguing-in-Publication Data
A catalogue record for this book is available from the British Library

ISBN 978 1 5261 5576 4 hardback

First published 2021

Typeset
by Sunrise Setting Ltd, Brixham

Contents

Figures

Acknowledgements

This project has been a long time in the making, and during this period I acquired many intellectual debts to a great number of people. The roots of this project lay in the research which I conducted for the University of Melbourne. Therefore, I would like to extend my gratitude to Dr Julie Fedor for her support, patience and encouragement throughout the course of the project. I would also like to thank Professor Sean Scalmer for his continual faith in me and words of encouragement. While working on my book manuscript and proposal, I received immense support from Professor Dan Healey. He not only advised me on the location of some of the sources for my research but also was kind enough to read my whole manuscript and book proposal, offering detailed comments and encouraging me to be more ambitious with my arguments and academic pursuits. I would also like to thank Professor Deborah A. Field, who also gave me extensive comments on the book manuscript.

I am immensely grateful to the people who agreed to consider my work for publication in the volumes and journals they edited, as well as providing useful feedback on my work – Professors Melanie Ilič, Harriet Murav and Richard Mole. I am also grateful to the anonymous reviewers of *Slavic Review*, who offered incisive comments and assisted greatly in improving one of my articles which formed part of this book. I am also grateful to writers like Masha Gessen and Professor Dennis Altman for taking their time in their busy schedules to discuss my project.

Obtaining sources for this project was an arduous task, and I am grateful to the many scholars who answered my queries on possible archives to consult and people to interview. Among these scholars, I want to mention Professors Ben de Jong and Laurie Essig, as well as Kateřina Lišková and Ineta Lipša. I am also grateful to the sexologists of the Moscow Research Institute of Psychiatry and especially Yan Genrikhovich Goland, a psychiatrist from the city of Nizhnii Novgorod, for sharing materials and documents from his collection. Whatever the differences I have with these doctors about the question of whether homosexuality is a disease or not, I realise that, without their aid, some chapters of this book would never have come into existence. I am also indebted to Russian, Ukrainian, Lithuanian and Estonian archivists for their immense help and guidance.

I am grateful to my friends and colleagues who offered their help and words of encouragement while I was writing this book. Among them are Samuel Gomes, Adam Elm and Mia Shouha. A special thanks to Peter McKerrow, who helped me fathom the differences between Russian and English legal terms and definitions; Konstantin Fillipenok and Anton Shubin, who tirelessly went to the libraries and archives to find the relevant materials for the book; and Megan Ivory, who helped me with the final changes.

Finally, I am indebted to my friend Rhett Miller, who on a rainy autumn day of 2013 in Moscow Propaganda Café pitched me what at the time seemed to me a crazy idea to live in Australia and do research on Russian homophobia. Without his initial encouragement, my life in this beautiful country, as well as the research and subsequent book, would never have come into being. This book is, therefore, my modest expression of gratitude to him.

Melbourne, 2020

Abbreviations

AIDS	acquired immunodeficiency syndrome
GARF	Gosudarstvennyi arkhiv Rossiiskoi Federatsii (State Archive of the Russian Federation)
GDR	German Democratic Republic
GULAG	Glavnoe upravlenie lagerei (Main Camp Administration)
ITK	ispravitel'no-trudovaya koloniya (corrective labour camp)
ITU	ispravitel'no-trudovoe uchrezhdenie (corrective labour institution)
KGB	Komitet gosudarstvennoi bezopasnosti (Committee for State Security)
MVD	Ministerstvo vnutrennikh del (Ministry of Internal Affairs)
RSFSR	Rossiiskaya Sovetskaya Federativnaya Sotsialisticheskaya Respublika (Russian Soviet Federative Socialist Republic)
SSR	Soviet Socialist Republic
STI	sexually transmitted infection

Archival citations are accompanied by the following abbreviations:

f.	fond (archive)
op.	opis' (inventory)
l.	list (page)

Introduction

The history of Soviet homosexuality is largely unexplored territory, especially during the Khrushchev and Brezhnev eras. We know very little about the Soviet state's attempts to control and regulate homosexuality during this period, while the historiography on this topic is extremely scant. Igor Kon, the pioneering scholar of Soviet and Russian sexuality, said that between 1934 and 1986 'a complete and utter silence on the subject had descended ... homosexuality was simply never mentioned', having acquired the status of an 'unmentionable vice' during this period.[1] In fact, there was a lot of talk about sex during this time and this book breaks through the seeming silence to uncover what was being said. It examines a range of previously unexplored sources that demonstrate that there were remarkable discussions on the issue among Soviet experts – doctors, jurists and educators – and police from 1956 until the collapse of the USSR. In their discussions, both experts and police defined homosexuality and elaborated on ways of dealing with it in the Soviet context.

The examination of these extraordinary and previously unknown discussions allows us to explore the relevance of Michel Foucault's complex writing on 'the history of sexuality' to Soviet homosexuality and to see whether the Foucauldian power-knowledge paradigm had the same implications for the issue of homosexuality in the USSR as it did in Western countries. According to Foucault, the modernisation of Western societies was strongly linked to the emergence of discourses on sexuality in them. These discourses acted as new means of control over the health and prosperity of the people. Sexuality became the object of analytical and scientific scrutiny, so that sexual abnormalities, which had hitherto been regarded as moral failures and crimes, now became the objects of disciplinary power, regulated by medical knowledge and institutional controls. Medical examination of same-sex-attracted people led to the construction of a new image of the homosexual: a species with its own history, character, psychology and physiology.[2] Similar trends appear to have occurred in the Soviet Union: educators, doctors and jurists embraced sexual modernity, by rationalising and modernising controls over homosexuality and abandoning simplistic understandings of it as an infraction and temporary aberration, while framing it in more 'modern' terms – a disease, a mental disorder or even just a variant of normal sexuality. These experts moved forward with bold proposals to decriminalise homosexuality and wrest it from police hands, relegating the issue to the sphere of medicine, even admitting that homosexual desire was not an ailment at all. Importantly, it was not only homosexuality that fell within these experts' purview, but the issue of sex more broadly. Doctors and educators, concerned with post-war demographic crisis, framed sex as a matter of economic and national significance, underscoring the importance of medical discourse and sex education, as well as the provision of sexological medical services to Soviet people. Fulfilling sexual lives, they argued, enhanced the labour productivity of Soviet citizens and were therefore essential for the development of society and the state.

Despite the existing similarities between the Soviet and Western modernisation of sex, this process had been different in the USSR. In fact, it has always been problematic for historians to apply Foucauldian theories to Russian and Soviet cases. Laura Engelstein expressed doubts about the relevance of Foucault's ideas to the Russian case, arguing that the power-knowledge paradigm never had the chance to thrive in Russia.[3] Oleg Kharkhordin expressed similar scepticism, contending that 'Soviet individualisation hardly happened in a way described by Foucault for the case of Western Europe' and noting that the practice of private confession was never a central feature of Russian society.[4] Kharkhordin's observation is a useful one for historians attempting to draw parallels between Foucault's writing and Soviet reality: in Western societies, it was precisely during the course of patients' confessions to their doctors that their sexuality (and homosexuality) was becoming the object of medical intervention and disciplinary controls. According to

Kharkhordin, political suppression of psychoanalysis in the 1930s and, more importantly, a 'lack of habit among Russians to discover one's own essence by means of confessing desires', as well as a 'wholehearted aversion to wordy outpourings', made confessions an unlikely feature of Soviet reality.[5]

Although confession didn't seem to play a central role in Russia, this book reveals that Soviet same-sex desiring men and women did in fact discuss their sexual lives and desires with their doctors and in a very elaborate form. These patient–doctor interactions were often as striking as their settings – GULAG and prison infirmaries, as well as Soviet clinic consultation rooms. There, doctors listened to their same-sex-attracted patients and actively encouraged them to pronounce and reflect on their desires verbally and in writing. The extent of these practices is yet to be established, because most of the illuminating sources are still classified. In fact, the materials explored in this book may well be the tip of the iceberg, but so far it seems that the Soviet medicalisation of homosexuality was limited in scope, at least in the 'free' society, although interactions between doctors and same-sex-desiring inmates were more consistent. Unlike in the West and some Eastern European countries, Soviet sexology, only revived in the mid-1960s, received little support from the state and was too weak to produce powerful discourses to disseminate them across the vast territories of the country. The practitioners of this new discipline who seriously practised the psychotherapy of homosexuality could only be found in a handful of large Soviet cities and so were not widely available to Soviet same-sex-desiring men. The voices of sexologists who argued for the decriminalisation of homosexuality were feeble and unconfident in confronting the moralistic and ideological reasoning of Soviet key decision-makers. I will argue, then, that Soviet leadership remained reluctant to fully embrace sexual modernity, and this reluctance carried conflicting implications for Soviet gay and lesbian people. On the one hand, medical discourses encouraged a re-evaluation of homosexuality as a medical matter, lending support to arguments for decriminalisation. On the other hand, police officers, despite being influenced by medical models, continued to insist that homosexuality was a criminal act which should remain in their purview.

Apart from engaging with Foucauldian theories, this book also explores Soviet experiments on raising a special type of citizen – the

New Soviet Person. The creation of such a person was the cornerstone of Soviet plans to build a new society; with the help of this person, the Bolsheviks attempted to uphold their political decisions and promote social stability.[6] Scholars, training their gaze on this historical theme, have identified a set of characteristics that this New Soviet Person was expected to possess. John Haynes has argued that such a person was 'the figurehead of the people's government of the revolutionary Soviet Union, the populist proselytiser of a qualitative change in human nature'.[7] Soviet leaders expected such a person to have 'a high-principled personality, placing the social, the public interest first, and sharing the aims and principles of the communist ideology'.[8] Other characteristic features of the New Soviet Person included 'youth, fitness and energy, particularly as expressed in the fields of manual labour and physical culture'.[9]

The moulding of the New Soviet Person, as Catriona Kelly has argued, was contingent on the inculcation of Soviet people with a set of behavioural ideals to conform and measure up to. These ideals were designed in the early years of Soviet power and they were 'clearly recognisable in later generations, even if they had started to seem controversial, or even absurd, to some members of these'.[10] The creation and proliferation of ideal models of 'new men' and 'new women' were 'to function as incentives to the creation of a new society' and 'to act as a proof that this society already existed'.[11] Scholars have pointed out that Soviet leaders used a variety of methods with a view to raising such a person – one such way was making the lives of Soviet people inseparable from the collective. Under Stalin, for instance, Soviet citizens were taught to 'sacrifice their personal interests for the sake of the collective', and the official propaganda linked personal fulfilment with a close association with the collective.[12] Under Khrushchev, as Oleg Kharkhordin shows, the collectivisation of life was further intensified, and its role in the formation of a consciousness of the New Soviet Person continued to be important.[13] Apart from instilling collectivist values and consciousness in Soviet people, the government relied on educational methods. One of these consisted of encouraging people to 'work on oneself', that is, to work towards self-transformation and self-perfection. Popular Soviet brochures on 'working on oneself' started to appear in the late 1950s and proliferated during the late Soviet era.[14] The authors of the brochures offered a variety of methods on how one should work on oneself, and according to Kharkhordin they all included three main stages: 'self-evaluation', which included 'the realisation of certain personal deficiencies', then 'self-compulsion or self-stimulation' and finally 'self-control and self-command'.[15] Building on these insights, this book attempts to discern the ethos of Soviet man in discussions of homosexuality between GULAG officials, sex educators and Soviet sexologists, suggesting that the eradication of homosexuality was also part of the Soviet project of creating a New Soviet Person, albeit one that was discussed mostly behind closed doors.

This book also enhances our understanding of public and private boundaries in the Soviet society of the Khrushchev and Brezhnev eras. Earlier scholarly works noted that, from the onset of the Soviet state, its leaders sought to appropriate private realms for public needs. Eric Naiman shows that, during the early Soviet years, Bolshevik leaders sought to subject the personal life of their citizens to societal needs.[16] During the Stalin period, as Jeffrey Brooks argues, collectivisation significantly diminished private space; Brooks goes so far as to argue that 'the press shrank private space still further during these years by enlarging and sacralising public places and structures'.[17] Vladimir Shlapentokh asserts that since the mid-1950s the Soviet state had begun to gradually lose its authority over 'all strata of the population', and the process of 'privatisation' of society had commenced.[18] Such 'privatisation' manifested itself in the emergence of 'totally private institutions' of family and friends, the growth of 'unofficial public life' in civil society and the exploitation of Soviet citizens' positions for personal gains.[19]

More recent studies of Soviet private and public boundaries have offered a more nuanced examination of this theme. Deborah A. Field argues that, despite the growing aspirations of the Khrushchev government to introduce new types of social control, during this time Soviet people managed to find new ways 'to evade, to resist, and make use' of the state's interference.[20] Field also challenges Shlapentokh's view whereby Soviet public and private were sharply distinct, proposing that there was a fluid relationship between them.[21] Further, Lewis H. Siegelbaum contends that Soviet private spheres were 'neither hermetically sealed nor necessarily in antagonistic relation to public spheres', as opposed to being viewed as merely 'the beleaguered antithesis of state power'.[22] Drawing on Siegelbaum's framework, Juliane Fürst examines the networks of like-minded friendship circles among Soviet youth in the 1950s and 1960s, filled 'with a spirit of political and social reawakening'.[23] Although, as Fürst contends, one would be inclined to assign these networks to the private realm, they 'demonstrated a desire to "be" or "create" a public sphere'.[24] This book supports both Shlapentokh's argument about growing privatisation and more recent scholars' descriptions of a fluid relationship between public and private in Soviet society after Stalin's death. In fact, I show that these two positions are mutually inclusive rather than exclusive.

The lives and experiences of Soviet homosexual people is a particularly fitting object for the examination of public and private dynamics: male homosexuality was criminalised, which meant that Soviet same-sex-desiring men had to carve out private spaces in which to pursue their sexual desires. Dan Healey shows that homosexual men established their bonds through the use of 'private sites', which included 'all-male drinking parties (popoiki), workplace fraternisation, mentoring, and comradeship'.[25] Healey also argues that these men 'were helped by a strong and growing popular sense of entitlement to a private life that was less intrusively policed by the state and its agents'.[26] It was not only homosexual men who were helped by this growing 'privatisation': Soviet legal scholars and sexopathologists made extensive use of this trend, framing homosexuality not as a matter of the state's concern, but a private matter of a given individual. Indeed, as I show in Chapter 4, Brezhnev-era legal scholars who suggested decriminalising consensual sex between men implicitly appealed to the 'notion of privacy'; they stated that consensual homosexual relations were not worthy of penalising, since they were located in the private realm, unreachable for the state. In Chapter 5, I examine medical discussions of homosexuality by Soviet doctors in the 1970s, who underscored the importance of privacy for the treatment's success. Likewise, in this chapter I reflect on the place of such medical practice in public and private boundaries. Certainly, since male homosexuality was officially a crime and medical treatment of homosexuality was not an institutionalised practice, those doctors who administered these treatments had to do so in private.

What do we know about Soviet homosexuality?

It was only in the second half of the twentieth century that sexuality and homosexuality came to be globally accepted as valid topics of historical research. Inspired by the sexual revolution of the 1960s and with the help of Western feminist and gay liberation movements, historians began to conceptualise sex as a historical issue.[27] They dispelled the hitherto prevailing notion of sexuality as a mere biological category, contending that it was a socially constructed concept. Since then a large body of literature on the history of homosexuality and homosexual emancipation in the West has been produced.[28] Although an impressive number of scholarly works are also emerging on the history of homosexuality in the countries of Eastern Europe, scholarship on the history of Russian and Soviet homosexuality remains modest, and the paucity of sources is one of the chief reasons for the absence of systemic studies of homosexuality in Russia and the USSR.[29] Indeed, Russian archives do not allow historians to access personal files more recent than seventy-five years old, and it is in these files that the most illuminating information on the lives of Soviet homosexual people can be found. The access to archival materials on homosexuality can be even more difficult, despite the expired privacy limitations of the requested files.[30] On some occasions, as Ira Roldugina explains, Russian archival workers may even deny historians permission to peruse materials whose content they consider to be 'inappropriate'.[31]

Another cause of the absence of historical studies on Soviet homosexuality is scholars' reluctance to seriously engage with the topic. Unfortunately, the field of Russian and Soviet studies is still prone to evade, trivialise and under-theorise homosexuality, so scholars generally fail to adequately examine examples of same-sex desire in the sources they find. It appears that most historians simply view homosexuality as a sexual act which lacks any emotional or intellectual dimension, and therefore, according to their line of reasoning, it does not deserve serious historical thinking.[32] Jeffrey S. Hardy, for example, in his study *GULAG after Stalin: Redefining Punishment in Khrushchev's Soviet Union, 1953–1964* (2016) completely ignores the topic (the word 'homosexuality' itself was not included in the monograph's index), despite the ample discussions between GULAG officials and doctors on the subject during the period, as well as their availability in the archives.[33] Miriam Dobson's monograph *Khrushchev's Cold Summer: Gulag Returnees, Crime, and the Fate of Reform after Stalin* (2011) also makes no mention of the topic.[34] Be it benign neglect or intentional oversight, the avoidance of the issue by historians has implications both for the existing body of knowledge on Russia and for our understanding of the present-day homophobia in the region. When we omit homosexuality from the historical narrative, we risk confining ourselves to a reductive understanding of how the relations of power were ordered in the USSR.[35] Undoubtedly, for example, the examination of how GULAG managers and doctors attempted to control homosexuality with disciplinary mechanisms, rather than criminal sanctions, would have significantly amplified the scope of Hardy's discussion on the redefinition of punishment in the Khrushchev-era GULAG and society. Likewise, an examination of Soviet homosexuality from a historical perspective would broaden our scant understanding of the homophobia rampant in most countries of the former Soviet bloc.

Although modern Russian homophobic sentiment had been brewing since the early 2000s, it intensified after the adoption of a notorious federal law in 2013 banning propaganda of 'non-traditional sexual relations'.[36] As Alexander Kondakov explains, this law rendered 'the repression of sexualities' an 'official policy'.[37] In the wake of its adoption, the Russian government unleashed a campaign of hatred towards gay people in Russia, legitimised gay bashing and censored any media that did not cover homosexuality in a negative way.[38] This hostility extended to the realm of academia, where research on homosexuality came under attack from Russia's conservative activists, while academics accused of 'promoting sodomy' were even forced to leave their jobs and the country.[39] Russian homophobia took a more sinister turn in April 2017, when reports appeared about the brutal torturing and killing of gay people in the Russian region of Chechnya, sanctioned and condoned by the regional leaders.[40] Russian homophobia remains a serious issue which needs addressing. But in order to address it, we need, in Dan Healey's words, 'historical information about the mechanisms and scale of Soviet homophobic persecution', since such knowledge is able to 'provide a much-needed evidence base for arguments in favour of strengthening the human rights of LGBT citizens in Russia' and to 'explain the dangers of official homophobic persecution to their fellow citizens'.[41]

In the Soviet era, the social-scientific study of homosexuality remained largely taboo until the final years of Soviet rule, and research on homosexuality was conducted through the lens of medicine.[42] Soviet historians and sociologists almost never examined the issue from a historical or sociological point of view. Igor Kon demonstrates the impossibility of historicising homosexuality under the Soviet regime, recalling how in 1974 he attempted to discuss homosexual relations in an article, 'The Concept of Friendship in Ancient Greece', for publication in a historical journal, *Vestnik Drevnei Istorii* (Ancient History Review). The censors demanded that he avoid using words such as 'pederasty', which referred to anal intercourse between two men, or 'homoerotic' in the article, and eventually Kon had to opt for a more appropriate euphemism: 'those specific relationships'.[43]

Considering such hostile attitudes towards any studies of homosexuality in the Soviet Union, it comes as little surprise that the first ground-breaking historical research on Soviet same-sex desire came from the West. One of the most notable scholars here was Simon Karlinsky, who began to examine the issue in Russian history and literature from the late 1970s. Karlinsky's primary focus was literary: for example, he explored the depiction of homosexual love in the work of a Russian poet, Mikhail Kuzmin.[44] Karlinsky also provided a historical overview of how homosexuality was handled in Russia from the Petrine era to the post-Stalinist decades.[45] Some of his findings, however, were subsequently called into question by scholars who approached Russian history via new sources.[46]

It was only following the demise of the Soviet Union that Russian scholars turned to the topic. In 1995 Igor Kon published *The Sexual Revolution in Russia: From the Age of the Czars to Today*, which, by his own admission, draws on 'literary and scientific data' from various areas of knowledge.[47] Kon's discussion of homosexuality largely concentrates on the criminalisation of sodomy under Stalin and its framing under Khrushchev and Brezhnev. As a scientist and key contributor to Soviet studies of gender and sexuality, he presents an 'inside story' on how the Soviet authorities treated homosexuality, relaying curious episodes from his interactions with Soviet doctors, police and censors. Despite the uniqueness of Kon's work, it contains various contradictory generalisations. He argues, for example, that since the 1930s 'a complete and utter silence on the subject [homosexuality] had descended', that 'homosexuality was simply never mentioned' and that it 'had become an "unmentionable vice" in the full sense of the term' throughout the Soviet period.[48] Yet, contradicting his own statement that homosexuality was never mentioned, Kon notes that the first sexopathology books appearing in the USSR in the 1970s labelled homosexuality a 'sexual perversion'.[49]

The fall of the 'iron curtain' and the opening up of Soviet state archives attracted Western scholars and prompted them to approach the history of Russian and Soviet homosexuality with the newly available sources.[50] Unpacking Foucauldian ideas of knowledge and power, Canadian historian Dan Healey examines how they shaped the regulation of homosexuality in tsarist and communist Russia in his pioneering study *Homosexual Desire in Revolutionary Russia: The Regulation of Sexual and Gender Dissent* (2001).[51] Healey has persuasively argued that disciplinary mechanisms employed by tsarist and communist Russia's experts in relation to homosexuality were significant, despite the constraints of the authoritarian regime imposed on them. The decriminalisation of tsarist sodomy statutes in 1922 by Bolsheviks gave rise to the proliferation of medical discourses on homosexuality, which held a promise of reframing the issue as a matter of medical concern. Yet, after Stalin recriminalised male sodomy in 1934, male same-sex desire acquired a criminal status, and the state imposed 'compulsory heterosexuality' on its citizens.

Healey's more recent monograph *Russian Homophobia from Stalin to Sochi* (2018) departs from an entirely Foucauldian approach and explores the historical roots of contemporary Russian homophobic sentiment. It discusses the history of the GULAG, underscoring its crucial role in producing homophobia under and after Stalin. The monograph also shifts its focus from regulatory discourses on homosexuality to examine the lived experiences of Soviet same-sex-desiring people in the rural and urban areas in the 1950s, revealing that some of them possessed homosexual self-awareness. Finally, it discusses the Brezhnev era, a time of comfortable economic growth accompanied by the growing availability of housing and general improvements in people's standards of living – developments that expanded opportunities for Soviet homosexual people to have a relatively comfortable life and enjoy urban gay male cruising in the largest cities.[52]

In *Russian Homophobia* Healey argues that in the 1950s, as the dismantlement of the GULAG was under way, its authorities were worried about the possibility of homosexuality spreading into wider society.[53] It was one of these anxieties, as I show in Chapter 1, which apparently triggered a host of measures against homosexuals and lesbians in the GULAG from 1956 to 1959. Healey also considers the handling of same-sex love in the late Soviet penitentiary system, arguing that 'the late Soviet decades appear to have hardened the homophobia in prisoner subcultures, especially among male convicts'.[54] This homophobia was most evident in the proliferation of homosexual violence, wherein 'degraded' men – passive partners in anal intercourse – were raped by other prisoners and branded with shaming tattoos, which underscored their low status.[55] Building on these foundations, I demonstrate in Chapter 5 that throughout the 1970s, Soviet MVD (Ministerstvo vnutrennikh del, Ministry of Internal Affairs) officials were worried about these practices and were eager to resolve the problem of homosexual sex in prisons with the help of a newly established medical science – sexopathology, which emerged in the mid-1960s and included homosexuality in its research agenda. MVD officials commissioned sexopathologists to produce manuals on medical treatment of homosexuality in prisons; they did so on numerous occasions in the 1970s and despite the official status of male homosexuality as a crime.

Although Healey's monographs present numerous innovations, some of their arguments are problematic. For instance, reflecting on the fate of the Stalin-era sodomy statute, Healey noted that the 'energetic renewal of "socialist legality"' under subsequent Soviet leaders did not 'lead to an examination of the value of the 1934 anti-sodomy statute'.[56] More recently, he provides a new perspective on this issue, arguing that the decision to retain the anti-homosexual legislation after Stalin's death was made by a decree on the struggle with sodomy issued by the officials of the Interior Ministry in 1958. Healey construes this decree as 'rare evidence that Khrushchev's reformers deliberately discussed Stalin's law against male homosexuality, and chose to keep it'.[57] I will, however, demonstrate that it was Soviet legal scholars, drafting the new Republic Criminal Codes in 1959, rather than MVD officials, who were responsible for retaining the anti-sodomy statute. These legal scholars did examine the law on sodomy, and some of them even suggested eliminating the article penalising consensual homosexual relations between men. Likewise, commenting on the issues of medicalisation of homosexuality under

Khrushchev and Brezhnev, Healey notes that lesbians were the primary objects of medical intervention during these periods, due to the absence of legal penalties for female same-sex relations, while same-sex-desiring men were pursued with the existing sodomy laws.[58] Even so, medical treatment of homosexual men did occur in the Khrushchev and Brezhnev eras, despite the existing criminal penalties, and such treatments, as I show in Chapters 3 and 5, were no less common than medical treatment of lesbians.

Regrettably, the medicalisation of homosexuality in the USSR, and under Khrushchev and Brezhnev in particular, remains largely unexplored terrain. The unavailability of illuminating sources and stringent confidentiality rules imposed on medical materials dated from the mid-1960s onwards have prevented scholars from engaging with the topic satisfactorily.[59] The few existing scholarly discussions of the medicalisation of Soviet homosexuality usually start with a nod to the report *The Rights of Lesbians and Gay Men in the Russian Federation: An International Gay and Lesbian Human Rights Commission Report* (1994).[60] In her report, Masha Gessen observes that during Soviet times 'punitive psychiatry was employed against homosexuals and lesbians' and that it was often the relatives of a homosexual person that initiated such treatment.[61] Gessen bases her conclusions on a range of interviews with Soviet lesbians which she conducted in Russia in the period from 1991 to 1993. The interviewees revealed that the medical treatment of lesbianism typically occurred thus: a parent or any other guardian learnt that there was a sexual relationship between two young women and initiated hospitalisation of one or both of them in a psychiatric hospital. There, the women would typically be subjected to treatment with psychotropic drugs for about three months, and after discharge from hospital they were registered as psychiatric outpatients and assigned a local psychiatrist for regular monitoring.[62]

Echoing Gessen's account and drawing on her own interviews with eight Soviet lesbians, American sociologist Laurie Essig, in her monograph *Queer in Russia: A Story of Sex, Self and the Other* (1999), argues that apart from being forcibly hospitalised, Soviet lesbians succumbed to medical treatment, 'secure in the knowledge that only with medical intervention could they go on living'.[63] According to Essig, in order to conform to societal norms, Soviet lesbians even consented to undergoing same-sex operations, while homosexual men who wished to avoid prosecution for sodomy did likewise (Igor Kon subsequently criticised these conclusions, questioning the reliability of Essig's data).[64] More recent studies have shifted from the narratives of compulsory hospitalisation, presenting a more complex account of Soviet lesbians' everyday life during the late Soviet era. Francesca Stella, for example, suggests that forced psychiatric treatment of lesbians was not 'a universally accepted practice among medical practitioners' and that some of them, upon learning of their female patients' homosexuality, could offer the option of 'heterosexual re-education', rather than a medicated approach.[65] Some doctors, Stella reveals, even 'ruled out medical treatment as ineffective in changing an individual's sexuality'.[66]

If the existing literature, albeit very sketchily, reveals how medical treatment of female homosexuality was conducted in the Soviet Union, this is not the case when it comes to male homosexuality. Indeed, the literature says very little about the issue, especially with reference to the Khrushchev and Brezhnev periods.[67] Many questions remain unanswered. Could a medical diagnosis of homosexuality save those accused of sodomy from incarceration? How did Soviet courts distinguish between the disease and the crime? Did the regular police know about the existence of medical treatments for homosexuality? Was it a crime to go to the doctor and confess one's homosexual desires? Some scholars have argued that it was indeed possible for Soviet gay men to obtain legal immunity with the help of doctors. Sonja Franeta tells of an interviewee who in the 1980s escaped criminal punishment for sodomy due to his 'diagnosis' – he shared his problem with a local psychiatrist, who sent him to psychiatric hospital for medical examination. The medical examination revealed that he was indeed a homosexual; from now on this new status rendered him immune to the police.[68] In her book *My Pink Road to Russia: Tales of Amazons, Peasants, and Queers* (2015), Franeta quotes a man who deliberately underwent medical treatment for homosexuality to escape criminal prosecution.[69] French historian Arthur Clech confirmed the testimonials of Franeta's interviews in his article 'Between the Labor Camp and the Clinic: *Tema* of the Shared Forms of Late Soviet Homosexual Subjectivities' (2018), revealing that both women and men were subjected to medical treatment and that in some cases psychiatric treatment could save homosexual men from prosecution.[70]

Drawing on the existing work on the medical treatment of homosexuality, this monograph explores discussions and practices of Soviet sexopathologists who spearheaded Soviet sexological science. Although male homosexuality remained a crime, they examined it through a 'scientific' lens, seeking to provide medical treatment for such individuals. Some sexopathologists sought to claim homosexuality for their profession by arguing for the decriminalisation of sodomy and pointing out that existing criminal sanctions prevented homosexuals from seeking medical help due to fear of prosecution. Some made less explicit attempts to change the status of homosexuality from crime to disease, proposing to establish medical treatment of homosexuality as an official practice. Others theorised on the issue of whether a homosexual could be spared a prison sentence and instead be sent to a psychiatric hospital for treatment of his 'disease'.

Soviet homosexuality and new sources

The majority of documents and files I draw on have hitherto been unexplored by scholars and therefore it is worth elaborating on their provenance. The sources in question fall into three groups by their location – first, archival material; second, sources that I located in Russian libraries; and third, materials that I acquired through my personal interaction with former Soviet doctors who performed medical treatment on same-sex-desiring people.

The files from the first group of sources come from the State Archive of the Russian Federation (GARF) and the State Archive of Latvia. Most of these sources are GULAG documents produced between 1956 and 1959, and I examine them in Chapter 1. They include decrees by GULAG directors on the struggle against homosexuality, their internal correspondence and reports on the measures taken to prevent it, reports of GULAG doctors on venereal disease and an unpublished brochure by a GULAG psychiatrist on lesbianism. Another intriguing archival source in this group is a manual on 'physical education', produced in 1958 for the officials of juvenile colonies. In this manual, which is considered in Chapter 2, the author gives recommendations on how to prevent 'sexual perversions' among adolescents in places of confinement. Other archival materials include the minutes of the RSFSR (Russian Soviet Federative Socialist Republic) Legislative Commissions which participated in the drafting of a new RSFSR Criminal Code in 1959 – these commissions considered the first part of the law on consensual sodomy, and some of its members proposed eliminating it altogether. This group of sources also encompasses archival materials located in the State Archive of Latvia – a draft of the Latvian Criminal Code, proposed by the Latvian SSR's law commission in 1960, containing a proposal to criminalise lesbianism and a draft proposal of the Supreme Court of the Latvian SSR to introduce harsher penalties for 'perverted' sexual practices such as oral and anal sex in 1977. I obtained these files during my fieldwork in Russia and Latvia in autumn 2016, yet I was unable to find similar files in the state archives of Ukraine, Belarus, Lithuania and Estonia, which I also consulted in the course of this research trip.

The second group of sources comes in the main from the Russian State Library and the Russian National Library, specifically, from a reading room containing materials designated 'for official use only' (dlya sluzhebnogo pol'zovaniya). In this room I discovered manuals and handbooks for Soviet investigators and cadets of the MVD Higher School on the investigation of sex crimes, which featured debates on the criminal status of homosexuality in the USSR: these sources are considered in Chapter 4. Sources from this group also include brochures, intended for Soviet penal officers, with recommendations on how to combat sexual perversions in prisons, and these are considered in Chapter 5. I have also consulted the Central Scientific Medical Library, where I located monographs on sexopathology with medical discussions on homosexuality, as well as unpublished dissertations on treating lesbianism – these files are considered in Chapter 3.

The third group of sources is represented by materials that I obtained in the course of my communication with Soviet sexologists. Some of these scholars still work in the Department of Sexopathology of the Moscow Institute of Psychiatry, whose establishment dates back to 1965. This institution was the main sexological centre in the USSR where research on sexopathology was conducted and patients with sexual disorders, including homosexuality, were treated. During my fieldwork in Moscow in March 2017, I had an informal communication with the doctors of the department, who kindly shared some of the documents that they stored in their bookcases. These documents included an unpublished dissertation, 'Materials on the Sex Life of Male Workers of an Industrial City of Central Kazakhstan' (1968), by Soviet sexopathologist I. A. Popov. This dissertation was the first study to examine sexual behaviour of Soviet people, where the author compared the prevalence of homosexuality in Soviet and Western societies. Another source in this group is a typewritten outline of scientific tasks, put before the doctors of the Department of Sexopathology by the MVD in 1973, requiring sexologists to design methods of medical treatment of homosexuality to be used in Soviet prisons. One more illuminating source here is a report produced in 1973 by the doctors of the department, where they documented their meetings that year with the KGB and MVD officials on the issue of homosexuality, as well as their work on designing new drugs for the treatment of homosexuality.

Another doctor I approached is Yan Goland, a Soviet psychiatrist-sexopathologist, who has been practising the medical treatment of homosexuality in the city of Gorkii since the mid-1960s. After decades of medical practice, Goland accumulated a sizable collection of files and documents, which he kindly allowed me to use. These included his unpublished papers on homosexuality, his correspondence with Moscow sexopathologists, his letter to the Soviet journal *Zdorov'e* on the subject of homosexuality and many others. Patients under his treatment were required to keep a diary in which they described their lives prior to the start of the treatment and documented its progress. These diaries were meant to be part of the treatment – the documented progress would be discussed with Goland, who would then decide what course of action to take. Once the treatment was over, Goland typed out these handwritten testimonials, anonymising the diarists' identities and eliminating any other personal details. These former patients' typewritten testimonials were then shown to other patients, who were expected to be encouraged by them, and in this monograph I use some excerpts from these. I also use an excerpt from Goland's interview with a former patient conducted in the 1990s and recorded on a videotape. Finally, I rely on an interview with Goland himself, which I conducted with him in April 2017 in Nizhnii Novgorod.

A few words should be said about the limitations of the sources I have described above. The aim of this monograph is to document discussions on homosexuality held between Soviet officials and specialists, rather than identify the authentic voices of Soviet queer people – therefore my analysis is mostly state- and intelligentsia-centred. I also examine the officially published sources, considering the individuality of the views expressed in them and the authoritative regime and censorship constraints within which they existed. I analyse diaries from Goland's collection with great caution: I am aware that since he promoted his treatment using these diaries, some information, especially on the treatment outcomes, cannot be considered totally trustworthy – some of his patients would certainly report positive results just to meet the doctor's expectations. However, in my analysis of these diaries, I focus not on technical questions of treatment efficacy, but the patients' stories of how they first came to sexologists with the 'problem' and how they first consulted the doctor.

Each of the five main chapters of this book examines discussions on homosexuality within a specific realm and timeframe. The timeframes chosen are dictated by the available sources. In Chapter 1 I examine how homosexuality was dealt with in the GULAG in the period from 1956 to 1959. Chapter 2 looks at how Soviet educators discussed sex and homosexuality in a series of manuals published under Khrushchev in the period from 1956 to 1964. In Chapter 3 I consider how same-sex desire was explained and constructed within the field of Soviet psychiatry – sexopathology, which emerged in the 1960s. Chapter 4 examines manuals, textbooks and dissertations on sex crimes and on the sodomy law, produced by Soviet experts in crime and law in the period from 1959 until 1975, along with their discussions on the value of the existing sodomy statutes in them. Chapter 5 examines discussions of homosexuality among Soviet sexopathologists and MVD officials in the 1970s as well as their attempts to regulate homosexuality in prisons during this period. A conclusion reflects on the implications of these discussions and provides a brief overview of how Soviet experts and police tackled the issue after Brezhnev and up until the collapse of the Soviet Union.

A note on the Soviet sodomy law

A few words should be said about the existing anti-sodomy law in the USSR. Male homosexual acts became illegal under Stalin in

1934 with the adoption of the anti-sodomy law – Article 154a of the USSR Criminal Code.[71] The article consisted of two parts: the first (154a – I) criminalised consensual sodomy (punishable by deprivation of liberty for a term of three to five years), while the second (154a – II) criminalised so-called 'forcible' sodomy (with a more severe penalty of five to eight years).[72] Female homosexuality was never criminalised.

The few historical accounts of the adoption of this law point out that no announcement was made explaining the rationale for its introduction. The existing sources are too scant to deduce with certainty why the Stalinist leadership brought it in.[73] Historians have made some attempts to investigate this question. Dan Healey and Laura Engelstein agree that political reasons were an important factor and link the adoption of the law to the Stalinist leadership's drive to tighten control over the Soviet people's intimate lives and to deter political disloyalty, which the Stalinist leadership associated with homosexuality.[74] Healey also suggests that anxieties about the declining birth rate were relevant.[75] He has also pointed out that the leadership under Stalin deemed it unnecessary to criminalise lesbianism, preferring instead to reinforce the motherhood cult and using it as an important reminder of the purpose of women's sexuality, and in the later Soviet period resorted to medical controls.[76]

Notes

1 Igor Kon, *The Sexual Revolution in Russia: From the Age of the Czars to Today* (New York: Free Press, 1995), p. 241.
2 Michel Foucault, *The History of Sexuality.* Volume 1: *An Introduction* (New York: Pantheon, 1978), p. 43.
3 Laura Engelstein, 'Combined Underdevelopment: Discipline and the Law in Imperial and Soviet Russia', *American Historical Review* 98, no. 2 (1993): 338–53.
4 Oleg Kharkhordin, *The Collective and the Individual in Russia: A Study of Practices* (Berkeley: University of California Press, 1999), pp. 5–7.
5 Ibid.
6 Maja Soboleva, 'The Concept of the "New Soviet Man" and Its Short History', *Canadian – American Slavic Studies* 51, no. 1 (2017): 84.
7 John Haynes, *New Soviet Man: Gender and Masculinity in Stalinist Soviet Cinema* (Manchester and New York: Manchester University Press, 2003), p. 1.

8 Lynne Attwood, *The New Soviet Man and Woman: Sex-Role Socialisation in the USSR* (Basingstoke and London: Macmillan, 1990), p. 33.
9 Catriona Kelly, 'The New Soviet Man and Woman', in *The Oxford Handbook of Modern Russian History*, ed. Simon Dixon (Oxford: Oxford University Press, 2015), p. 4.
10 Ibid., p. 3.
11 Ibid.
12 David L. Hoffmann, *Cultivating the Masses: Modern State Practices and Soviet Socialism, 1914 – 1939* (Ithaca and London: Cornell University Press, 2011), p. 228.
13 Oleg Kharkhordin, *The Collective and the Individual in Russia: A Study of Practices* (Berkeley and London: University of California Press, 1999).
14 Ibid., p. 241.
15 Ibid., p. 242.
16 Eric Naiman, *Sex in Public: The Incarnation of Early Soviet Ideology* (Princeton and New Jersey: Princeton University Press, 1997).
17 Jeffrey Brooks, *Thank You, Comrade Stalin: Soviet Public Culture from Revolution to Cold War* (Princeton: Princeton University Press, 2000), p. 74.
18 Vladimir Shlapentokh, *Public and Private Life of the Soviet People: Changing Values in Post-Stalin Russia* (New York: Oxford University Press, 1989), pp. 153–4.
19 Ibid., p. 154.
20 Deborah A. Field, *Private Life and Communist Morality in Khrushchev's Russia* (New York: Peter Lang, 2007), p. 55.
21 Ibid., p. 102.
22 Lewis H. Siegelbaum, 'Introduction: Mapping Private Spheres in the Soviet Context', in *Borders of Socialism: Private Spheres of Soviet Russia*, ed. Lewis H. Siegelbaum (New York: Palgrave Macmillan, 2006), p. 3.
23 Juliane Fürst, 'Friends in Private, Friends in Public: The Phenomenon of the Kompaniia among Soviet Youth in the 1950s and 1960s', in *Borders of Socialism: Private Spheres of Soviet Russia*, ed. Lewis H. Siegelbaum (New York: Palgrave Macmillan, 2006).
24 Ibid., p. 244.
25 Dan Healey, *Russian Homophobia from Stalin to Sochi* (London and Oxford: Bloomsbury Academic, 2018), p. 62.
26 Ibid., p. 26.
27 John D'Emilio, *Sexual Politics, Sexual Communities: The Making of a Homosexual Minority in the United States, 1940–1970* (Chicago and London: University of Chicago Press, 1983), p. 3.
28 Among the most recent are the following: Sean Brady, *Masculinity and Male Homosexuality in Britain, 1861–1913* (Basingstoke and New

York: Palgrave Macmillan, 2005); Scott Gunther, *The Elastic Closet: A History of Homosexuality in France, 1942 – Present* (Basingstoke: Palgrave Macmillan, 2008); Richard Cleminson and Francisco Vasquez Garcia, *'Los Invisibles': A History of Homosexuality in Spain, 1850–1939* (Cardiff: University of Wales Press, 2007); Brian Lewis, ed., *British Queer History: New Approaches and Perspectives* (Manchester and New York: Manchester University Press, 2013); Jeffrey Meek, *Queer Voices in Post-War Scotland: Male Homosexuality, Religion and Society* (Basingstoke and New York: Palgrave Macmillan, 2015).

29 The existing historical and sociological scholarship on Russian homosexuality is largely confined to the post-Soviet period. See for example: Brian James Baer, *Other Russias: Homosexuality and the Crisis of Post-Soviet Identity* (New York: Palgrave Macmillan, 2009); Brian James Baer, 'Now You See It: Gay (In)visibility and the Performance of Post-Soviet Identity', in *Queer Visibility in Post-Socialist Cultures*, ed. Narcisz Fejes and Andrea P. Balogh (Bristol: Intellect, 2013). On representations of homosexuality in post-Soviet music, see: Stephen Amico, *Roll Over, Tchaikovsky! Russian Popular Music and Post-Soviet Homosexuality* (Urbana and Chicago: University of Illinois Press, 2014). On gay visibility in post-Soviet Russian films, see: Kevin Moss, 'Straight Eye for the Queer Gay: Gay Male Visibility in Post-Soviet Russian Films', in *Queer Visibility in Post-Socialist Cultures*, ed. Narcisz Fejes and Andrea P. Balogh (Bristol: Intellect, 2013), pp. 197–220. On the challenges facing historians writing the history of homosexuality in the USSR, see: Healey, *Russian Homophobia*, pp. 151–77. See also Dan Healey, 'Homosexual Existence and Existing Socialism', *GLQ: A Journal of Lesbian and Gay Studies* 8, no. 3 (2002): 351–2.

30 Irina Roldugina, 'Pochemu my takie lyudi? Rannesovetskie gomoseksualy ot pervogo litsa: Novye istochniki po istorii gomoseksual'nykh identichnostei v Rossii', *Ab Imperio*, no. 2 (2016): 183–7.

31 Ibid. The archives holding the most illuminating materials, namely those of the Federal Security Service (successor to the KGB) and the Archive of the President of the Russian Federation, are also likely to remain inaccessible in the foreseeable future. My attempts to approach these institutions, even under the guise of a more 'appropriate' research topic, were unsuccessful.

32 Healey, *Russian Homophobia*, p. 174.

33 Jeffrey S. Hardy, *The Gulag after Stalin: Redefining Punishment in Khrushchev's Soviet Union, 1953–1964* (Ithaca and London: Cornell University Press, 2016).

34 Miriam Dobson, *Khrushchev's Cold Summer: Gulag Returnees, Crime, and the Fate of Reform after Stalin* (Ithaca: Cornell University Press, 2009).

35 Dan Healey, *Homosexual Desire in Revolutionary Russia: The Regulation of Sexual and Gender Dissent* (Chicago and London: Chicago University Press, 2001), p. 9.
36 Alexander Kondakov, 'Teaching Queer Theory in Russia', *QED: A Journal in GLBTG Worldmaking* 3, no. 2 (Summer 2016): 107.
37 Ibid.
38 Ibid., 108.
39 Ibid., 113.
40 Elena Milashina, 'Ubiistvo chesti: Kak ambitsii izvestnogo LGBT-aktivista razbudili v Chechne strashnyi drevnii obychai', *Novaya gazeta*, 3 April 2017, www.novayagazeta.ru/articles/2017/04/01/71983-ubiystvo-chesti (accessed 17 December 2020).
41 Healey, *Russian Homophobia,* p. 154.
42 Daniel P. Schluter, *Gay Life in the Former USSR: Fraternity without Community* (New York and London: Routledge, 2002), p. 4.
43 Kon, *Sexual Revolution in Russia*, p. 328.
44 Simon Karlinsky, 'Death and Resurrection of Mikhail Kuzmin', *Slavic Review* 38, no. 1 (March 1979): 92–6.
45 Simon Karlinsky, 'Russia's Gay Literature and Culture: The Impact of the October Revolution', in *Hidden from History: Reclaiming the Gay and Lesbian Past*, ed. Martin Duberman, Martha Vicinus and George Chauncey (New York: NAL Books, 1989), pp. 347–64.
46 Healey, *Homosexual Desire*, p. 3.
47 Kon, *Sexual Revolution in Russia,* p. 4.
48 Ibid., p. 242.
49 Ibid.
50 See for example: Eve Levin, *Sex and Society in the World of the Orthodox Slavs, 900–1700* (New York: Cornell University Press, 1989); Laura Engelstein, *The Keys to Happiness, Sex and the Search for Modernity in Fin-de-Siècle Russia* (Ithaca and London: Cornell University Press, 1992); Laura Engelstein, 'Soviet Policy Towards Male Homosexuality: Its Origins and Historical Roots', in *Gay Men and the Sexual History of the Political Left*, ed. Gert Hekma, Harry Oosterhuis and James Steakley (New York and London: Haworth, 1995), pp. 155–78. More recent works include: Dan Healey, *Bolshevik Sexual Forensics: Diagnosing Disorder in the Clinic and Courtroom, 1917–1939* (DeKalb: Northern Illinois University Press, 2009); Frances Lee Bernstein, *The Dictatorship of Sex: Lifestyle Advice for the Soviet Masses* (DeKalb: Northern Illinois University Press, 2007).
51 Healey, *Homosexual Desire*.
52 Healey, *Russian Homophobia,* pp. 93–147.
53 Ibid., pp. 27–51.

54 Ibid., p. 45.
55 Ibid., pp. 45–6.
56 Healey, *Homosexual Desire*, p. 258.
57 Healey, *Russian Homophobia*, p. 43.
58 Ibid.
59 Catriona Kelly, 'White Coats and Tea with Raspberry Jam: Caring for Sick Children in Late Soviet Russia', in *Soviet Medicine: Culture, Practice and Science*, ed. Frances L. Bernstein, Christopher Burton and Dan Healey (DeKalb: University of Illinois University Press, 2010), p. 258.
60 Masha Gessen, *The Rights of Lesbians and Gay Men in the Russian Federation: An International Gay and Lesbian Human Rights Commission Report* (San Francisco: Gay & Lesbian Human Rights Commission, 1994).
61 Ibid., p. 16.
62 Ibid., p. 17.
63 Laurie Essig, *Queer in Russia: A Story of Sex, Self and the Other* (Durham and London: Duke University Press, 1999), p. 29.
64 Igor Kon, 'Amerikanskaya aspirantka otkryvaet golubuyu Rossiyu', (1999), http://az.gay.ru/articles/reviews/kon_essig.html (accessed 11 March 2018).
65 Francesca Stella, *Lesbian Lives in Soviet and Post-Soviet Russia: Post/Socialism and Gendered Sexualities* (New York: Palgrave Macmillan, 2015), p. 47.
66 Kon, 'Amerikanskaya aspirantka otkryvaet golubuyu Rossiyu', p. 48.
67 Vladimir Volodin, *Kvir-istoriya Belarusi vtoroi poloviny XX veka: Popytka priblizheniya* (Minsk, 2016), pp. 35–49.
68 Sonja Franeta, *Rozovye flamingo: 10 sibirskikh interv'yu* (Tver': Kolonna, 2004), pp. 70–1.
69 Sonja Franeta, *My Pink Road to Russia: Tales of Amazons, Peasants, and Queers* (Oakland: Dacha, 2015), pp. 203–31.
70 Arthur Clech, 'Between the Labor Camp and the Clinic: *Tema* of the Shared Forms of Late Soviet Homosexual Subjectivities', *Slavic Review* 77, no. 1 (2018): 6–29.
71 Healey, *Homosexual Desire*, p. 185.
72 Mark I. Yakubovich and Vladimir F. Kirichenko, *Sovetskoe ugolovnoe pravo* (Moscow: Gosyurizdat, 1958), p. 342.
73 Healey, *Homosexual Desire*, p. 186.
74 Ibid., p. 221. Laura Engelstein, 'Soviet Policy', pp. 169–70.
75 Healey, *Homosexual Desire*, pp. 202–3.
76 Ibid., p. 204.

1

Homosexuality in the Soviet GULAG (1956–59)

On 27 January 1956 the head of the corrective and labour camps and colonies of the MVD, Sergei Yegorovich Yegorov, signed a new decree featuring an unusual subject.[1] The document drew the attention of GULAG directors to the growing problem of homosexuality in colonies and prisons, which, as Yegorov wrote, was 'likely to have serious consequences', if measures to prevent it were not taken:

> The Central Administration of prison camps and colonies of the MVD USSR has information about increased instances (among both male and female prisoners) of sodomy (muzhelozhstva), lesbian love and other types of sexual perversion, including rape and syphilis infections resulting from this. Considering that this state of affairs is abnormal and that it is likely to have serious consequences, I request that you study this phenomenon on the ground and in detail and then submit an elaborate report (dokladnaya) to the Central Administration of prison camps and colonies of the MVD USSR by 15 March 1956.[2]

Yegorov went on to specify a list of the issues which he expected the chiefs of the GULAG colonies across the Soviet Union to address in their reports. Among other matters he required that they provide statistics on 'frequency of the instances of sexual perversions among prisoners', 'types of sexual perversions' and 'instances of mental, venereal and other illnesses due to this (na etoi pochve)' and information on 'the cohort of prisoners engaging in sexual perversions, their age, gender, physical state and the type of conviction'.[3] Furthermore, Yegorov sought suggestions on 'the measures of the regime (rezhimnyi), educative or whatever measures of influence on prisoners, required to be employed in the struggle with sexual perversions'.

The head of the GULAG also suggested that apart from prison officers, specialists in psychiatry, forensic medicine and venereology should also be engaged in the effort to eradicate homosexuality in the GULAG system.[4]

Yegorov's decree represented, in Michel Foucault's words, an 'institutional incitement' to speak about homosexuality and a 'determination on the part of the agencies of power to hear it spoken about'.[5] It was also apparently one of the first serious and massive attempts of the Soviet officials to bring same-sex desire 'under the authority of the language' and 'take charge' of it through discourse after Stalin's death. Indeed, Yegorov's decree gave rise to fruitful discussions on homosexuality among GULAG directors and doctors which I will explore in the sections to follow. In their reports GULAG directors framed homosexuality as not just a crime against morality, but a problem that had implications for the inmates' health and the GULAG's economic productivity. Same-sex activity was a source of sexually transmitted infections (STIs) which threatened to go beyond the barbed wire and spread to society at large. It also provoked gruesome acts of violence among prisoners, fomenting the establishment of informal prisoner hierarchies and destabilising camp discipline and work. GULAG directors proposed to tackle homosexuality with discourse: they stressed the importance of educational work with prisoners and individual discussions between the doctor and the prisoner on the harm of this phenomenon. GULAG doctors, often underestimated and neglected, seized the opportunity to demonstrate the utility of their profession to the GULAG leadership by studying lesbianism, offering scientific solutions to the problem and, most importantly, emphasising the crucial role they played in the fight against it.

Yet, despite their use of discourse against homosexual activity, some GULAG directors still contended that camp authorities should continue to punish male same-sex activity in the camps with prison terms, and that lesbianism should be criminalised too. Doctors, while not opposing the prosecution of male homosexual activity, had a different opinion on lesbianism, preferring to examine it through a scientific lens. According to them, female homosexuality was a temporary phenomenon which in most cases would disappear once the prisoner was released, and only hardened lesbians should be tackled with punitive measures.

GULAG crackdown on homosexual sex: reasons and background

So why did the issue of homosexuality become a matter of urgency for the GULAG leaders in early 1956? Dan Healey tells us that the sexual culture of the Soviet GULAG was no different from that of tsarist prisons, where same-sex activity flourished and was deplored by penal experts.[6] In the Stalin GULAG, male and female homosexual activity was highly visible too. Although male homosexual relations were often marked with rape and sexual abuse of younger inmates at the hands of older or more 'criminal' inmates, some same-sex liaisons could be consensual.[7] Lesbian relationships, according to the GULAG memoirists, were less violent and often gendered – 'masculinised', tougher women cohabited with more submissive 'feminine' partners – and such couples mounted stiff resistance to the authorities' attempts to separate them.[8]

A handful of indictments and terse summaries of GULAG sodomy cases from 1943 to 1953 demonstrate that camp authorities routinely prosecuted same-sex relations between men. Such cases were tried in special camp courts, which were created in 1944 and dealt specifically with the crimes committed in the corrective labour colonies.[9] Courts relied on the testimonies of eyewitnesses and camp guards who caught the defendants red-handed. Medical examinations of the suspects appear to have been conducted occasionally: only one indictment contains a reference to this procedure.[10] It also seems that inmates playing an 'active' role in sexual intercourse were likely to be penalised more severely than their 'passive partners'. For instance, inmates Sherbakov and Golubev from the Khabarovsk GULAG, who were found guilty of consensual sodomy which they engaged in during January and February 1951, received different sentences. Sherbakov, who played an active role, received five years in prison and Golubev three years.[11] Sherbakov twice tried to appeal the court's decision, arguing in his complaint to the USSR Supreme Court that his ill-wishers deliberately gave false testimony against him, but his complaints were eventually rejected.[12] Judicial decisions in sodomy cases could also be affected by special state occasions: Mark Dubovitskii, convicted for sodomy with minors in one of the prisons of the city of Nal'chik in August 1945, had the charges against him revoked and was released as part of Stalin's 1945 amnesty.[13]

After Stalin's death it became obvious to his heirs that the GULAG was in urgent need of reform. The system of prison camps and colonies was indeed in deep crisis: it was economically inefficient, and due to the rapid growth of the prison population, it was becoming more difficult to control. Prisoners actively sought to undermine the camp administration's authority, taking part in acts of mass disobedience, refusing to work and instigating uprisings.[14] Messages about the GULAG system's degradation were quickly reaching the Party leaders, who received numerous complaints from prisoners about their dire living conditions and the rampant criminality in the camps.[15]

One of the Party's earliest responses to this crisis was the amnesty decree in 1953, which triggered the release of 1.2 million prisoners from the camps and colonies.[16] Far from resolving the GULAG crisis, this led to more problems and concerns. The mass exodus of an able-bodied 'positive contingent' (polozhitel'nogo kontingenta) from camps and colonies led to a deficit of a qualified labour force in the camp system, while the sharp increase in the remaining cohorts of especially dangerous criminals (osobo opasnykh prestupnikov) further intensified tensions in the GULAG and led to more prisoner uprisings.[17] A wave of crime overwhelming the entire country was another undesirable consequence of the mass exodus of prisoners.[18] Despite this, the Soviet leadership continued reducing the size of the GULAG, placing the blame for the crime wave on the camp officials, who had ostensibly failed to re-educate prisoners and prepare them for life outside the GULAG.[19]

Yegorov's decree was a product of these massive reforms: it reflected the GULAG leadership's anxiety about the mass release of prisoners into the society, which could have unforeseen consequences. In particular, camp authorities and medics were anxious about the possible spread of the prisoners' homosexual relations beyond the barbed wire, along with a spread of STIs such as syphilis, believed to be a consequence of sodomy.[20] Yegorov's call for educative measures also appears to be a result of Stalin's heirs' determination to 'diminish the economic focus' of the GULAG 'in favour of re-education' of prisoners, as demonstrated by Jeffrey S. Hardy.[21] GULAG inmates were no longer to be perceived as merely a labour force; instead, camp administrators were encouraged to view them as 'wayward citizens in need of encouragement, support, trust, training and education'.[22] As part of this 're-education' shift, the party leadership adopted other decrees between March and July 1954. These required that GULAG officials prepare inmates 'for an honest working life' through the improvement of the use of labour, education and political work.[23] Yet, as Hardy has argued, Stalin's heirs did not have a clear strategy on how to transform the GULAG into a place of re-education.[24] The lack of such a strategy is palpable in the GULAG commandants' approach to homosexuality, which I will examine further: although they reported the usefulness of 'educative talks' with prisoners engaging in same-sex activities, some of them still suggested that criminal sanctions were more efficient.

Yegorov circulated the decree to the directors of the corrective labour camps across the entire Soviet Union.[25] However, only one short memorandum responding to his call is available in the archives – signed by the head of the Siberian GULAG, Velikanov.[26] Addressing his report to the new director of the GULAG, Pavel Nikolaevich Bakin, who took over from Yegorov on 4 April 1956, Velikanov admitted that in the Siberian corrective labour camp there were instances of 'lesbian love' among women:

> In the MVD Siberian corrective labour camp there are instances of sexual perversions in the female camp sections. So-called lesbian love is common among female prisoners. This type of sexual perversion is mainly prevalent among women prisoners at the age of twenty to forty years, who come from criminal-bandit and thief cohorts (ugolovno-banditstvuyushchii i vorovskoi element) with multiple convictions for various crimes… [In the camp sections], where thieves-recidivists and criminal-bandit cohorts with multiple convictions are housed, 50–60% of all prisoners engage in sexual perversions. In other camp sections that house inmates convicted for the first time and those convicted under article 58 the instances of sexual perversions are also present, but they are not widespread (ne nosyat massovogo kharaktera).[27]

This report is unique documentary evidence of the camp authorities' understanding of the distribution and nature of homosexual activity in the GULAG. Velikanov believed that homosexuality was more characteristic of common prisoners with multiple convictions, rather than political prisoners from the educated intelligentsia. The latter, relating their GULAG experiences in memoirs, demonstrated a similar perception of GULAG homosexuality, also suggesting that it was widespread among common criminals and distancing themselves from it.[28]

Out of four suggestions offered by Velikanov to tackle lesbianism, two recommended punitive measures. He suggested imposing administrative penalties on lesbians who violated the camp order: 'Sexual perversions are to be considered a breach of the camp regime and the perpetrators are to be punished administratively as in cases of other breaches of camp discipline.'[29] Most importantly, he advocated criminalising female homosexual acts by going as far as to petition the Presidium of the Supreme Soviet of the USSR 'for imposition of a penalty for individuals engaging in sexual perversions'.[30] As I will show further, other GULAG directors also called for criminalisation of female homosexuality, arguing that no other measures against lesbians were as effective, yet their proposals never became law.

Among other proposals in Velikanov's report were the enforcement of nocturnal surveillance over prisoners' barracks and 'conducting of regular competent conversations (kvalifitsirovannykh besed) on the harm of sexual perversions' among them. As Yegorov's decree dictated, Velikanov consulted with the doctors on the issue too. In their opinion, the root of the problem was women's isolation from men: 'The medical personnel believe that the main reasons for sexual perversions among women are physiological needs, arising as a result of their long isolation from men.'[31] As I will show further, other GULAG doctors held similar opinions on the origins of homosexuality – they argued that female homosexuality would disappear on its own once women engaging in lesbianism had access to men.

Homosexuality in the reports of GULAG officials

Fresh scholarship reveals that in the late 1950s the GULAG leadership was deeply concerned about the rise in criminal activity in the camps, and particularly criminal gangs that undermined the camp order. As early as 5 April 1956 the MVD leadership observed that more than 25 per cent of all camp prisoners were recidivists, who committed robberies, murders and other grave crimes, adversely influencing the camp life.[32] The guard department of the GULAG was so worried about these problems that it wrote more than a thousand pages on the issue between October 1957 and July 1958.[33]

It was precisely in the context of anxiety about the growing criminal activity in the GULAG that its directors started to problematise the phenomenon of homosexuality.

Party officials frequently released decrees in which they urged GULAG officials to tackle crime in the camps more effectively, and these decrees apparently mentioned homosexuality too. On 25 October 1956 the Council of Ministers and the Central Committee of the Communist Party issued one such decree. The text is not available, but the responding reports by camp directors on its enforcement suggest that sodomy and lesbianism were listed among crimes to be tackled. On 1 July 1958 the head of the Corrective Labour Colonies of Belarus, Soblov, summarised the tasks set out by the decree in his report:

> The Decree of the Council of Ministers of the USSR and Central Committee of the Communist Party of the Soviet Union of 25 October 1956 that focused on the struggle with crime in camps and colonies demanded that the leadership of the UITK [Upravlenie ispravitel'no-trudovykh kolonii, Directorate of Corrective Labour Camps] and corrective labour colonies undertake the most energetic measures to prevent sodomy and other sexual perversions among prisoners.[34]

Soblov reported that the colony's administration had increased surveillance over prisoners' behaviour to identify those 'inclined to sodomy and other sexual perversions', enforced nocturnal surveillance over bunk beds (spal'nye mesta) and conducted systematic 'educational' (vospitatel'naya) and 'sanitary-educational' (sanitarno-prosvetitel'skaya) work among prisoners.[35] Soblov also suggested that the prisoners' collective was an important means of struggling with sodomy – 'to fight this evil, the societal forces of the collective have been engaged to create an environment of intolerance and condemnation of these instances [of sexual perversions]'.[36]

Other GULAG directors stressed the importance of repressive measures. The head of the corrective labour colonies of Udmurtskaya ASSR, Lieutenant Colonel Kuznetsov, revealed in his report of 2 July 1958 that male prisoners caught in homosexual acts were prosecuted under the Soviet Criminal Code, while women engaging in lesbianism were punished administratively.[37] Kuznetsov noted that 'all services of the camp have been mobilised for the struggle with "lesbian love" and primarily operational personnel (operativnyi sostav)'.[38] As a result, the camp administration identified and punished forty lesbians: 'Due to a variety of agent-operative (agenturno-operativnykh) and investigative measures, forty individuals were revealed to have committed sexual acts in perverse forms and strictly punished administratively. Some of them were transferred to the strict regimen (perevedeny na strogii rezhim).'[39] Kuznetsov observed that 'lesbian love' spawned quarrels and fights between women, undermining the camp regime and discipline.[40]

In response to the increasing demands from the top to address the problem of homosexuality, some GULAG directors sought to demonstrate that they had bolstered the enforcement of the sodomy law in their colonies. In his report to the GULAG directorate on 24 July 1958 the head of the Usol'skii labour camp, Colonel Varakin, presented a table of convictions for various crimes in the colony from 1956 to 1958, which demonstrated an increase in sodomy convictions.[41] Varakin noted that this increase was due to the camp authorities' crackdown on this type of crime, rather than by its growth.[42]

Varakin's report also reveals how inmates' homosexual sex came to the attention of the GULAG administration. The sentinels and camp workers of the Usol'skii labour camp made an effort to detect inmates engaging in sodomy: they conducted nocturnal surveillance over prisoners in penalty cells and inspected secluded spots amenable for sex at night. As a result, several inmates were caught in the act of committing sodomy. Suspicious lingering of two or more inmates in the male toilets also caught the camp guard's eye: they immediately investigated to sometimes find a man being coerced into sex by other inmates. Some prisoners got caught because of their indiscretion: for instance, Varakin reported that inmates Kravtsov and Fedorenko attempted to commit consensual sodomy on the doorsteps (na kryl'tse) of the camp canteen but were quickly apprehended.[43]

Varakin revealed that when spotting male same-sex activity, the GULAG administration acted promptly: inmates were taken to the medical units of the camp for forensic examinations, normally conducted by GULAG doctors. In the 1950s, forensic expertise on the crime of sodomy was slowly reviving, with more elaborate instructions on how to deal with such crimes appearing in books on forensic medicine. Even so, forensic experts argued that the traces of homosexual intercourse found on perpetrator's bodies should be construed as evidence of sodomy only in conjunction with other pieces of evidence. Forensic examination results alone did not provide sufficient grounds to establish that sodomy had taken place.[44] Catching prisoners in flagrante delicto together with prompt medical examinations during the first hours after the prisoners' intercourse enabled GULAG doctors to find fresh signs of sodomy on their bodies and apparently streamlined the handling of such cases.

While violent sex between male prisoners certainly predominated, some of them did engage in homosexual sex by mutual consent. This was the case in at least four out of six sodomy cases from 1957 to 1958 reported by Varakin.[45] Prisoners Dobrovol'skii and Fedorov, who committed consensual sodomy in a boiling chamber of the colony on 23 April 1957, received three years, while prisoners Zarubin, Yakobuk and Sorokin, prosecuted for the same type of crime, were sentenced to five years. Indeed, the Stalinist anti-sodomy law punished consensual sodomy by deprivation of liberty for a term of three to five years and apparently the severity of the sentence was determined by factors that authorities perceived as aggravating. In the case of Zarubin, Yakobuk and Sorokin, a higher penalty could have been warranted because Zarubin infected his partners with syphilis and Yakobuk consented to sodomy with Zarubin for a reward of five rubles.[46] These actions were perceived as threats to both the physical and moral health of other prisoners.

Between 1956 and 1958 the GULAG leadership constantly urged camp directors to step up measures against homosexuality and prodded them to provide updates on the issue. On 31 May 1958 a new GULAG director, Mikhail Nikolaevich Kholodkov, who had been in office for one month, signed a decree code-named '128-c', which reaffirmed the 'dangerousness' of homosexual acts between men and women and the urgency of dealing with them.[47] Reporting to Kholodkov on 8 July 1958, Colonel Ivanov, the deputy head of Vladimir corrective labour colonies, reiterated that the 128-c decree concentrated on three major tasks: the fight with 'organised distribution of narcotic substances' among prisoners; sodomy; and the struggle with 'organised warring groups'.[48] Ivanov reported that two prisoners, Koryagin and Ganabin, who attempted to commit sodomy with other inmates on 11 June 1958 were prevented from doing so and eventually removed from the colony, and that the camp administration conducted 'explanatory work' (razyasnitel'naya rabota) with other male prisoners.[49] As far as lesbianism was concerned, Ivanov reported the use of police and 'explanatory work':

> Among the women prisoners held at Golovinskii ITK there were instances of 'lesbian love', that is, cohabitation of a woman with a woman. In order to reveal the fact of such a liaison between prisoners, the entire net of agents (agentura) was mobilised. On receiving the information from agents, individual explanatory work is conducted, social organisations of the colony (obshchestvennye organisatsii kolonii) condemn worst offenders of the regime (zlostnye narushiteli rezhima) and those cohabiting are confined to a strict regimen and prosecuted. Thus, five individuals were transferred to a strict regimen in 1957–8 and prisoners Karpova and Berezovskaya were prosecuted. Out of jealousy (na pochve revnosti) towards other prisoners, they were engaging in hooliganism (sovershali khuliganskie deistviya).[50]

Other camp directors were worried that female homosexual relations not only undermined camp discipline but led some lesbians to suicide. Reporting to Kholodkov, Colonel Kisilev from Saratov wrote: 'these acts of sexual perversions exert a rather harmful influence on most women prisoners. Because of homosexuality, so-called lesbian love emerges among women, and the accompanying jealousy leads to fights, scandals and in some cases the suicide of cohabiting women (sozhitel'nits).'[51] Kisilev produced a familiar spiel on the effectiveness of 'explanatory work' in the struggle with lesbianism: 'the struggle with homosexuality in subdivisions of the OITK [Otdel ispravitel'no-trudovykh kolonii, Department of Corrective Labour Camps] is conducted by means of explanatory talks on the harm of this act of sexual perversion, constant surveillance over cohabiting women, and measures of a political and educational character and disciplinary action'.[52] Yet, Kisilev deplored the inefficacy of these measures, arguing that they did not 'produce a positive effect to the full extent' and that it was impossible to prosecute lesbians in the absence of relevant criminal penalties.[53] Kisilev was determined to punish them anyhow, by removing the most trouble-making women from the colony altogether: 'On 25 June 1958 in GUITK MVD RSFSR we raised a petition №2/I-328 to convoy a group of prisoners, Bystrova, Bubnova, Tikhonova, Tsiligina, Chertoeva,

Chernyshova, Kartushina and Gorshkova, engaging in homosexuality to the camps of strict regimen outside Saratov oblast'. We ask that this petition not be declined.'[54]

Apparently, GULAG directors attached little importance to explanatory work with prisoners, preferring a hard-line approach. Many only briefly discussed the effectiveness of educative measures towards homosexuality, affording much more attention to the descriptions of the punitive measures they had taken. Some of them went as far as to openly suggest criminalising lesbianism. It is likely that by their allusions to the efficacy of educative measures, GULAG directors merely paid lip service to the educational efforts promoted from above, while trying to punish lesbians with the available legal tools. Hardy tells us that the GULAG leadership was struggling to promote the importance of education among GULAG directors. While some GULAG directors demonstrated promising results in this area, still others neglected the importance of educational work with prisoners.[55] To all intents and purposes, despite the GULAG directors' preference to treat lesbianism as a crime, it was never criminalised.

GULAG doctors and 'lesbian love'

Unlike GULAG commandants, who mostly advocated for the use of legal sanctions, GULAG doctors called for a more differentiated approach to the problem of 'sexual perversions'. From their discussions it appears that their attitude to sodomy was as hostile as that of the GULAG directors, yet when it came to lesbianism, doctors espoused different views. In order to better understand how doctors handled the question of homosexuality we need to consider the broader history of medical service in the GULAG, which, as scholars of the GULAG note, has not been given proper scholarly attention.[56]

Few existing examinations of the GULAG medical service emphasise its inconsistency with the harsh treatment of prisoners in the camps. For example, Anne Applebaum characterises the GULAG medical service as one 'of the many absurdities found in camp life'.[57] Dan Healey has recently challenged Applebaum's understanding of the GULAG medical service as an 'absurdity', arguing that its existence had a purpose.[58] Drawing on a Foucauldian framework,

Healey argues that GULAG medicine constituted a form of 'bio-power', geared at exercising tighter surveillance mechanisms over the GULAG prisoners' bodies and thus increasing their productivity.[59] Healey also notes that after Stalin's death, the GULAG medical service 'adumbrated an ostensibly more humane view of the prisoner as meriting medical rather than "sanitary" attention'.[60] This shift to a more 'humane' approach to prisoners after Stalin's death is discernible in the camp doctors' discussions of sodomy and its detrimental effect on young newcomers, which will be examined further.

Scholars have also elucidated the power relationships between GULAG doctors and directors and the extent to which the GULAG's medical-sanitation department could influence the decisions of the latter. Golfo Alexopoulos suggests that, despite a range of functions that GULAG doctors had to perform, they had little power compared to the camp's production-managers before and following World War II.[61] The relationships between camp directors and doctors were fraught with tensions, and doctors complained that their work was often neglected and undervalued.[62] Instead of acknowledging the existing problems and difficulties that doctors faced in regional camps and colonies, the Central GULAG leadership in charge of medical services scolded them for the high rates of illness and mortality and criticised them for not being resourceful enough to find solutions to the problems themselves.[63] Directors of medical services across camps and colonies resented such pressure and expressed frustration with their bosses.[64] Later in 1944–45, however, the GULAG leadership began issuing decrees which emphasised the importance of improving the physical condition of prisoners. Health officials working for GULAG medical services welcomed these decrees, arguing that they enhanced their authority and rendered their work easier.[65] The 1956 decree by Sergei Yegorov on the importance of involving doctors in the efforts to combat homosexuality, along with the leaders' desire to re-educate prisoners and prepare them for release, also enhanced GULAG doctors' authority and influence. The Central GULAG leadership now held medical expertise in higher regard and expected doctors to provide extensive contributions on the problem of homosexuality, with concrete solutions to the problem as well as scientific opinions on the origin of sexual perversions in camps. Male homosexuality in the GULAG was framed by doctors as the main cause of STIs. At a conference for directors of medical departments of corrective labour camps held between 6 and 11 March 1956, one camp health official noted that ‘the number of those infected with syphilis in some camps is significant’ and that the problem was urgent ‘especially against the backdrop of the decrease in syphilis rates among civilian populations’.[66] Attributing the rise of syphilis to sodomy, the official deplored the prevalence of both phenomena in various labour camps:

> According to numerous oral and written reports by medical workers of the camps and colonies, the spread of syphilis among prisoners is largely due to sodomy. It is transmitted by recidivist criminals who, because of their long stint in camps and prisons, without families, indulging in casual sex, acquired the vice in the form of sodomy … as well as syphilis. Their partners, or rather victims, are young inmates whom recidivist criminals under the threat of punishment (pod ugrozoi raspravy) rape and [whom they] convert into passive pederasts and infect with syphilis. In some camps like Ust’vymlag, USVITL, Yuzhkuzbasslag and Sevkuzbasslag sodomy among recidivist criminals and the ensuing infection of the youth with syphilis have become widespread.[67]

GULAG medical departments’ shift to a ‘humane approach’ is palpable here: doctors appear to be genuinely concerned about the younger inmates, whom older criminals abused, drawing them into homosexuality.[68] As I will show in Chapter 2, Khrushchev-era educators and physicians were worried about the vulnerability of the younger generation to homosexual influences and sought to inculcate in them correct ‘sexual morality’.[69] Apart from issues of sexuality, party officials were also troubled by the increasing juvenile delinquency and its apparent appeal to young people.[70] The concern that ‘criminal recidivists’ were drawing young inmates into sodomy can be interpreted as a reflection of these broader anxieties. Perhaps doctors perceived the homosexual acts between a hardened criminal and a young newcomer as an act of initiation of the latter into the prison world. Moreover, the act of rape, making someone a ‘passive pederast’, signified their firm incorporation in the lowest caste of the prison hierarchy with all corresponding consequences. Other prisoners would ostracise such a ‘pederast’ and in order to survive he would have to come to terms with his new role as a sexually accessible object, further losing his dignity and stepping deeper into the criminal underworld.[71]

In a conference report for the chief GULAG doctors in Kiev on 11 September 1956, Colonel of the Medical Service Ustinchenko expressed similar anxiety about the harmful influence of hardened criminals on newcomers.[72] He underscored the link between sodomy, STIs and moral corruption:

> the proliferation of syphilis occurs mainly through sodomy, and active pederasts are usually criminals from the cohorts of physically strong criminal-recidivists. As a rule, they don't work, they take drugs and finally they rape young inmates who don't belong to the criminal underworld, infect them with syphilis and corrupt them morally and physically.[73]

Although Yegorov's 1956 decree emphasised the importance of tackling both sodomy and lesbianism, GULAG doctors showed little interest in the former. What really fascinated them was homosexual sex between women prisoners. Dan Healey has suggested that the interest in lesbianism could be explained by the existing criminal statute for sodomy, which criminalised male same-sex relations and thereby rendered studies of same-sex relations between men 'rare and subordinate to police requirements'.[74] Lesbianism, which was not technically a crime, was to be dealt with medically.[75] Furthermore, lesbianism was a promising domain which GULAG doctors could claim and utilise to prove their usefulness to the GULAG leadership and reinforce their positions within the GULAG system.

In 1958 a doctor from a psychiatric hospital of the Yaroslavl' corrective labour colony, V. S. Krasuskii, presented his treatise 'On the issue of the study of perverse forms of sexual relations among women prisoners' to the MVD leadership. The treatise spanned sixty-eight pages and examined 'lesbian love' in the camps, providing lengthy recommendations on how to tackle the issue.[76] Krasuskii underscored the GULAG doctors' skills and abilities to engage lesbians during individual appointments in frank conversations about their sexual lives, thereby highlighting the utility of the medical profession for the leadership's plans. During these appointments, doctors sought to dissuade women prisoners from engaging in sexual perversions. Elaborating on these prisoner–doctor interactions, Krasuskii wrote:

> Doctors of female units (podrazdelenii) can do particularly significant work and usually do it during medical check-ups and when administering treatment, by individually influencing women prisoners who engage in unnatural forms of sexual relations and often turn to them for help. In the private and intimate setting of the consultation room of the ambulatory, infirmary and especially of the gynaecologist, honest confessions about perverse forms of sexual relation may lay the groundwork for conducting conversations with prisoners with detailed descriptions of the amorality of such behaviour and its negative impact on one's health. We had the opportunity to verify the significant effect of these type of conversations in a number of cases.[77]

The infirmary consultation room was an important site, where new understandings of homosexuality were negotiated and Foucualdian controls over sexuality were forged through confession and medico-educational discourse. There, GULAG doctors examined and listened to their same-sex-desiring patients, giving them an inducement to speak and integrating their confessions into the nascent scientific discourse about homosexuality. From these doctor–patient interactions homosexuality derived new meanings – it was not a simple act of perversion, but a complex and multifaceted phenomenon.

Apart from underscoring the doctors' potential to assist the GULAG authorities in combating homosexuality, Krasuskii criticised some camp officials for their indulgent attitude towards lesbianism:

> We know about a case when a newly appointed head of the women's camp unit energetically took on the task of eradicating the perverted forms of sexual relations between women prisoners ... He combined strict administrative measures with political and educational work. However, his promotion changed everything, since the new chief who replaced him was quite tolerant and indifferent towards the issue.[78]

Indeed, not all camp directors believed that female homosexual relations were problematic. Dan Healey has argued that their indulgence of queer relations between women could be explained by the fact that, 'in theory, queer relations did not disrupt the GULAG economic model as drastically as heterosexual relations did' because they did not lead to pregnancy.[79] It is possible that GULAG directors adhered to the same line of reasoning, but doctors like Krasuskii saw it differently, arguing that lesbian relationships significantly disrupted the GULAG's productivity in many important ways.

To begin with, Krasuskii argued that lesbianism had adverse effects on women prisoners' physical and mental health: such prisoners were 'lethargic (vyalye)' and 'considerably lose their appetite and weight'.[80] Other camp doctors observed that lesbians suffered from genital illnesses (zabolevaniya polovoi sfery) which were resistant to treatment.[81] These diseases prompted women prisoners to request medical internment in prison hospitals and exemption (osvobozhdenie) from work.[82] The widespread disdain for homosexuality among women prisoners, and the necessity to hide lesbian relationships from fellow inmates, worsened the psychological well-being of lesbian prisoners and by extension their capacity to perform labour:

> Apart from the direct impact of perverted forms of sexual relations on the health of women prisoners, the socio-psychological aspect also plays a role in this regard. This group of people constantly has to experience the condemnation of a certain element of the prisoners surrounding them. Moreover, these individuals are constantly forced to reconcile the desire to be together, to eat together, to wear each other's clothes, to share the received money and products, with the continuous denial that there is cohabitation between them. Naturally, this kind of continuous need to hide, to deceive everyone, and also the constant threat of being separated and punished, has an impact on the health of cohabiting women. As a rule, in these persons there is a decrease, and in some cases a loss, of working capacity.[83]

Another problem with lesbians was their propensity to disrupt camp discipline because of the quarrels and fights which accompanied their relationships. It is no wonder that Krasuskii, as well as the camp directors, used the language of emotion to describe women's same-sex activity, calling it 'lesbian love'. It appears that such a designation reflected the nature of homosexual relations between women in prisons and the deep ties that lesbian women cultivated. Krasuskii noted that lesbian relationships often resembled marriage with all the accompanying attributes: 'Observing perverse forms of sexual relations between women prisoners sometimes it is striking how … their relationships bear all the characteristics of conjugal life (supruzheskaya zhizn').'[84] Lesbians courted their partners and wrote poems to their lovers.[85] Krasuskii was also struck by the loyalty that some lesbians displayed towards their partners by waiting for their release outside their penalty cells.[86] In some cases love between women was so enduring that it continued after their release from the GULAG: 'Some women prisoners get accustomed to same-sex forms of cohabitation to such an extent that they seek to retain them after their release from the camp – in some cases, this leads to family dissolution and perverse forms of same-sex cohabitation go beyond places of confinement.'[87] Yet, apart from loyalty and affection, lesbian relationships displayed severe intensity at times and fights arose: 'Quarrels, fights, scenes of jealousy alone between these persons lead to a number of violations of the camp regime and discipline. To this we must add that it is not uncommon for these individuals to refuse to work, drink cologne, enter into conflicts and disobey orders of supervisory service.'[88]

Soviet psychiatrists' engagement with the prison lesbian in the second half of the 1950s coincided with the mass anti-homosexual crackdown in the United States, launched by the American government shortly after World War II.[89] Amidst the anti-homosexual policies of the McCarthy era, prison lesbianism was placed under increased surveillance and condemnation too.[90] Just like Soviet gaolers, American legislators deplored the fact that some parolees were spreading homosexuality beyond the barbed wire.[91] In the Soviet case, however, fears about homosexual contagion were especially intense and were worsened by the profound anxieties and dilemmas characteristic of the de-Stalinisation campaign launched by Khrushchev.[92] The declining birth rates were still a significant concern and the Khrushchev leadership sought to settle this problem by strengthening the family institution.[93] Former prisoners who carried their apparent perversions into society threatened to undermine these plans.

Krasuskii argued that homosexual relations between women prisoners were not of a biological nature and were merely due to the absence of sexual outlets:

> We may consider it an established fact that women prisoners involved in perverted forms of sexual relations do not possess any pathology of a biological nature and have normal physical development. Their perversity in sexual relations is the result of unfavourable social and living conditions, and in some cases, under normal conditions, they switch to normal sexual relations with men.[94]

He argued that occasional meetings with spouses could alleviate the lack of sexual fulfilment which women prisoners experienced in the camps.[95] Yet, he lamented that only a limited number of inmates enjoyed such a privilege and prisoners usually 'settled the sex question themselves, doing it exceptionally poorly, resorting to unnatural forms of sex life'.[96] Most who were inclined to homosexual relations were 'morally degraded recidivists with a record of multiple convictions' who enticed and seduced other prisoners. This perspective on lesbianism overlapped with that of GULAG directors who, as I have shown, linked sexual perversions with criminality.

What were Krasuskii's proposals in regard to the issue of lesbianism? He observed that women upon becoming mothers tended to forgo their homosexual proclivities: 'It is interesting that pregnancy and child-bearing, evoking the woman's biologically inherent aspiration to become a mother, even after lasting perverted forms of cohabitation with women before pregnancy, decisively eliminate these abnormal forms of sexual relations'.[97] As an example, Krasuskii related a case of one female prisoner who maintained sexual relations with many fellow prisoners, until she entered a sexual relationship with a man and got pregnant. Krasuskii wrote: 'It is interesting that after her release, the prisoner Mirovaya wrote a letter to the head of the camp subdivision, in which she expressed condemnation of her behaviour during her stint, writing that now she was leading a normal way of life and would continue to do so from now on.' Krasuskii's certainty that maternal instinct would overshadow lesbian proclivities in women was not unique – other GULAG doctors emphasised the necessity of heterosexual relationships for women and their potential to eradicate perversions.[98] Such views were in line with the official pronouncements of the Khrushchev leadership. As Susan E. Reid has argued, despite the Party's commitment to engage more deeply with the problem of women's equality, gender stereotypes continued to prevail and Khrushchev's speeches and policies from 1958 only emphasised the woman's biological role as a mother and a housekeeper.[99] Another important measure in the struggle with lesbianism was involving prisoners in labour, rechannelling their sex drive into a more productive activity: 'The first and foremost task in the struggle with the emergence of unnatural relations among women prisoners is to create conditions for rechannelling of the sexual drive (polovoe vlechenie) to productive labour activity.'[100] Such a strategy was also nothing new – the Stalin-era *Great Soviet Encyclopaedia* (1940) mentioned the efficacy of labour in distracting people from sex and sublimating their sexual energy into work.[101]

Unlike GULAG operatives who believed that female homosexuality could be disciplined most effectively by means of punitive measures, Krasuskii was more inclined to believe in the efficacy of the educational approach and collective intervention. He wrote: 'It is beyond doubt that all forms of administrative measures, particularly various forms of punishment, are inferior in their influence to societal condemnation exerted by the prisoners themselves.'[102] Krasuskii argued that public shaming and exposure of lesbians to the gaze of the collective of fellow prisoners would help eradicate sexual perversions. He recommended 'issuing leaflets with caricatures, depicting different sides of life between cohabiting women prisoners such as "the partition of property" (razdelenie imushchestva) between quarrelling women, scuffles and fights (draka i ssora) between them'. Krasuskii went so far as to suggest that prison radio should broadcast talks by prisoners who formerly engaged in sexual perversions, encouraging other similar inmates to follow suit.[103] Wall newspapers with articles highlighting the negative influence of lesbianism on the colony regime were also suggested.[104]

One of the most effective ways to shame lesbian prisoners into stopping the practice of homosexuality was the use of activist councils (sovety aktiva). These were one of the various 'self-governing' institutions established by the GULAG leadership in 1954 in order to facilitate the management of the corrective labour camps. Activist councils were elected by inmates themselves.[105] Krasuskii pointed out that the influence of the activist council on the struggle with homosexuality was most effective when the chairman of the council summoned a 'cohabiting couple' (sozhitel'stvuyushchaya para) for a reprimand at the council's meeting. Krasuskii explained: 'It is precisely the fact that they have to confront not just the camp administration, but their own comrades, where all things are called as they are and merely denying the guilt bears no results, that in some cases makes them promise to stop maintaining perverse forms of sexual relations'.[106] The educative effect of such meetings, he argued, was significant.

Krasuskii's proposal to mobilise the collective against lesbians and encourage prisoners to police themselves was not a unique initiative and was a reflection of Soviet policies on deviance beyond the barbed wire. Indeed, in the 1950s, the Soviet authorities attempted to delegate the policing and prosecution of deviants to the public, by creating 'a mass infrastructure of grassroots volunteer organisations'.[107] One such organisation was the druzhina – the people's auxiliary police.[108] LaPierre tells us that one of the most important instruments for the druzhina's fight with deviants was 'the use of public shaming techniques, such as exposing offenders to the gaze of the assembled collective through satirical cartoons, wall newspapers, and public displays of offenders' photographs'.[109] These measures had a profound meaning, for 'being publicly displayed as a hooligan, the deviant was stigmatised in the court of public opinion, exposed to the ridicule of his collective, and started on the long road to rehabilitation'.[110] The Soviet authorities encouraged social self-policing and comprehensive mutual surveillance, by consolidating and strengthening so-called 'people's patrols' and the 'comrades' courts', which had existed since the early Soviet years.[111] These bodies of societal surveillance were not meant to punish transgressors, but correct their behaviour and admonish them to live righteously.[112] The effectiveness of 'people's patrols' and 'comrades' courts' was high, since they 'were more meticulous and closer to the people: they were the people policing itself, and thus escape was hardly possible from their omniscient gaze and omnipresent power'.[113]

While arguing that punitive measures were ineffective for disciplining lesbians, Krasuskii acknowledged the existence of the view whereby lesbians should be punished with legal sanctions and lesbian couples forcefully separated:

> The proposals of practitioners of the camps and corrective labour colonies addressed to the ministry aimed at a more efficient fight against this phenomenon deserve interest ... These proposals especially emphasise the more severe measures of influence in relation to persons performing a male role, so-called kobly. Considering that they are usually the main distributors of this evil, it is proposed that they be decisively removed from the women's units and then isolated in special camps or transferred to the prison regime.[114]

Krasuskii also acknowledged that several camp directors proposed to criminalise lesbianism: 'The Directorate of the ITK of the Ministry of Internal Affairs of the Ukrainian SSR and the Uzbek SSR, as well as the Directorate of the Siblag, raises the question of the necessity to introduce a criminal penalty for women conducting perverse forms of sexual relations among themselves, just as men are prosecuted for homosexual forms of sexual relations.'[115] However, Krasuskii refrained from commenting on these proposals, neither refuting nor supporting them. From this text, it is difficult to establish whether he was in favour or against legal sanctions. Judging by the context of his manual and his arguments he indeed could have been against such initiatives. Yet apparently he could have been compelled to acknowledge the importance of punishment, paying lip service to the still-powerful camp managers, who were reluctant to invest resources in re-educating prisoners and allowing doctors to claim broader jurisdiction over the issue.

Indeed, GULAG bureaucrats did not readily accept all the proposals that doctors made regarding prison lesbianism. One point of divergence between them was whether or not doctors should lecture prisoners on the harm of sexual perversions, and Krasuskii mentioned that in his treatise: 'The expediency of holding lectures by doctors in the female sections of the camp on the harm of perverse forms of sexual life between women prisoners is often a matter of debate between the camp administration and doctors of the female sections of the camp.' He concluded that such lectures were harmful: 'it is important to say that such form of struggle with perverse forms of sexual relations among women prisoners is not justified and cannot be recommended: such a lecture on the harm of these relations may turn into a lecture sparking interest in such forms of relations'.[116] Krasuskii's statement did not necessarily reflect his own views on this issue, but could have been a result of pressure from the GULAG leadership to state such a view in the brochure. Having their own views on the problem, the leadership may have been reluctant to allow doctors to take charge of the issue.

Conclusion

On 13 May 1959 a conference for the heads of the GULAG operative departments (operativnyi apparat) took place to share the experiences of dealing with crime in the GULAG.[117] The head of the first directorate of the Karaganda ITL MVD, Lieutenant Colonel Chekin, prepared a conference report in which he announced that the year 1959 'had seen changes in the operative environment (operativnaya obstanovka) in the camp and colonies of the MVD'.[118] These changes were due to the decisive crackdown (reshitel'noe nastuplenie) on the 'criminal-bandit element'.[119] Yet, despite these changes, Chekin noted that there were still some problems to solve. The first was the remaining issue of drug addiction (narkomaniya).[120] Another was lesbianism:

> The second problem on which I would like to dwell is the struggle with lesbianism that has become widespread in the camp. Because of jealousy, women create a scene, fight, knife one another and commit a range of crimes, drawing the youth into this and corrupting the latter. This also prevents other inmates from serving their sentences in peace.[121]

Chekin suggested taking the following measures:

> We need to step up repressions. From the talks with women convicts, engaging in this activity – engaging very actively, talks with medical staff and other GULAG operatives, we have concluded that stable lesbians (ustoichivye lesbiyanki) need to be isolated and put in the facilities ... which may be called 'isolation wards' (meditsinskii izolyator), whose harsh incarceration conditions (zhestkie usloviya soderzhaniya) would serve as a deterrent. We are contemplating creating such an organisation (takaya organizatsiya) in the whole republic, if financial considerations do not thwart our plans (esli opyat' vopros 'bezdotatsionnoi' raboty ne zakroet etomu dorogu).[122]

Yet it appears that Chekin's proposition was never announced at the conference, since the whole section on lesbianism was crossed out in his report – and apparently this happened before the meeting. The reasons are difficult to establish; they could include the reluctance of camp officials to admit that they were still unable to fight homosexuality, or their conviction that overall the problem was solved. Indeed, Jeffrey Hardy tells us that in 1958 camp authorities were very keen to report that criminal activity in the GULAG was no longer a problem; for example, this year the head of the GULAG, Kholodkov, reported to the Central Committee that 'the criminal gangs are for the most part liquidated, they don't exist as an organised force'.[123]

The elimination of this part may also signal ministry officials' willingness to turn to medical solutions to the problem of homosexuality, triggered by the GULAG doctors' contributions in response to Yegorov's decree. We certainly do not have enough evidence to measure how much medical knowledge was produced in the GULAG in the 1950s and the extent to which it shaped the handling of same-sex desire there – access to new sources will enable us to shed more light on the issue. Yet, as I have shown in this chapter, some doctors made significant attempts to present the issue of lesbianism as a matter which should be dealt with by doctors and not criminal penalties. Krasuskii argued that doctors were the key when it came to dealing with lesbianism – they predisposed them to a frank conversation, listened to their confessions and directed their desires. They meticulously studied homosexual prisoners' behaviour, and the MVD leadership was also willing to listen to doctors and their proposals. In fact, they set off a whole machinery of producing discourse on sex. A new image of the homosexual was being born. Even so, the MVD authorities were apparently unwilling to relegate the issue to the medical field and, most importantly, invest resources and time into re-educating prisoners. Although they did not openly challenge medical views in their reports, they made no mention of them either, signalling their reluctance to engage with them.

Notes

1 For a brief biography of Yegorov, see: Aleksandr Kokurin and Nikita Petrov, eds, *GULAG: (Glavnoe Upravlenie Lagerei), 1917–1960* (Moscow: MFD, 2000), p. 815.

2 GARF, f. P-9414, op. 1, delo 2882, l. 78. The original typed text read '15 February' but has been changed by hand to '15 March.' Yegorov's untitled decree.

3 Ibid.

4 Ibid.

5 Foucault, *History of Sexuality*, p. 18.

6 Healey, *Homosexual Desire*, p. 230.

7 Healey, *Russian Homophobia*, pp. 35–6.

8 Ibid., p. 37.

9 Denis Shkarevskii, 'Spetsial'nye lagernye sudy v SSSR (vtoraya polovina 1940-kh gg.)', *Lex Russica*, no. 4 (April 2017): 209–12.

10 GARF, f. 9474, op. 18, delo 2415, l. 2.

11 GARF, f. 9474, op. 18, delo 1748, l. 2.

12 Ibid., l. 9.
13 GARF, f. 9474, op. 18, delo 30, l. 1.
14 Steven A. Barnes, *Death and Redemption: The Gulag and the Shaping of Soviet Society* (Princeton and Oxford: Princeton University Press, 2011), pp. 202–3.
15 Vladimir Kozlov, ed., *Istoriya stalinskogo GULAGa: Konets 1920-kh – pervaya polovina 1950-kh godov.* Tom 6. *Vosstaniya, bunty i zabastovki zaklyuchennykh* (Moskva: ROSSPEN, 2004), p. 88.
16 Barnes, *Death and Redemption,* p. 205.
17 Kozlov, *Istoriya stalinskogo GULAGa*, p. 86.
18 Dobson, *Khrushchev's Cold Summer*, p. 39.
19 Barnes, *Death and Redemption,* p. 207.
20 Healey, *Russian Homophobia*, p. 44.
21 Hardy, *GULAG after Stalin*, p. 33.
22 Ibid., p. 73.
23 Ibid., p. 33.
24 Ibid.
25 GARF, f. P-9414, op. 1, delo 2882, l. 79. Among other corrective labour colonies where Yegorov's decree was circulated were the following: Karagandinskii, Vorkutinskii, Kargopol'skii, Angarskii, Ivdel'skii, Severo-Kuzbasskii, Unzhen'skii, Usol'skii, Sibirskii, Vyatskii and North-Eastern corrective labour camps. The decree was also circulated to the Directorate of Corrective Labour Camps and Colonies (UITLK) of Kazakhstan, Ukraine and Khabarovskii krai.
26 GARF, f. P-9414, op. 1, delo 2896, l. 144. The document is undated.
27 Ibid. For a brief biography of Bakin, see: Kokurin and Petrov, *GULAG*, p. 800. Political crimes, that is, 'counterrevolutionary crimes', were prosecuted under Article 58. See: Oleg V. Khlevniuk, *The History of the Gulag: From Collectivisation to the Great Terror* (New Haven and London: Yale University Press, 2004), pp. 365–6.
28 Adi Kuntsman, '"With a Shade of Disgust": Affective Politics of Sexuality and Class in Memoirs of the Stalinist Gulag', *Slavic Review* 68, no. 2 (Summer 2009).
29 GARF, P-9414, op. 1, delo 2896, l. 144.
30 Ibid.
31 Ibid.
32 Barnes, *Death and Redemption*, p. 250.
33 Hardy, *GULAG after Stalin*, p. 89.
34 GARF, f. P-9414, op. 1a, delo 604, l. 78. The document did not mention Soblov's name.
35 Ibid., l. 79.
36 Ibid.

37 Ibid., l. 64.
38 Ibid., l. 65.
39 Ibid., l. 66.
40 Ibid., l. 65.
41 GARF, f. P-9414, op. 1 dop., delo 606, l. 153.
42 Ibid., l. 158.
43 Ibid., l. 162.
44 Rustam Alexander, 'New Light on the Prosecution of Soviet Homosexuals under Brezhnev', *Russian History* 46 (2019): 16–18.
45 GARF, f. P-9414, op. 1 dop., delo 606, ll. 159–62.
46 Ibid., l. 160.
47 For a brief biography of Kholodkov, see: Kokurin and Petrov, *GULAG*, p. 854.
48 GARF, f. P-9414, op. 1 dop., delo 605, l. 106.
49 Ibid.
50 Ibid.
51 GARF, f. P-9414, op. 1 dop., delo 606, l. 11.
52 Ibid.
53 Ibid., l. 12.
54 Ibid.
55 Hardy, *GULAG after Stalin*, p. 85.
56 Dan Healey, 'Lives in the Balance: Weak and Disabled Prisoners and the Biopolitics of the GULAG', *Kritika: Explorations in Russian and Eurasian History* 16, no. 3 (2015): 528.
57 Anne Applebaum, *GULAG: A History* (New York and London: Doubleday, 2003), p. 369.
58 Healey, 'Lives in the Balance', p. 533.
59 Ibid.
60 Ibid., p. 535.
61 Golfo Alexopoulos, *Illness and Inhumanity in Stalin's GULAG* (New Haven and London: Yale University Press, 2017), p. 160.
62 Ibid., p. 162.
63 Ibid., p. 164.
64 Ibid., p. 168.
65 Ibid., p. 175.
66 GARF, f. P-9414, op. 1, delo 2888, l. 91. The last name of the author at the end of the report is illegible.
67 Ibid.
68 Similar anxiety about the younger inmates being drawn into homosexuality was voiced by scholars studying American prisons in 1955: John Bartlow Martin, *Break Down the Walls* (New York: Ballantine, 1954), pp. 168–9.

69 Deborah A. Field, 'Communist Morality and Meanings of Private Life in Post-Stalinist Russia, 1953–1964' (PhD dissertation, University of Michigan, 1996), p. 116.
70 On the concern of the Khrushchev leadership about juvenile delinquency, see: Ann Livschiz, 'De-Stalinizing Soviet Childhood: The Quest for Moral Rebirth, 1953–58', in *The Dilemmas of De-Stalinisation: Negotiating Cultural and Social Change in the Khrushchev Era*, ed. Polly Jones (London and New York: Routledge, 2006), p. 117. On hooliganism under Khrushchev, see: Brian LaPierre, *Hooligans in Khrushchev's Russia* (Wisconsin: University of Wisconsin Press, 2012).
71 On Russian and Soviet prison subcultures, see: Healey, *Homosexual Desire*, pp. 230–7. On the fate of 'degraded' persons in Soviet prison, see: Essig, *Queer in Russia*, pp. 7–13. On homosexual relations in Russian and Soviet prisons, see: Vladimir Kozlovskii, *Argo russkoi gomoseksual'noi subkul'tury: Materialy k izucheniyu* (Benson: Chalidze Publications, 1986), pp. 88–118. On the 'stigma of bottom-status' in Russian gay culture, see: Dan Healey, 'Active, Passive, and Russian: The National Idea in Gay Men's Pornography', *Russian Review* 69, no. 2 (April 2010): 210–30.
72 GARF, f. P-9414, op. 1, delo 2888, l. 186.
73 Ibid., ll. 205–6.
74 Healey, *Homosexual Desire*, p. 241.
75 Dan Healey, 'From Stalinist Pariahs to Subjects of "Managed Democracy": Queers in Moscow, 1945 to the present', in *Queer Cities, Queer Cultures: Europe Since 1945*, ed. Matt Cook and Jennifer V. Evans (London and New York: Bloomsbury Academic, 2014), p. 99.
76 GARF, f. P-9414, op. 1, delo 2896, ll. 234–5.
77 Ibid.
78 GARF, f. P-9414, op. 1, delo 2896, l. 216.
79 Healey, *Russian Homophobia*, p. 34.
80 Ibid., p. 214.
81 Ibid.
82 Ibid.
83 Ibid., p. 215.
84 Ibid., p. 194.
85 Ibid., p. 207
86 Ibis., p. 208.
87 GARF, f. P-9414, op. 1, delo 2896, ll. 234–5.
88 Ibid., p. 215.
89 On the crackdown during the McCarthy era, see: David K. Johnson, *The Lavender Scare: The Cold War Persecution of Gays and Lesbians in the Federal Government* (Chicago and London: University of Chicago Press, 2004).

90 Estelle B. Freedman, 'The Prison Lesbian, Race, Class and the Construction of the Aggressive Female Homosexual, 1915–1965', in *Sex, Love, Race: Crossing Boundaries in North American History*, ed. Martha Hodes (New York and London: New York University Press, 1999), p. 428.
91 Ibid., p. 430. Freedman tells us about a book on prison lesbianism by Katherine Sullivan in 1956, which argued that after engaging in homosexuality in prison, former women prisoners developed an addiction to lesbianism and built their life around such practices on the outside.
92 On anxieties of de-Stalinisation, see: Polly Jones, ed., *The Dilemmas of De-Stalinisation: Negotiating Cultural and Social Change in the Khrushchev Era* (London and New York: Routledge, 2006). Melanie Ilič argued that under Khrushchev 'the Soviet government was keen to increase the overall birth rate'. See: Melanie Ilič, 'Women in the Khrushchev Era: An Overview', in *Women in the Khrushchev Era*, ed. Melanie Ilič, Susan Reid and Lynne Attwood (Basingstoke: Palgrave Macmillan, 2004), p. 6.
93 Deborah A. Field, 'Irreconcilable Differences: Divorce and Conceptions of Private Life in the Khrushchev Era', *Russian Review* 57, no. 4 (1998): 599–613.
94 GARF, f. P-9414, op. 1, delo 2896, ll. 233–4.
95 American prison officers also framed the problem of lesbianism in prison as a 'sexual problem'. Freedman tells us that, by the 1960s, psychologists and criminologists writing on lesbianism suggested that homosexuals 'present the greatest sexual problem' in women's prisons. See: Freedman, 'Prison Lesbian', p. 423.
96 GARF, f. P-9414, op. 1, delo 2896, l. 172.
97 Ibid., l. 193.
98 See Velikanov's report, where he stated the opinion of medical professionals working in Siblag under his leadership. GARF, f. P-9414, op. 1, delo 2896, l. 144.
99 Susan E. Reid, 'Women in the Home', in *Women in the Khrushchev Era*, edited by Melanie Ilič, Susan E. Reid and Lynne Attwood (Basingstoke: Palgrave Macmillan, 2004), p. 160.
100 GARF, f. P-9414, op. 1, delo 2896, l. 218.
101 Kon, *Sexual Revolution in Russia*, p. 101. The stress on the necessity to 'rechannel' sexual energy of Soviet people for the good of the collective work and life was a common trope in the Khrushchev-era sex education campaign, which will be examined in Chapter 2.
102 GARF, f. P-9414, op. 1, delo 2896, l. 222.
103 Ibid., l. 227.
104 Ibid., l. 228.

105 Hardy, *GULAG after Stalin*, p. 82.
106 GARF, f. P-9414, op. 1, delo 2896, l. 228.
107 LaPierre, *Hooligans in Khrushchev's Russia*, p. 145.
108 Ibid., p. 132.
109 Ibid., p. 151.
110 Ibid.
111 Ibid., p. 282.
112 Ibid.
113 Ibid., p. 286.
114 GARF, f. P-9414, op. 1, delo 2896, l. 231.
115 Ibid., l. 232.
116 Ibid., l. 225.
117 GARF, f. P-9414, op. 1 dop., delo 608, l. 72.
118 Ibid.
119 Ibid.
120 Ibid., l. 74.
121 Ibid., ll. 75–6.
122 GARF, f. P-9414, op. 1 dop., delo 608, l. 76.
123 Hardy, *GULAG after Stalin*, p. 91.

2

Same-sex desire and sex education under Khrushchev (1956–64)

During the Khrushchev thaw, from the early 1950s to the early 1960s, the Soviet state launched a campaign on sex education, publishing a whole series of manuals on the subject. This represented a significant shift in the official Soviet policy towards sex: from prevailing silence on sex issues of the Stalin era to their examination in sex education brochures aimed at Soviet young people. These manuals were introduced in the hope of restricting the sexual activity of Soviet young people and in order to raise their awareness of venereal diseases, abortion and human physiology. In addition, some of these publications featured passages on homosexuality, labelling it a 'sexual perversion'.

The emergence of these sex education manuals represented the Foucauldian 'pedagogisation of children's sex' and a genuine attempt by the Soviet state to impose a 'medical-sexual regime' on Soviet families in the 1950s and 1960s. Doctors and educators, who wrote these manuals, urged parents and teachers to put children's sexuality under close surveillance, looking out for any sort of suspicious behaviour and signs of sexual deviance.[1] As Foucault argued, European governments of the eighteenth century took charge of sex through medical and pedagogical discourse because they perceived it to be a vital element of economic and political development. The question of sex had multiple facets: birth and death rates, life expectancy, fertility, demographics and people's individual health, so governments sought to exercise control over these issues to maximise the collective and individual forces of their societies.[2] Similar considerations animated the Soviet pedagogisation of sex during the Khrushchev era: post-demographic crisis and the need for repopulation of the country warranted greater controls over the sexual lives of the young Soviet generation, especially non-productive sexual practices such as masturbation and homosexuality. The pedagogic discourse on sex and homosexuality, which I examine in this chapter, was to become an instrument of such control.

The Soviet sex education campaign was not merely about the economy of population. During the Khrushchev period, the main focus of sex education manuals shifted from an attempt to eliminate 'the vestiges of the capitalist past' to a focus on confronting 'ideological diversions' of the West. Soviet sex education also assisted Soviet leadership in its continued attempts to raise a generation of New Soviet People, who would adhere to the principles of communist morality, abstain from premarital sex and promiscuity and avoid sexual perversions. The latter issue was especially difficult to address.

Although homosexuality was practically unmentionable in almost all public sources of the time and was a very uncomfortable topic to discuss, the authors of some of these sex education manuals felt compelled to comment on it in their texts. Censorship and reluctance to admit that such phenomena existed in Soviet conditions certainly prevented them from addressing this topic at length and thus their thoughts on homosexuality do not easily lend themselves to scholarly analysis. Other authors were silent on the issue altogether. Yet their silence transmitted unspoken anxieties about possible sexual perversions in which adolescents could engage. In reading these manuals, I am guided by Michel Foucault, who wrote: 'Silence itself – the things one declines to say, or is forbidden to name, the discretion that is required between different speakers is … an element that functions alongside the things said, with them and in relation to them.'[3] Indeed, those authors who chose not to speak about homosexuality in the manuals did speak about adolescents' 'early sexual arousal' and the importance of curbing it. When trying to decipher the ambiguities and the silences surrounding the issue of homosexuality in the manuals, I turn to Khrushchev- and Brezhnev-era specialist books on medicine, and other sources hidden from the public eye, where homosexuality was discussed with candour. The authors of these manuals emphasised the strong connection between 'early sexual arousal' and homosexuality, suggesting that the authors of sex education manuals indeed sought deflection from homosexuality.

Stalinist sexophobia and failed attempts to talk about sex

Before we proceed to the Khrushchev era, it is useful to say a few words about discussions on sex under Stalin. Scholars have argued that the Stalin era was a period of repressive sexual policies and gender ideology: abortion and homosexuality became a crime; psychoanalysis had been banned and Sigmund Freud denounced as a bourgeois scientist.[4] Those few Stalin-era public sources discussing the issue of sex downplayed its significance in Soviet society. *The Great Soviet Encyclopaedia* (1940) proclaimed: 'In Soviet society there is no sex question as a complex problem of relationships between sexes, because everything necessary is provided to eliminate disharmony between biological demands and needs of a personality, which is inherent in the capitalist society.' According to the author, there was no need for sex education either:

> The system of upbringing of children and adolescents in the USSR is based on cultivation of ardent love for the motherland, comradeliness (tovarishchestvo), love of labour, respect for the woman as a comrade in labour. A mass of creative impulses is created, diverting the youth's attention from excessive sexual pursuits (chrezmernoe polovoe uvlechenie) and rechannelling its energy to joyful labour (radostnyi trud) and healthy recreation (zdorovyi otdykh), combined with physical culture.[5]

Yet, despite the severe sexual conservatism and official downplaying of the issue of sex, Stalin-era doctors made attempts to pitch their manuscripts on sex education manuals to editors. We can find one such manual, which was never published, in the State Archive of the Russian Federation. The manuscript was titled 'On Sex Education' (1946) and was produced by K. M. Kushnirchuk, a doctor from Poltava. It dealt with a variety of issues, ranging from sexual hygiene to marital life, with 'sexual perversions' discussed in the last section, which spanned as many as fourteen pages.[6]

Kushnirchuk asserted that there were two types of homosexuality – 'congenital' (vrozhdennaya) and 'acquired' (priobretennaya). The latter manifested itself 'in the form of pederasty', which 'had a negative effect on one's behaviour'.[7] While the author was pessimistic about medical treatment of 'congenital homosexuality', arguing that in such cases 'the prognosis was negative', he added that 'acquired' homosexuality was merely a 'bad habit' and could be eradicated with the same methods employed for combating masturbation: 'Acquired homosexuality is perfectly correctable (vpolne ispravim) under the influence of the similar methods employed for correction of masturbation.'[8] In cases of 'malignant pederasty' (zlokachestvennaya pederastiya), the author recommended psychotherapy and hypnosis.[9] Kushnirchuk mentioned lesbianism too, using an archaic term, 'sapphism' (safizm): 'One of the types of homosexuality is safizm and lesbian love, which can be encountered among women and only among adults.'[10] The manuscript, however, was sharply criticised by the reviewer – professor of biology V. Efimov. On 30 May 1946 Efimov produced a two-page review of Kushnirchuk's book, blasting the author for daring to speak about sexual perversions in a manual intended for a young audience: 'And then the author proceeds to sexual perversions. A question arises here – does the author really cover sexual perversions in his lectures on sex education?'[11] Efimov concluded that the author's manuscript 'cannot be and must not be used in sex education of the youth' and 'can only bring harm to the youth'.[12]

Kushnirchuk's treatment of sexual perversions is illuminating and we should consider it when examining the content of the Khrushchev-era sex education manuals. The most noteworthy point here is that this Stalin-era sex educator, writing about sex education, equated homosexuality with masturbation, framing both as part of the same construct – sexual perversion. He also believed that homosexuality, just like masturbation, could be 'acquired' and was a 'bad habit', and therefore could be eradicated with the same techniques. As I will show, Khrushchev-era sex educators, who discussed masturbation but preferred to avoid discussions of homosexuality, could have similar views.

The publication of the first Soviet sex education manual, *Healthy Marriage and Healthy Family* (1948), with a print run of 200,000 copies, written by Soviet doctor L. A. Zalkind, is also striking.[13] It attests to the fact that despite the rigid ideological controls and total silence about sex peculiar to the Stalin era, there were still professionals who expressed the need for sex education among young people. The publication of this manual appears to be the result of the government's aspiration to boost the declining birth rate. As Mie Nakachi has shown, the issue became especially acute following the war: living conditions were poor, there were significantly fewer men, and the privations and horrors of war led to increased infertility rates among women.[14] Zalkind's manual gave instructions on how to have a long, fulfilling marital life. It reminded readers that families with multiple children were given extensive support by the government; mothers who managed to give birth to as many as ten children were awarded an honorary title of 'mother heroine'.[15] Masturbation was framed as a pernicious habit that deprived young people of their energy and ability to have a healthy sexual life. Zalkind also covered the issue of abortion, framing it as a significant threat to women's health and an act against the state.[16] There was a substantial ideological component in his manual too: he treated questions of sex education with an overt Marxist gloss, heralding the victory of socialism in Soviet society and crediting it with women's liberation and equality of rights with men.[17] According to Zalkind, the victory of socialism had raised public consciousness and the cultural level of Soviet people; the old 'communist morality' and its emphasis on the building of communism replaced 'bourgeois morality'.[18] However, to Zalkind's chagrin, some of its features – adultery, the disrespectful treatment of women, even depravity, still ailed Soviet society and needed to be eliminated through communist sex education.[19]

Zalkind contrasted the achievements of the socialist revolution and communist morality to life in the West and the 'hypocritical' bourgeois morality, which supposedly permeated Western society. He claimed that Western youth resorted to the services of prostitutes and was generally prone to promiscuity and sexual depravity.[20] The lifestyle of Soviet young people, according to Zalkind, was completely antithetical: Soviet adolescents were more concerned with the interests of the collective and society, their approach to marriage and family was more 'critical and conscious' and their sexual attitudes were more restrained.[21] Three years later, *Healthy Marriage and Healthy Family* (1951) was republished with a print run of 100,000 copies, having undergone several changes in its content. The revised edition further emphasised the dangerousness of the 'vestiges of the capitalist past' lingering in Soviet people's consciousness and reframed some chapters accordingly. Whereas the first chapter of the first edition was simply titled 'Marriage in Bourgeois Society and in Our Country', the title of the first chapter in the second edition was more elaborate:

'Marriage in Bourgeois Society and the Fight against the Vestiges of Bourgeois Attitudes towards Marriage in Our Country'.[22]

These two editions of the same-sex education manual were the only successful attempts by Soviet doctors to examine sex education and bring their ideas within the reach of the Soviet reading public under Stalin. Their publication suggests that different perspectives regarding sex education were apparently allowed within a tolerable range of discord. While Zalkind deplored parents' inability to engage in the sex education of their children due to their own ignorance, he was also cautious not to challenge the official Soviet policy towards sex, which sought to prevent young children from reaching early sexual maturation. Zalkind constantly reminded his readers that sex education, if conducted improperly, might trigger premature sexual curiosity.[23] His inconsistent views on sex education, as well as his repetitive warnings about the existing 'capitalist vestiges of the past', are discernible also in the narratives of the first Khrushchev-era sex education manuals.

After Stalin's death in March 1953, the so-called period of the 'thaw' set in. This was characterised by important transformations in Soviet society distinct from the Stalinist period: millions of Soviet political prisoners were amnestied and released from labour camps, and the Soviet Union became more open to the outside world. Khrushchev's Secret Speech to the XX Communist Party Congress in February 1956 launched the process of de-Stalinisation, which manifested itself in the significant relaxation of censorship and gave more freedom of information in the media. This freedom extended to issues surrounding sexuality, gender and the family: the Khrushchev leadership decriminalised abortion in 1955 and embarked on further 'pedagogisation' of the issue of sex by publishing more sex education manuals. The primary focus of these was the physiology of female bodies and pregnancy, as well as the undesirability of abortion and the associated medical complications.[24] Apart from demonising abortion, Soviet educators attempted to control the sexual behaviour of Soviet young people and inculcate sexual morality in them. Health officials observed and deplored Soviet people's romantic trysts with foreigners, clandestine abortions, adultery, pregnancy out of wedlock and thriving venereal diseases.[25] Concerns about the sexual immorality of young people were an extension of broader anxieties about the perceived failure of the younger generation to meet the Soviet leadership's expectations for the New Man and Woman.[26]

'Hands above the blanket': anxieties about sexual perversions in Khrushchev-era sex education manuals (1956–60)

Sex education was a difficult goal to accomplish. The Stalin-era attitudes towards sex were still fresh in people's minds, including those of Soviet officials responsible for this sex education campaign. The reluctance of sex educators of the early Khrushchev era to talk about topics even distantly related to sex is obvious in the archival transcript of a discussion of the board meeting of the RSFSR Ministry of Education held on 29 December 1955. The agenda for the meeting was a manuscript of a new manual on biology titled *Human Anatomy and Physiology*.[27] During the discussion, one of its participants, V. N. Belyaeva, noted that the book had one significant flaw – it featured an 'excessively detailed description of sex cells and reproduction'. She went on to say:

> It seems to me that we should be more cautious with issues related to sex education. We are talking here about schoolchildren who are fourteen years old … A detailed description of sex cells in the process of fertilisation may invite a host of extra questions in the classroom – they are unnecessary and undesirable.[28]

Belyaeva also argued for a less explicit description of the human body and recommended ignoring the most sensitive topics: 'It seems to me that we may skip the descriptions of buttocks and the pelvic area.'[29] She also suggested that the process of reproduction should be sketched out in general terms and preferably using the example of animals: 'It is enough to indicate that the human fertilisation process is like that of mammals, in general terms, ignoring spermatozoon, egg cells, fertilisation.'[30]

Apparently, it was this continued reluctance of Soviet officials to provide explicit information on sexual issues to adolescents that delayed the publication of sex education manuals during the first years under Khrushchev. In 1958 a rural doctor from Ukraine, Anatolii Stankov, published a manual, *Sex Life and Family*, with a print run of 200,000 copies, which instructed parents and teachers on how to deal with issues of adolescent sexuality.[31] Stankov alerted his readers: 'Educators and parents should be able to notice the earliest deviations in sexual behaviour of adolescents, as they are easier to prevent than fix.' He also argued that parents should direct children's and adolescents' sexual instinct from an early age in 'the right direction', raising their awareness of the 'vestiges of the past' and helping them protect themselves from moral degeneration, sexual disorders and venereal disease.[32] Stankov made a number of striking statements: he proclaimed that family and marriage were not private matters in the Soviet Union, that young men and women were fully developed for sexual lives by the age of twenty-five and that they should start having sex only after they were married.[33]

Stankov also instructed parents on how to prevent the 'early awakening' of sexual desire in their children. It was especially important because, as a result of such an awakening, adolescents, both boys and girls, engaged in masturbation. If girls engaged in masturbation for a long time, then it would be difficult for them to feel sexual pleasure during 'normal' sexual intercourse. Furthermore, in rare cases, masturbation could lead some females to develop an 'increased sexual need' (povyshchennaya polovaya potrebnost') or 'nymphomania'. As for boys, masturbation could deprive them of energy, lead to sexual impotence and negatively affect their behaviour in society: 'Focusing their thoughts on various sexual experiences, masturbators (onanisty) often seek solitude, avoid people, become secretive and shy.'[34] To prevent early sexual awakening, Stankov advised parents to avoid touching children's genitals when drying them off in the bathroom and to make sure that they wore comfortable clothes. It was crucial that adolescents had their hands above the blanket during sleep and that they got up immediately from bed after waking.[35] Stankov's recommendations ended with a categorical piece of advice: 'Under no circumstances should two children or an adult with a child be allowed to share one bed.'[36] This advice apparently reflected the author's anxiety about the crowded conditions in which many Soviet people lived and the unwanted sexual experimentation that it could trigger between adolescents. Indeed, as scholars have shown, the problem of living space was still acute under Khrushchev: despite the massive housing campaign, apartments of the time were small and remained in 'multiple occupancy', typically because of sets of parents cohabiting with relatives.[37] A child sharing a bed with an adult was an even more disturbing product of housing overcrowding – since the latter might be a homosexual.

Although Stankov did not mention the issue of sexual perversions in his manual (such discussions were considered inappropriate for young audiences, and even if his initial manuscript had such references, they would have probably been cut out by censors), we may discern unspoken anxieties about same-sex attraction in his narrative. As I noted, Stalin-era doctors deemed both masturbation and homosexuality as sexual perversions. Under Khrushchev, doctors discussing masturbation and 'early sexual awakening' in their medical articles argued that these phenomena were conducive to sexual perversions. For instance, Soviet doctor Yevgenii Popov wrote in the *Soviet Medical Encyclopaedia* that sexual perversions stemmed from the early 'arousal' of 'children's and adolescents' sexuality'.[38] Brezhnev-era police officers underscored the link between masturbation and 'early sexual awakening' and homosexuality even more explicitly. They did so in classified handbooks for law-enforcement agencies which were not available for regular Soviet readers. The author of one wrote:

> Taking the path of homosexuality is undoubtedly facilitated by early sexual life, which leads to satiation and leads an individual to seek new emotions. It is also facilitated by protracted masturbation, which psychologically alienates the individual engaging in it and makes him seek fulfilment of sexual desire with individuals of the same sex.[39]

The fear that masturbation could cause homosexuality was not unique to Soviet sex educators and doctors – as Dagmar Herzog has shown, East German moralists in the late 1950s also warned that excessive sexual activity and self-pleasuring could drive people to 'perversities'.[40]

Workers and directors in Soviet juvenile colonies also developed a concern about sexual perversions among young prisoners and insisted on the importance of sex education. In 1958, the same year that Stankov's manual was published, Doctor Enver Mamedovich Rakhimov wrote a manual, *On the Question of Physical Development of Wards in Juvenile Colonies* (1958), for the workers of the Department of Juvenile Colonies of the Interior Ministry of the

USSR.[41] The manual dealt with questions of health, hygiene and the sexual maturation of the children in colonies. Rakhimov, apparently, staked his entire career on the sexuality of inmates in juvenile colonies and lesbianism in particular. I have been unable to find any biographical information on him, but I came across a reference to an unpublished manuscript of his work on lesbianism between underage female inmates. It was titled 'On the Question of Sexual Perversions in the Juvenile Corrective Labour Institutions of the MVD' (1952) and found in a manual, *Sexual Perversions and Criminal Liability* (1972), aimed at Soviet investigators.[42] Rakhimov's work provides another piece of striking evidence that under Stalin doctors and sex educators engaged with the issue of homosexuality.

Unlike Stankov's book, which was published and available for the readers of 'free society', Rakhimov's manual was intended solely for the official use of prison wardens and therefore featured more frank discussions on sexual perversions. His handbook explicitly emphasised the link between 'early awakening of sexual desire' and sexual perversions, claiming that correct sex education was the best way to prevent them. Advising the workers of the juvenile colonies on how to prevent 'masturbation (onanism) and other sexual perversions', Rakhimov wrote:

> In the conditions of juvenile colonies, one of the main reasons for masturbation and other sexual perversions may be considered breaches of sanitary and hygienic norms: overcrowded dormitories (skuchennost' v obshchezhitiyakh), two pupils sleeping in the same bed or three pupils sleeping in two beds, insufficient supervision over the adolescents, especially at night when sexual perversions become critical (prinimayut ostryi kharakter).[43]

Rakhimov's belief that adolescents sharing the same bed was conducive to sexual perversions lends further credence to my argument that sex educators like Stankov sought to prevent homosexuality among adolescents in 'free society' by advising parents to disapprove of such a practice.

According to Rakhimov, it was important that underage convicts received proper information on sex education:

> Educators, teachers, masters and medical professionals must consistently, truthfully and carefully talk with youngsters about sex life (polovaya zhizn') considering their understanding and age. It should

> be done so as not to focus their attention on unnecessary details and wake unhealthy curiosity. At the same time, they should be protected from dishonest (nedobrosovestnyi) and vulgar (poshlyi) information emanating from various sources.[44]

Rakhimov maintained that good hygiene 'plays an important role in the prevention of sexual perversions'.[45] He advised excluding any external factors that might cause sexual arousal in children. For example, he recommended against hot baths as 'they cause a strong rush of blood to sex organs and predispose to sexual perversions'.[46] Finally, in order to prevent sexual perversions, Rakhimov advised taking special care with the young people whose 'sexual maturation (polovoe sozrevanie) outruns (operezhat') other features of physical maturation (fizicheskaya zrelost')'. He advised his readers to keep such children away from any external sexual stimuli, both physical and verbal. He also urged the operatives of the colony to refrain from 'juicy talks' (pikantnye razgovory), 'salacious anecdotes' (pokhabnye anekdoty) and 'seductive dress' (soblaznitel'nye kostyumy) that could lead to 'premature development of sexual feelings in children and adolescents'.

Another Soviet physician, Tigran Atarov, gave somewhat similar advice in his manual *Questions of Sex Education* (1959), published with a print run of 100,000 copies. Certainly, he did not talk about sexual perversions explicitly, but he did stress the point that adults should refrain from inappropriate behaviour in the presence of children. According to the author, if parents allowed themselves to demonstrate excessive affection to one another in front of their child, this might infringe on the moral development of their offspring.[47] Atarov was also concerned about the early awakening of sexual desire and masturbation. He recommended that parents prevent their children from 'contemplating the sex life of domestic animals and birds' and not allow children to spend time on their own (uedinyat'sya). He advised parents not to leave children unattended and keep them close to the collective.[48] Young people's dietary habits had to be healthy as well: excessive consumption of sweets, spices and smoked food might trigger 'increased sexual arousal'.[49] Working conditions were also of paramount importance: those young people who worked in restaurants or cafes were particularly susceptible to premarital liaisons and the unhealthy awakening of sexual feelings. Atarov advised employers to hire only adults to work in such places.[50] It is worth noting that some law-enforcement operatives believed that 'public catering facilities' (predpriyatiya obshchestvennogo pitaniya) were often used by homosexuals to find new acquaintances: 'many homosexuals deliberately seek employment in public catering facilities, because it gives them an opportunity to establish a wide circle of acquaintances, discern homosexuals among them and draw new individuals in sodomy.' It is therefore possible that Atarov's prescriptions about the inadmissibility of hiring young people to work in cafes and restaurants were informed by similar anxieties.

'Homosexuals … satisfy themselves with adolescents and youngsters'

In 1960 the Soviet State Medical Publishing House brought out more brochures on sexual education: *The Youth Becomes a Man* (1960), written by a Czechoslovakian professor of sexology, Josef Hynie, with a print run of 200,000 copies, and *Questions of Sex* (1960), by East German hygienist Rudolf Neubert, with a print run of 100,000 copies.[51] These books stood in stark contrast to the previously published Soviet manuals on sex education. They dared to open a relatively frank discussion on sex with young readers without lengthy discussions of 'capitalist vestiges of the past' and 'communist morality'. Most importantly, they explicitly discussed homosexuality. The authors of these books came from Czechoslovakia and East Germany and were sexologists with a solid international reputation. Indeed, by the late 1950s, sexology was already an established and legitimate field of academic and scientific inquiry in Czechoslovakia. At the time of the publication of his manual in the USSR, Josef Hynie directed the Czech Institute of Sexology in Prague, which had been functioning for over forty years.[52] As I will show in the following chapters, sexological science from other socialist countries such as Czechoslovakia and East Germany exerted significant influence on the discussions of homosexuality not only among Soviet sex educators, but among Soviet doctors and legal scholars too.

It is striking that censors allowed discussions on homosexuality to appear in the Soviet versions of Hynie's and Neubert's manuals, considering their anxieties about the potential of such discussions to spark 'unhealthy interest' in children. We know, however, that the inclusion of these discussions was not merely due to the Soviet censors' and editors' oversight: they abridged the original versions and edited out some details.[53] Apparently, there was a faction of Soviet censors and editors who saw value in bringing the issue of homosexuality to the attention of young people. Hynie's manual, for example, depicted homosexuals as insidious and dangerous individuals who preyed on youth. The author encouraged young people to report such individuals to the police:

> One can find people who have abnormal attraction to individuals of the same sex; they are called gomoseksualisty (homosexuals). Gomoseksualisty are aroused by and satisfy themselves with adolescents and youngsters, even though the latter have a normal interest in girls. Gomoseksualisty go all out to gain young people's affection; they buy sweets and cigarettes for youngsters, tickets to the cinema, give them money, help them to do homework and generally pretend that they unselfishly love youngsters. However, after such preparation, they sooner or later proceed to act. Do not let them touch you! Do not be shy about reporting them to your parents or educators, do not hesitate to report such attempts aimed at you or other young men! Both parents and educators will willingly help. Homosexuality is a punishable crime, and gomoseksualisty are perfectly aware of that: that is why it is not difficult to get rid of them![54]

Similar anxieties about predatory homosexuals permeated Khrushchev-era manuals on forensic medicine. One of them, *Forensic Medicine* (1960), related a sodomy case involving a man who seduced adolescents with the help of sweets and alcohol, and had sex with them in a park in a Soviet city from September to December 1959. The investigators established that one of the adolescents spent the entire night with the man, committing three acts of sodomy as a passive partner.[55] It is worth noting that in 1960 US educators framed homosexuality in the same way, presenting homosexuals as child molesters. The controversial findings of Kinsey's studies and the growing Cold War hysteria over homosexual subversion made homosexuality a matter of nationwide concern, urging American educators to tackle the problem. In 1961 the police department of Englewood, California, made an educational film *Boys Beware*, which depicted homosexual men as child molesters.[56]

Neubert's *Questions of Sex* presented homosexuality in a different way.[57] Unlike Hynie's alarmist tone and warnings about the danger presented by predatory homosexuals, Neubert framed homosexuality as a medical matter, expanding on its presumed causes and suggesting some ways to treat it. He emphasised the biological nature of homosexuality: 'the reason for such a deviation is the incorrect development of endocrine glands. There are people with alterations in the pancreas who suffer from childhood with diabetes. In the same way, there are people whose sex glands develop incorrectly from childhood.'[58] Even in suggesting the congenital nature of homosexuality, Neubert deemed it necessary to treat homosexuality with hormone preparations, surgery and psychotherapy: 'Medical science has found ways to treat this anomaly partially with hormonal drugs or by means of surgery through the transplantation of glandular tissue. However, more often, an already tried medical method is employed – psychotherapy, that is, an educative influence imposed by the doctor on the patient.'[59] Unlike Hynie, who advised his readers to report homosexuals to law-enforcement agencies, Neubert's attitude seems to be somewhat more lenient: homosexuals had to be treated, rather than just removed from society – a similar point of view would be promoted by Soviet sexologists later in the 1960s, as I will show in Chapter 3. Neubert did, however, note that such treatment was essential: 'People with such deviations from the norm cannot have healthy relations with people around them and that is why they are to be subject to serious treatment.'[60]

Neubert also argued that incorrect upbringing could be a possible cause of the development of sexual perversions, although these cases were encountered less frequently than those where sexual perverts were genetically predisposed: 'Perverted inclinations may appear in individual cases as a result of a depraved upbringing or under some other unfavourable circumstances.' These 'circumstances' might occur as a result of parents' irresponsible attitude to their children: 'Deviations from the norm can be prevented provided that parents pay enough attention to their children. If parents are busy with their own business and amusements while children are on their own ... there is a danger that this will produce some undesirable phenomena.'[61] Lack of occupation was another reason for homosexuality and sexual perversions: 'A person whose life is not filled with joyful labour seeks to make use of his energy in various follies (sumasbrodstvo).' Thus, in a socialist society, where collective labour was of the utmost importance, instances of perversions were an exception: 'All these phenomena are more characteristic of the obsolete, decaying capitalist world, rather than a developing and growing society. Often various perversions are the consequence of satiety and a frivolous way of life. In the majority of cases this can be said about the perverted progeny of rich families or antisocial elements.'[62]

Detrimental Western influences: sexual perversions and anti-Western propaganda

Despite Soviet health officials' understanding of the importance of sex education, manuals with advice on how to lead one's sex life were not published frequently. As Soviet professor of psychology V. N. Kolbanovskii explained in the medical journal *Soviet Healthcare*, there was a significant divergence of opinion on the issue among doctors.[63] This was coupled with the institutional sluggishness of the Ministry of Education and other related governmental bodies.[64] The publication of sex education manuals, however, was somewhat expedited in the wake of the June 1963 Plenum of the Central Committee of the Communist Party. The decision to organise the Plenum was related to specific political developments in Soviet society in 1961 and 1962 that led the Soviet leadership to believe that 'detrimental Western influences' were seeping into the Soviet Union, corrupting Soviet people's minds. What seemed particularly disturbing for Soviet officials were the 'negative' effects of Western culture, to which Soviet people were now exposed, either on their trips overseas or even at home mingling with foreign tourists visiting the Soviet Union.[65]

The Khrushchev government became concerned about the potentially undesirable consequences that the exchange of tourists between the Soviet Union and the United States might entail as early as 1955, when for the first time Soviet citizens received permission to apply to travel overseas, including to capitalist countries. Only those Soviet citizens 'politically prepared' and 'stable from the perspective of morality and everyday life' were permitted to travel abroad. Accordingly, to prevent Soviet citizens from excessive mingling with foreigners, the Soviet press warned Soviet citizens about Americans engaging in anti-Soviet behaviour. As I will show, there was also anxiety that these increasing interactions with foreigners could result in a greater prevalence of homosexuality in the Soviet Union.

According to Khrushchev himself, some prominent Soviet cultural workers, instead of propagating socialist ideals, had fallen prey to the 'ideological diversion of the West', imitating 'inferior bourgeois traits' in their art which were alien to the Soviet people. On 1 December 1962 he attended an exhibition of paintings and sculptures, organised by the Moscow branch of the Union of Soviet Artists, where he expressed his infuriation at a number of abstract works, which according to him were 'alien' to Soviet people. Khrushchev even suggested that homosexual influences might be at work, calling the art 'pederasty'.[66] On the following day the main Soviet newspaper *Pravda* denounced 'inferior bourgeois traits' in the works of those Soviet cultural workers, labelling them traitors to Soviet 'realistic art'.[67] These anxieties essentially legitimised Khrushchev's move for greater ideological propaganda against bourgeois influences from the West and made him backpedal on almost every front.

To the dismay of the Soviet authorities, Western countries were not the only source of perverse influences. As some criminal cases of that period demonstrate, visitors from African countries with which Khrushchev sought to establish friendly relations exerted no less 'perverse' an influence on Soviet people. On 15 May 1962 the procuracy of the city of Moscow initiated a criminal case against two male students – Ahmed and Khafid, who came to study at the Moscow State University from Zanzibar. The investigation established that on 17 February 1962, at a party in one of the university's dorms, Ahmed met fifteen-year-old Sasha Bolotin, whom he invited to his room. After treating Sasha to cognac, Ahmed committed sodomy with him as an active partner. Several days later, on the university campus, Sasha ran into Ahmed's friend Khafid, who also inclined him to sodomy on several occasions.[68] Sasha's mother, who discovered these homosexual liaisons of her son from an entry in his diary, promptly reported these incidents to the police. After conducting a forensic examination and collecting evidence from eyewitnesses, investigators indicted the African students with sodomy. Hesitant about how to deal with students from Africa, and scholarship holders at that, investigators sent a secret note to the Foreign Ministry for clarification. Eventually the criminal file ended up on the desks of Soviet high-ranking officials Deputy Foreign Minister S. G. Lapin and Deputy Prosecutor General N. V. Zhogin, who ordered the African students to be deported, and closed the criminal case.[69]

The June 1963 Plenum was arranged to tackle the problem of perverse Western influences, while preparing Soviet citizens for ideological confrontation. It was devoted to the 'tasks of ideological battle in contemporary conditions' and stressed the importance of fortifying propaganda in the face of 'the bitter ideological fight in the international arena'.[70] It was decided to 'increase political vigilance' against 'imperialist sabotage' whose displays had already manifested themselves in Soviet society, in the art of some prominent Soviet cultural workers and in some 'depraved' Western theatrical plays shown in Moscow theatres.[71] The delegates of the Plenum coincided in the opinion that 'imperialist ideologies are trying in every way possible to influence Soviet people; their main objective is unstable elements, that is, individuals who are not politically and ideologically case-hardened'.[72] Educational work was claimed to be the most effective means of confronting this malevolent capitalist ideology.[73]

The Plenum led Soviet sex education authors to reframe their discussions of sex education. Soviet physicians were now expected to address issues of sex in a similar anti-Western vein. From this point on, sex education discourse became more defensive: it essentially became an instrument for the dissemination of anti-Western propaganda. While earlier sex education manuals were merely expected to set their narratives around communist morality and 'capitalist vestiges', the authors of sex education manuals published in the wake of the Plenum were apparently expected to extrapolate the Plenum's decisions to their discussions of sex education, suggesting that the main threat to the healthy sex life of the Soviet people was now coming from the West. In fact, one brochure on this point overshadowed all others: the foreword to *On Sex Education* (1964) explicitly stated that the task of sexual education was to prevent young people from acquiring 'deleterious views' on sex, as the 'deleterious ideological influence of the West with its propagation of the animal importance of sexual attraction is still insinuating itself into our country in different forms'.[74] The authors of another manual, *Marital Hygiene* (1964), stated: 'Unfortunately the pernicious influence of bourgeois ideology, dominating the literature and arts of the capitalist countries, is taking its toll on a group of less stable representatives of Soviet youth in regard to morals.'[75] The eradication of negative bourgeois influence required the joint work of parents, educators and doctors.[76] The anxieties about homosexuality and sexual perversions as a result of Western pernicious influence were also incorporated in the sex education narrative.

Following the Plenum, the authors of sex education manuals devoted significant energy to descriptions of Western society's inherent degeneracy. They suggested that it was the economic structure of the capitalist system that was inherently perverted – they contended that with the emergence of capitalist society and the prevalence of a 'buy and sell' attitude, economic inequality had become widespread, and this forced women to indulge in prostitution as the only means they could resort to in order to survive.[77] The authors of sex education manuals also claimed that young people in the West, having at their disposal such a wide assortment of potentially corrupting institutions (nightclubs, rampant prostitution, cinema and television), became increasingly susceptible to vice.[78] In contrast to Soviet young people, Western youth was merely interested in deriving a transient pleasure from sexual relations.[79] Although these narratives were not new (Zalkind's *Healthy Marriage and Healthy Family* had depicted Western society in a similar way), they had become more pronounced and elaborate, as it was now especially important to expose the 'perverse ideological influence' coming from the West.

Soviet physicians depicted the professedly high level of unemployment in Western society as the root of various kinds of antisocial behaviour: 'Obvious and veiled vices of the social realm corrupt young people in capitalist countries physically and morally and they often adopt the path of a criminal. This is fostered by the prevailing unemployment in the West, which provokes a desire to live for the day.'[80] Soviet conditions, then, were presented as an effective and healthy alternative to the depraved Western world. The aptitude of Soviet institutions to help Soviet people engage more deeply in productive labour and social life was contrasted with Western institutions, which allegedly facilitated the pleasure-seeking desires of the individual: 'Sexual continence in our country can be feasibly achieved, for we have a variety of possibilities for sublimation. Devotion to work, studying, science or social activities alleviate the problem of sexual continence before solemnising a marriage.'[81]

Sex educators now explicitly framed homosexuality as a product of Western societies in line with the June 1963 Plenum's pronouncements. A manual *Hygiene of Sex Life* (1964) presented homosexuality as a result of unemployment in the West:

> the most important reason for homosexuality lies in those conditions of the capitalist countries which prevent starting a family ... unemployment, the uncertainty about the future, lack of housing or its unaffordability, the uncertainty about whether one will be able to provide sustenance for future children – all these factors provide conditions for sexual perversions.[82]

Even though this particular passage does not plainly set out the logic of how homosexuality and uncertainty about the future are linked, a section from another sex education manual published in the same year discloses the inferential link between homosexuality and allegedly precarious social conditions in Western society:

> Sexual debauchery and promiscuity are rooted in a deeply erroneous logic about the necessity to 'get everything out of life' (vzyat' ot zhizni vse) ... in bourgeois countries such thoughts are based on uncertainty about the future, the constant threat of unemployment and the absence of any room for growth for young people in the future.[83]

Promiscuous sexual activity resulting from uncertainty about the future was believed to be the key reason for sexual perversions: 'Promiscuous sexual activity is always related to excess, which leads to satiety, which prompts a desire to irritate the nervous system more actively. This, in turn, leads to sexual perversions.'[84] In the face of ostensibly unreliable Western social institutions and lack of occupation, therefore, young people were believed to become more desperate and sceptical about their future. According to Soviet physicians, they had no other option but to live their lives to the full and welter in endless sexual pleasure (since they could not afford to have a family), which drove them to seek new and sophisticated ways of appeasing their sexual desire, with homosexuality being one of the best options to do that.

The authors of *Hygiene of Sex Life* reluctantly admitted that homosexuality was a phenomenon that might also be found in Soviet society, although very rarely: ‘Along with normal (sexual) attraction, in very rare cases an attraction to the same sex is observed, so-called homosexuality.’ They continued:

> The latter is … the result of the psychopathic alteration of the personality. Socially created reasons for mental perversions, for homosexuality in particular, are military barracks, prisons of the capitalist countries, where many men lead an unhealthy life. The breeders of homosexuality are also private male institutions, which are very common in the West.[85]

The authors made sweeping claims about the roots of homosexuality, not providing any credible evidence for their claims and hampering understanding of the logic of their descriptions. Yet, if one places these claims in the overall narrative on sex and sexual perversions contained in this manual, it becomes clear that the authors did not just randomly refer to homosexuality as a ‘psychopathic alteration of the personality’. An explanation for what might trigger such a condition was essentially provided in the preceding section of *Hygiene of Sex Life*, where the authors discussed ‘excessive sexual desire’, which was an indication of ‘neurasthenia, hysteria and psychasthenia with signs of sexual obsession’.[86] Since, allegedly, homosexuality, like other sexual perversions, stemmed from ‘sexual excess’, then it comes as no surprise that a ‘psychopathic alteration of the personality’ (that is, homosexuality) was its direct result.

Although Soviet physicians did not explain how Western influences could encourage Soviet citizens to become homosexuals, Soviet doctors expressed such fears in their correspondence. For instance, in 1964 the chief venereologist of the Moscow Health Department A. Obukhova observed in her report on venereal disease: ‘Widespread exchange of tourists, long overseas trips, acquaintance with perverted customs of the bourgeois countries have a negative impact on some morally unstable Soviet citizens. Therefore, various sexual perversions, primarily homosexuality and sodomy, have seeped into our country.’[87] A manual for sex crimes from the Brezhnev era further elaborated on the link between Western influences on Soviet people and how exactly it contributed to homosexuality:

> One of the factors contributing to the spread of homosexuality is the influence of corrupt bourgeois ideology on morally unstable people. Such people are intensely searching for foreigners and other persons who have various kinds of pornographic literature, pornographic photographs, products etc. In the future, these objects are used as a means of involving new persons, including minors, in criminal activity.[88]

Conclusion

Although it might appear surprising, Soviet doctors actually attempted to make a case for sex education during the extremely conservative Stalin era. They pitched manuscripts of manuals to editors in which they discussed the issues of children's and adolescents' sexual development. Editors and reviewers were very careful in selecting appropriate materials for publication, censoring and rejecting anything that could be deemed harmful to the younger generation. Homosexuality was one such dangerous topic and any mentions of it in the context of sex education were believed to be inadmissible. The first Stalin-era sex education manual, *Healthy Marriage and Healthy Family* (1948), dealt with the issues of human psychology, sexual relations between men and women, and venereal diseases, avoiding any discussions of 'sexual perversions'. It also delineated the overarching goal of Soviet sex education: the fight against the 'vestiges of the capitalist past', a term that embraced all of the undesirable sexual phenomena existing in Soviet society at the time: venereal disease, extramarital sex and adultery.

With the abolition of criminal penalties for abortion in 1955, Khrushchev attempted to bring the issue of sex and reproduction under the tighter controls of disciplinary discourse. During clinic appointments doctors were expected to educate their patients on the harm of abortion and discourage them from such a practice, while sex education manuals, which were now published more frequently, deployed medical discourse on a larger scale. Apart from tackling abortion, these manuals instructed young people on how to properly lead sexual lives, encouraging them to wait until they were married and to engage in sex only for procreation. The authors of these manuals advised parents to preclude any early sexual awakening of their children by depriving them of any sexual stimuli and redirecting their attention from sex to more productive activities. Some recommendations given in these manuals point to the authors' anxiety about homosexuality and their concern about the emergence of such activity among children with heightened sexual desire. Some manuals, mainly those written by sexologists from communist countries, openly discussed the issue.

As cultural contacts between the Soviet Union and the US expanded under Khrushchev and the Soviet government became more anxious about the consequences, Soviet sex education manuals saw corresponding changes. After the June 1963 Plenum, which was devoted to strategies for confronting the 'ideological influence of the West', Soviet sex education changed its focus from the goal of eliminating 'vestiges of the past' to the fight against the 'advancing bourgeois ideology' that allegedly sought to influence 'unstable elements' in Soviet society. These changes affected the discourse on sexual perversions and homosexuality. Rather than emphasising 'early awakening of sexual desire' as a core rationale for sexual perversions, the authors of sex education manuals published in 1964 claimed that it was Western influences that were the real reason for sexual perversions.

After Khrushchev's removal from power, Soviet sex education manuals continued to be published in the Soviet Union, but with their content now less influenced by anxiety about the 'ideological influence of the West'. Instead, Brezhnev-era sex manuals became more focused on increasing young people's awareness of the physiological aspects of their bodily maturity. Throughout the ensuing 'stagnation' period, homosexuality was mentioned even less frequently and the few allusions to it were apparently informed by Soviet 'sexopathology', which emerged in 1964 and defined it as a medical condition. The emergence of a medical definition of homosexuality will be explored in the following chapter.

How serious were the attempts of the Khrushchev and Brezhnev governments to bring adolescent and adult sexuality under disciplinary controls of discourse? It is certainly difficult to gauge the magnitude of these attempts with complete certainty, yet considering that the sex education manuals were published across the Soviet Union's various republics (despite their somewhat modest print runs, which usually did not exceed 200,000 copies), one may draw the conclusion that these attempts were significant.[89]

Notes

1 Foucault, *History of Sexuality,* p. 42. On the 'pedagogisation' of sex, see p. 104.
2 Ibid., pp. 24–5.
3 Ibid., p. 27.
4 Anna Rotkirch, 'What Kind of Sex Can You Talk About? Acquiring Sexual Knowledge in Three Soviet Generations', in *Living through the Soviet System*, ed. Daniel Bertaux, Paul Thompson and Anna Rotkirch (New Brunswick: Transaction, 2005), p. 99.
5 See D. Gorfin, 'Polovaya zhizn'', in *Bol'shaya sovetskaya entsiklopediya*, 1st edn, vol. 46 (Moscow: Sovetskaya entsiklopediya, 1940), pp. 163–9.
6 GARF, f. 10049, op. 3, delo 98, ll. 1–65.
7 Ibid., ll. 62–4.
8 Ibid., l. 65.
9 Ibid.
10 Ibid.
11 Ibid., ll. 66–7.
12 Ibid.
13 Lev A. Zalkind, *Zdorovyi brak i zdorovaya sem'ya* (Moscow: Medgiz, 1948).
14 Mie Nakachi, 'Abortion Is Killing Us: Women's Medicine and the Dilemmas for Post-war Doctors in the Soviet Union, 1944–48', in *Soviet Medicine: Culture, Practice and Science*, ed. Frances L. Bernstein, Christopher Burton and Dan Healey (DeKalb: Northern Illinois University Press, 2010), pp. 196–7.
15 Zalkind, *Zdorovyi brak*, p. 15.
16 Ibid., p. 21.
17 Ibid., p. 3.
18 Ibid., p. 4.
19 Ibid., p. 9.
20 Ibid., pp. 36–7.
21 Ibid., p. 37.
22 Lev A. Zalkind, *Zdorovyi brak i zdorovaya sem'ya* (Moscow: Medgiz, 1951), p.5.
23 Ibid., p. 62.
24 See for example: Ol'ga Nikonchik, *Abort i ego posledstviya* (Moscow: Medgiz, 1956). On sex education and abortion, see: Field, *Private Life and Communist Morality*.
25 Field, *Private Life and Communist Morality*, pp. 55–6.
26 Juliane Fürst, 'The Arrival of Spring? Changes and Continuities in Soviet Youth Culture and Policy between Stalin and Khrushchev', in

The Dilemmas of De-Stalinisation: Negotiating Cultural and Social Change in the Khrushchev Era, ed. Polly Jones (London and New York: Routledge, 2006), p. 135.

27 GARF, f. A-2306, op. 75, d. 1074, ll. 1–26. I was first alerted to this document by Deborah A. Field's book *Private Life and Communist Morality in Khrushchev's Russia* (2007).

28 Ibid., p. 1.

29 Ibid., p. 3.

30 Ibid.

31 Anatolii G. Stankov, *Polovaya zhizn' i sem'ya* (Kiev: Gosudarstvennoe meditsinskoe izdatel'stvo SSSR, 1958).

32 Ibid., p. 4.

33 Ibid., pp. 19–69.

34 Ibid., p. 90.

35 Ibid., pp. 92–3.

36 Ibid., p. 93.

37 Lynne Attwood, *Gender and Housing in Soviet Russia: Private Life in a Public Space* (Manchester and New York: Manchester University Press, 2010), p. 156.

38 Yevgenii A. Popov, 'Polovye izvrashcheniya', in *Bol'shaya meditsinskaya entsiklopediya,* 2nd edn, vol. 25 (Moscow: Sovetskaya entsiklopediya, 1962), p. 951.

39 Yurii V. Aleksandrov, *Polovye prestupleniya: Prestupniki i poterpevshie* (Kiev: Nauchno-issledovatel'skii i redaktsionno-izdatel'skii otdel Kiev-skoi vysshei shkoly MVD SSSR, 1975), p. 41.

40 Dagmar Herzog, *Sex after Fascism: Memory and Morality in Twenti-eth-Century Germany* (Princeton and Oxford: Princeton University Press, 2005), pp. 196–7.

41 GARF, f. P-9412, op. 2, delo 110, l. 48.

42 Boris V. Daniel'bek, *Polovye izvrashcheniya i ugolovnaya otvetstven-nost'* (Volgograd: Vysshaya sledstvennaya shkola MVD SSSR, 1972), pp. 106–7.

43 GARF, f. P-9412, op. 2, delo 110, l. 86.

44 Ibid., l. 89.

45 Ibid.

46 Ibid., l. 90.

47 Ibid.

48 Ibid., ll. 50–1.

49 Ibid., l. 54.

50 Tigran S. Atarov, *Voprosy polovogo vospitaniya* (Moscow: Medgiz, 1959), p. 54. See: Aleksandrov, *Polovye prestupleniya*, p. 45.

51 Iosif Gyne, *Yunosha prevrashchaetsia v muzhchinu* (Moscow: Medgiz, 1960); Rudolf Neubert, *Voprosy pola* (Moscow: Medgiz, 1960). Igor

Kon tells us that Neubert's *Questions of Sex* and his other book *A New Book on Wedlock* (published in 1969) 'became immediate best-sellers'. Kon also revealed that these books 'had been deliberately selected by the authorities for the Soviet reader as the least "offensive" and most moralistic'. See: Kon, *Sexual Revolution in Russia*, p. 96.

52 Věra Sokolová, 'State Approaches to Homosexuality and Non-Heterosexual Lives in Czechoslovakia during State Socialism', in *The Politics of Gender Culture under State Socialism: An Expropriated Voice*, ed. Hana Havelková and Libora Oates-Indruchová (Oxford: Routledge, 2014), pp. 85–6.

53 Rudolf Neubert, *Die Geschlechterfrage* (Greifenverlag, 1956), pp. 80–2. I am grateful to Kate Davison for translating some parts of Neubert's book for me.

54 Gyne, *Yunosha prevrashchaetsia v muzhchinu*, p. 36.

55 Mikhail I. Avdeev, *Sudebnaya meditsina* (Moscow: Gosudarstvennoe izdatel'stvo yuridicheskoi literatury, 1960), pp. 394–5.

56 Catherine A. Lugg, *US Public Schools and the Politics of Queer Erasure* (New York: Palgrave Macmillan, 2016), pp. 20–1.

57 Neubert, *Voprosy pola*.

58 Ibid., p. 44.

59 Ibid.

60 Ibid.

61 Ibid., p. 44.

62 Ibid.

63 Viktor N. Kolbanovskii, 'O polovom vospitanii podrastayushchego pokoleniya', *Sovetskoe zdravookhranenie*, no. 3 (1964): 19.

64 Field, *Private Life and Communist Morality*, pp. 56–7.

65 For more details, see: Anne E. Gorsuch, *All This Is Your World: Soviet Tourism at Home and Abroad after Stalin* (Oxford: Oxford University Press, 2011). On other kinds of socio-cultural interactions between the Soviet Union and the United States, see: Yale Richmond, *Cultural Exchange and the Cold War: Raising the Iron Curtain* (Pennsylvania: Pennsylvania State University Press, 2003).

66 For details, see Abraham Brumberg, 'Tempest in a Gallery', *New Republic* 148, no. 7 (1963): 17–20.

67 See: Anonymous, 'Iskusstvo prinadlezhit narodu', *Pravda*, no. 3 (December 1962): 1.

68 GARF, f. 8131, op. 34, delo 386, l. 2.

69 Ibid., ll. 4–21.

70 Boris P. Bortsov, *XXII s"ezd partii i iyun'skii (1963g.) Plenum TSK KPSS o zadachakh ideologicheskoi raboty v sovremennykh usloviyakh* (Kiev: Vyshaya partiinaya shkola pri TSK KP Ukrainy, 1964), p. 16.

71 Viktor A. Ageev, Ovsei G. Korogodzkii and Petr G. Novikov, *Iyun'skii /1963/ Plenum Tsentral'nogo Komiteta KPSS i ego istoricheskoe znachenie* (Moscow: Moskovskoe gorodskoe otdelenie obshchestva 'Znanie' RSFSR, 1963), pp. 10–13.
72 Bortsov, *XXII s"ezd*, p. 16.
73 Ibid., pp. 17–18.
74 Nikolai I. Chuchelov, *O polovom vospitanii* (Moscow: Meditsina, 1964), p. 4.
75 Aleksandr A. Gabelov and Elizaveta B. Derankova, *Gigiena braka* (Moscow: Meditsina, 1964), p. 67.
76 Ibid.
77 Serafim A. Artem'ev, Vasilii D. Kochetkov and German G. Shtan'ko, *Gigiena polovoi zhizni* (Moscow: Znanie, 1964), p. 5.
78 Ibid.
79 Chuchelov, *O polovom vospitanii*, pp. 24–25.
80 Gabelov and Derankova, *Gigiena braka*, p. 27.
81 Chuchelov, *O polovom vospitanii*, p. 19.
82 Artem'ev et al., *Gigiena polovoi zhizni*, p. 20.
83 Chuchelov, *O polovom vospitanii*, pp. 24–5.
84 Ibid., p. 25.
85 Artem'ev et al., *Gigiena polovoi zhizni*, p. 20.
86 Ibid., p. 19.
87 TsMAM [Central Archive of Moscow], f. 552, d. 1335, l. 69.
88 Aleksandrov, *Polovye prestupleniya*, p. 41.
89 See for example: Seranush Dashtayants, *O polovom vospitanii shkol'nikov* (Grozny: Checheno-Ingushskoe knizhnoe izdatel'stvo, 1966); Liliya Sanyukevich, *Polovoe vospitaniie detei i podrostkov* (Minsk: Nar. Asveta, 1979); Iosif Gyne, *Yunosha prevrashchaetsya v muzhchinu* (Tashkent: Ukituvchi, 1970); Lyudmila Timofeeva, *Vospitanie chuvstv: O nekotorykh voprosakh polovogo vospitaniya uchashchikhsya* (Frunze: Mektep, 1977).

3

From sodomy to homosexuality: same-sex desire and the rise of Soviet sexopathology in the 1960s

In 1967 a young woman named Nadezhda arrived at a psychiatric clinic in the city of Gorkii to seek medical advice from Yan Genrikhovich Goland, a psychiatrist and sexologist, on her relationship with her husband.[1] Her one-year marriage to Andrei was fraught with conflict and antagonism, teetering on the brink of collapse. Besides, there was no sexual intimacy in their relationship. Andrei had gone so far as to suggest a divorce, yet both decided to retain their legal status as spouses in order to keep their flat. Nevertheless, Nadezhda kept nurturing a hope of saving their marriage and this had brought her to visit Goland. Later, in a written account of her family life with Andrei, written at Goland's prompting, Nadezhda recalled:

> We have always had an 'interesting' relationship. We could talk or be silent for hours, but any sort of intimacy that happens between young people was out of the question. I thought he was modest. I was certain that he hadn't had an affair with another girl (devushka). Our town was small, and I would have known about that. Besides, I kind of knew (primerno znala) how he was spending his time. Always with young men ... At that time I was not paying attention to that. I was not thinking the worst, besides, I did not know that such things existed.[2]

The lack of sexual intimacy was not the most problematic aspect of her relationship with Andrei. In fact, what bothered Nadezhda most was her husband's unusual craving for the company of young men, which often took precedence over their family life. Andrei's friendships with men seemed far too intimate, a fact made clear when one evening in January 1966 she saw her husband kissing one of his young male friends at a party. Nadezhda sketchily described the unpleasant episode in her diary:

> I saw him kissing a boy – both were drunk. He had always been cold with me – and here he wasn't. I could barely restrain my temper. On seeing me, he was embarrassed. I started paying more attention to his relationships with boys. One of his admirers told me: 'He told me that he liked guys more than women.' And one day, after reading some literature, I asked him directly. He replied affirmatively. That drove me mad. I forbade him to talk with boys and I told him if I saw him again with them – I would report him to the procuracy ... I raised the question of treatment, but he was against it.[3]

After carefully listening to Nadezhda's complaints, Goland instructed her to bring her husband in for an appointment. In short order, Andrei turned up in Goland's office and his story confirmed Goland's suspicions: Andrei was a homosexual. After being assured that he could speak frankly without fear of being reported to the police, Andrei opened up completely, relating all his homosexual pursuits. He also confessed that he feared 'lack of prospects' (bezperspektivnost') and loneliness in the future, noting that he had 'become addicted to homosexuality' to the point that he lost his ability to 'feel the woman' (oshchushchat' zhenshchinu). The treatment was started immediately and after a series of sessions of psychotherapy, the situation improved: Nadezhda's husband started paying more attention to her and their sex life slowly normalised.[4]

This vignette illustrates the ongoing transformations of the Soviet handling of same-sex desire – a departure from prevalent understandings of homosexuality as a mere crime to viewing it as a medical matter. Crucial in the development of this trend was the emergence of a new branch of medical science in the 1960s – sexopathology. Underscoring the importance of sexological research and treatments, the proponents of the new discipline framed their arguments in Foucauldian fashion, contending that medical intervention into the sexual lives of Soviet people was of great interest to the public. Sex was crucial for productive labour and marriage stability. Most importantly, the practitioners of the new science approached the issue of homosexuality scientifically. In their writing, sexopathologists posited that homosexuality was a medical issue treatable with psychotherapy. Some of these doctors received homosexual patients in clinics, encouraging them to confess their desires in the privacy of consultation rooms and to work through them with a view to eliminating them. Others studied homosexuals and their lives, constructing a new image of the homosexual – a personality with its own history and physical and psychological characteristics.

Scholars have emphasised the complex relationship between Soviet medical experts and the state, arguing that the former were the patrons of the latter. They have also contended that, although the USSR was lacking liberal institutions and Soviet doctors could not boast professional autonomy, medicalisation was still happening there. Interestingly enough, the proximity of the Soviet medical professionals to the state did not necessarily preclude medicalisation, but allowed it to develop in unexpected ways.[5] Drawing on these insights, in this chapter I will enquire further into the extent of the dissemination of Soviet medical discourses and its potential to exercise disciplinary power over the sexuality of Soviet people. I will start this chapter with a brief examination of discussions of homosexuality in Stalin- and Khrushchev-era books on psychiatry and then I will proceed to the examination of Soviet sexopathology and the texts of its practitioners on homosexuality.

'Sometimes these psychopaths are even married': homosexuality and psychiatry under Stalin

The interest of Soviet doctors, especially psychiatrists, in the phenomenon of homosexuality can be traced to the onset of the Soviet state. As Frances Lee Bernstein and Dan Healey have shown, early Soviet-era psychiatrists examined the question of homosexuality's origins and pondered what exactly constituted male homosexual practice.[6] Female homosexuality was also a subject of early Soviet psychiatric inquiry.[7] Soviet psychiatrists, such as Vladimir M. Bekhterev, considered options for the medical treatment of homosexuality, offering psychotherapy as a possible solution.[8] Such scientific interest in homosexuality, as Dan Healey explains, was driven by discoveries in European sexology and endocrinology, as well as the absence of criminal penalties for same-sex relations in the new Soviet penal code.[9] However, medical discussions of homosexuality were discontinued after 1930, when Stalin outlawed homosexuality and introduced rigid ideological controls.

Despite homosexuality being deemed an 'unmentionable vice' under Stalin, Soviet psychiatrists did not lose interest in the topic completely.[10] For example, in 1935 Soviet psychiatrist Yevgenii Popov produced an article, 'On the Classification of Sexual Perversions', which featured in a compendium on psychiatry. Popov argued that homosexuality could be both congenital and acquired.[11] Even more unusual was another article, 'On the Psychotherapy of Homosexuality', published by Soviet psychiatrist Igor' Stepanovich Sumbaev from Irkutsk, in the scientific journal *Soviet Psychoneurology* in 1936.[12] In his article Sumbaev presented three cases in the early 1930s where he treated three homosexual men with psychotherapy in the psychiatric clinic of the East Siberian Medical Institute. After the treatment, the patients reported that their homosexual desire 'became weaker' and that they were now able to control it.[13] The article was published two years after male homosexual acts were deemed crimes yet approached homosexuality as a psychiatric disorder.

From the memoirs of one of Sumbaev's trainees, the prominent Soviet psychiatrist Aron Isaakovich Belkin, we know that at the time of the article's publication Sumbaev was providing psychotherapy to homosexuals, who turned to him for help from all over the Soviet Union. He did so with the help of his trainee Nikolai Ivanovich Ivanov, who would later emerge in the 1960s as one of the founders of Soviet sexology and a proponent of psychotherapeutic treatment of homosexuals.[14] In the 1930s Sumbaev's and Ivanov's practices made Irkutsk, in Belkin's words, a 'place of genuine homosexual pilgrimage'.[15] In order to undergo treatment and keep in constant touch with their doctors, many patients changed their lives drastically: they obtained residency permits in Irkutsk and settled there. Both Sumbaev and Ivanov conducted individual and group psychotherapy sessions with their patients despite the existing opprobrium and legal sanctions for such crimes. Having witnessed such practices, Belkin underscored their determination and courage: 'I would call Sumbaev's and Ivanov's position on homosexuality dissident. It was a quiet, secret dissidence that did not broadcast itself, but in fact it was very firm and unbending.'[16]

Sexual abnormalities in women occasionally interested Stalin-era psychiatrists. In 1939 Professor Manenkov from the Gynaecological

Clinic of the Kazan Medical Institute produced a short article, 'A Case of Unusual Cohabitation Between Two Women'. He related that in 1937 an editor of the local newspaper alerted him to the fact of two women cohabiting, whom Manenkov invited for medical examination. One of the women, T. A., claimed during a medical examination that before the age of twenty she was female, but after she began to develop 'male capabilities' (muzhskie sposobnosti). She then began to experience sexual arousal for women, wearing male clothes and engaging in sexual intercourse with women. She soon came to feel that she was a male and decided to marry one of her sexual partners.[17] The couple even attempted to legally register their marriage, but since both were female, officials denied them such a right. Despite this, they continued living together and considered their relationship a 'marriage'. After physical examination of both women Manenkov came to the conclusion that they were neither hermaphrodites nor sexual perverts, noting the complexity of the case and the importance of presenting it to the scientific community.

Other mentions of homosexuality as a medical matter appeared in texts on psychiatry towards the end of the 1940s. In a handbook for medical students entitled *Psychiatry* (1949), a Soviet psychiatrist, Mikhail Gurevich, framed homosexuality as a 'sexual psychopathy' (polovaya psikhopatiya), which, he believed, stemmed from a variety of factors, among which were 'the social conditions (sotsial'no-bytovoi), sexual impression from early childhood, bad example (durnoi primer) and temptations'.[18] Gurevich also acknowledged that 'endocrine disorders' could be at work.[19] Homosexuals with such disorders usually displayed 'endocrine stigmas' (endokrinnye stigmy), among which were 'female-like hair growth' (rastitel'nost' po zhenskomu tipu), 'soft skin', 'female-like breasts and waist' (grudi i taz zhenskogo teloslozheniya) and a 'high-pitched voice'.[20] The behaviour of these men, he said, also resembled that of women – Gurevich claimed that adult male homosexuals 'wear corsets, powder their face (pudryatsya) and engage in handcrafts (rukodelie)'.[21] Female homosexuals, on the contrary, he claimed, displayed male-like features and behaviour.[22] Gurevich's descriptions were accompanied with a photo of a 'typical' homosexual (see Figure 1).

After Stalin's death the psychiatric interest in homosexuality saw a gradual revival. It was in the GULAG, as I have demonstrated in

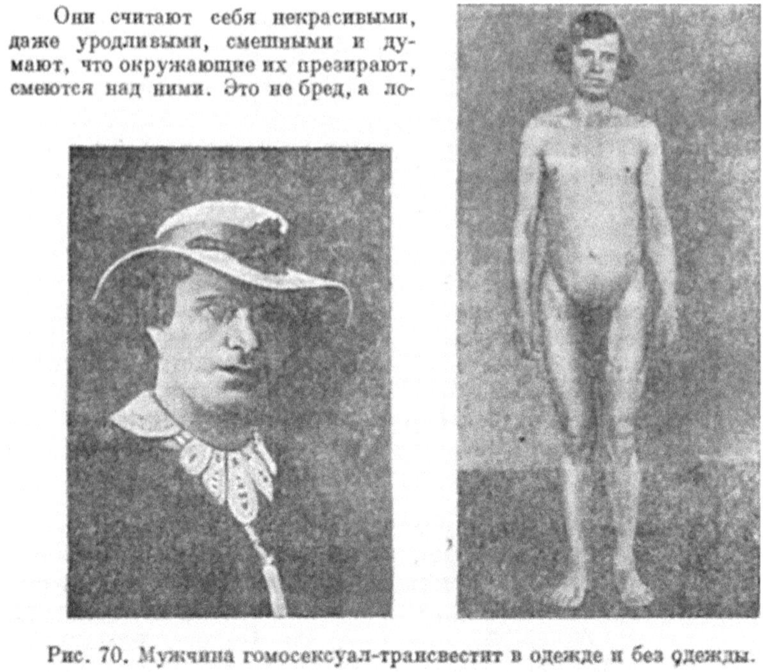
Они считают себя некрасивыми, даже уродливыми, смешными и думают, что окружающие их презирают, смеются над ними. Это не бред, а ло-

Рис. 70. Мужчина гомосексуал-трансвестит в одежде и без одежды.

Figure 1 'A man homosexual–transvestite dressed and undressed'

Chapter 1, where psychiatric interest in homosexuality was most evident. One of those scientists most concerned with homosexuality in this period was Elizaveta M. Derevinskaya, who began examining lesbian prisoners in the Karaganda corrective labour camp in 1954 and defended her doctoral dissertation on the topic in 1965; her dissertation will be explored later in this chapter. Outside the GULAG, psychiatrists continued to engage with the issue of homosexuality, albeit rarely. In a book titled *Psychiatry* (1957), Soviet psychiatrist Izmail Fedorovich Sluchevskii demonstrated the same distorted understanding of homosexuality as that presented by Gurevich in 1949. Sluchevskii also branded homosexuals as 'psychopaths' and described what he believed was their habitual way of life: 'When [the homosexual] man comes home, he puts on a female dress (zhenskii kostyum) and in this dress does all the housework. Sometimes these psychopaths are even married, because homosexuals may display bisexuality, that is, have sexual intercourse with women and simultaneously display homosexual tendencies.'[23]

Sluchevskii did not propose any treatment options for such individuals; if anything, he apparently believed that homosexuals were criminals rather than medical subjects deserving compassion and medical help. His description of a special category of psychopathic disorders – 'perverted psychopaths', to which he attributed homosexuals – attests to that. The representatives of this category were described thus:

> deceitful (lzhivyi) and immoral, merciless, indifferently cold to the sufferings of other people, egoistical, heartless and cruel. They are rude and shameless. In order to achieve their goals they go all out; to satiate their sexual and eating instinct they defy the societal norms of behaviour; they are oversexed (erotichnyi), inclined to sexual perversions.[24]

Such framing of homosexuality suggests that in the years immediately after Stalin's death little changed in Soviet mainstream psychiatric thinking on homosexuality. However 'medical' the context in which homosexuality was placed by Soviet psychiatrists, their attitudes remained moralistic and negatively judgmental. The conflation of homosexuality and transvestitism appeared to be conventional wisdom, and no attempts to suggest changing homosexuality's status from criminal to medical were made.

A more sophisticated discussion of homosexuality through the lens of psychiatry emerged only in the last years of the Khrushchev era, in the *Great Medical Encyclopaedia* (1962).[25] The entry 'Sexual perversions', written by Soviet psychiatrist Yevgenii Popov (who, as I have shown, had already discussed sexual perversions under Stalin in 1935), mentioned homosexuality, and for the first time in such a text discussed the possibilities of treatment. According to Popov, homosexuality could be treated with psychotherapy, although it was a 'difficult task': 'At the centre of the contemporary treatment of sexual perversions lies psychotherapy in all its various forms. Sometimes success can be achieved with hypnosis. It is important to remember the importance of "rechannelling" of sexual stimuli into other fields (physical work, sport, arts and so on).'[26] Popov's reference to the usefulness of rechannelling 'sexual stimuli' is illuminating, since it suggests the link between unrestricted sexual activity and its role in generating sexual perversions (as I have shown in the previous chapter) which were seen as related phenomena by Soviet sex educators. Popov too reminded his readers that male homosexuality was subject to criminal penalty.[27] Such was the verdict of the Soviet psychiatrists of the Khrushchev era: homosexuality was a medical aberration, but it still merited criminal sanctions. However, a new Soviet science – sexopathology, which emerged in 1963 and continued its development throughout the Brezhnev era – offered a different view on the problem of homosexuality.

Emergence of Soviet sexopathology (1963)

Igor Kon has argued that 'the establishment of [Soviet] sexopathology as a discipline was an attempt to bring sexuality under medical control'.[28] However, it appears that the new science was also concerned with the issue of male impotence and its perceived result, family dissolution. The first calls for the establishment of sexopathology were made by prominent Soviet urologist Il'ya Mironovich Porudominskii in his article 'Who Treats Sexual Disorders?' published on 29 November 1963 in *Meditsinskaya gazeta* (see Figure 2).[29] There, Porudominskii raised two key problems – the great social impact of male impotence and the virtual inaccessibility of its effective treatment in Soviet clinics.

Porudominskii warned that neglecting sexual disorders, especially in males, could have far-reaching consequences for Soviet society as a whole, for these disorders affected men's ability to work and have a family life: 'Male sexual disorder is a severe affliction (tyazhkoe stradanie), which often leads to the loss of ability to perform labour (poterya trudosposobnosti) and irreparable family tragedies (semeinye tragedii).'[30] In his view male impotence made it impossible for a Soviet man to have a family, which was crucial for one's well-being and productivity: 'Both the impossibility of creating a family and family conflicts have a negative bearing on the physical and psycho-nervous state of the patient, which eventually has negative bearing on his ability to perform labour and his labour productivity.'[31] Embedded in Porudominskii's arguments about the necessity to look into the sexual lives of Soviet people from a scientific perspective were not merely professional concerns about the well-being of his patients, but implicit suggestions to 'transform the sexual conduct of couples into a concerted economic and political behaviour'.[32] Dismissing the sexual lives of Soviet people as an

ПРОБЛЕМА, ПОДСКАЗАННАЯ ЖИЗНЬЮ

КТО ЖЕ ЛЕЧИТ ПОЛОВЫЕ РАССТРОЙСТВА?

Проф. И. ПОРУДОМИНСКИЙ

Figure 2 Il'ya Porudominskii's article 'Who Treats Sexual Disorders?'

object of scientific observation and study meant overlooking a whole range of issues critical to the economic and political development of the state: progression of propagation, boosting birth rates, fertility and productive labour. Porudominskii essentially proposed to administer sex to make it work for the benefit of the society, rather than simply ignoring it as had been done before.

Porudominskii's concern about the disastrous consequences of male impotence on family life and, most importantly, ability to perform labour reflected official anxieties on these issues and realities at the time of his article's publication. Peter H. Juviler tells us that between 1955 and 1965 the Soviet divorce rate increased by a massive 270 per cent.[33] Deborah A. Field has shown that Soviet experts under Khrushchev deemed divorce to be dangerous to Soviet society and so sought to avert it. They identified a variety of reasons that contributed to problems in family life: the inability of young wives to manage a household, material misfortune and adultery. In order to prevent divorce, they suggested that problems should be resolved through education, individual will power and community intervention.[34]

The lack of effective treatment for sexual disorders in the Soviet Union, Porudominskii argued, was a result of the absence of a relevant branch of medicine – sexual pathology (seksual'naya patologiya) – which was essential for the treatment of sexual maladies. Soviet medical university curricula did not include training on sexopathology, nor was there any specialised institution in the Soviet Union conducting related research. Porudominskii concluded that it was necessary to establish a research centre specifically dealing with sexual pathologies. To begin with, he suggested holding a symposium to attract medical professionals interested in the promotion of the new science: 'In order to coordinate research in this field, it is expedient to hold a special symposium.'[35] This call for action did not fall on deaf ears – Porudominskii's proposition materialised in a symposium that was held the next month.

That effective treatment of male impotence was a key objective of the new science is also clear from the introduction to the first compendium on sexopathology, *Contemporary Problems of Sexopathology* (1967). Its author was Pavel Posvyanskii, head of the Moscow Department of Sexopathology set up in 1965, the first research centre on sexopathology in the USSR. He observed that the establishment of sexopathology was, in part, a compassionate response to the desperate pleas for help coming from male patients suffering from impotence.[36] Embarrassed and desperate, some suicidal, they barraged doctors with letters in which they described their plight and confusion in the face of their ailment. Posvyanskii quoted one:

> I cannot call myself a coward, I fought in the war with dignity and I was decorated on numerous occasions, but now I can't and I don't want to live. In despair, I grabbed a rope and then I came to my senses – this is not worthy of a Soviet man. So I offer you to use me for any medical experiments needed by science.[37]

The sexological symposium which Porudominskii proposed took place in the city of Gorkii in December 1963.[38] Gorkii, not Moscow, appears to have been chosen as a venue for the seminar for at least one important reason: it was the home of Professor Nikolai Vladimirovich Ivanov (Figure 3), former trainee of the prominent psychiatrist Igor Sumbaev, and therefore a point of personal connection with earlier scientists who had treated homosexuals under Stalin. Since 1954 Ivanov had headed the Department of Psychiatry at the Gorkii State Medical Institute, where he led the research on sexual disorders.[39] In cooperation with Porudominskii, Ivanov helped organise the seminar and agreed to share his expertise with the aspiring sexologists. The 1963 seminar was followed by another in 1964. While little is known about the 1963 participants, a photograph of the participants of the 1964 seminar (Figure 4) shows an attendance of sixty-seven doctors from all over the Soviet Union. Among them were leading Soviet psychiatrists – Mark S. Lebedinskii, Il'ya M. Porudominskii, Vladimir M. Myasishchev, Pavel B. Posvyanskii and Nikolai V. Ivanov himself – as well as aspiring sexologists who would later become prominent in the field, Yan G. Goland, Aron S. Belkin and Sergei S. Libikh.[40]

The formal emergence of Soviet sexopathology was inaugurated on 29 June 1965, when the deputy health minister Aleksandr Sergeev decreed the establishment of a Department of Sexopathology within the Moscow Research Institute of Psychiatry.[41] Professor Pavel Borisovich Posvyanskii (Figure 5) was appointed department head.[42] Under his leadership, the department began coordinating efforts of aspiring sexologists across the Soviet Union, organising

Figure 3 Nikolai V. Ivanov

Figure 4 Medical Seminar on Psychotherapy and Sexology in Gorkii (1964)

seminars and conferences where doctors could receive training and exchange expertise. An undated and un-authored report from the Department of Sexopathology (Figures 6 and 7) reveals that from 1965 to 1969 the department organised several such conferences – a seminar in Gorkii in 1965 attended by 120 doctors; a conference in Moscow in 1967 (Figures 8, 9 and 10) attended by 250 doctors; a conference in Moscow in 1969 attended by 180 doctors and one in Riga attended by 200 doctors.[43] We also know that in 1966 another seminar on sexology, apparently coordinated by the department, was held in Gorkii (see Figure 11).[44] Once the department was established, the annual number of patients grew from 150 in 1966 to 461 in 1969.[45] Alongside therapeutic practice, the department's sexologists engaged in research work; although the number of their publications remained modest throughout the 1960s, it was growing steadily – from three publications in 1965 to seventeen in 1969.[46] Some of these publications were devoted to sexual perversions, mainly homosexuality, which, as I will show, was presented as a treatable condition in the 1960s.

Figure 5 Pavel B. Posvyanskii

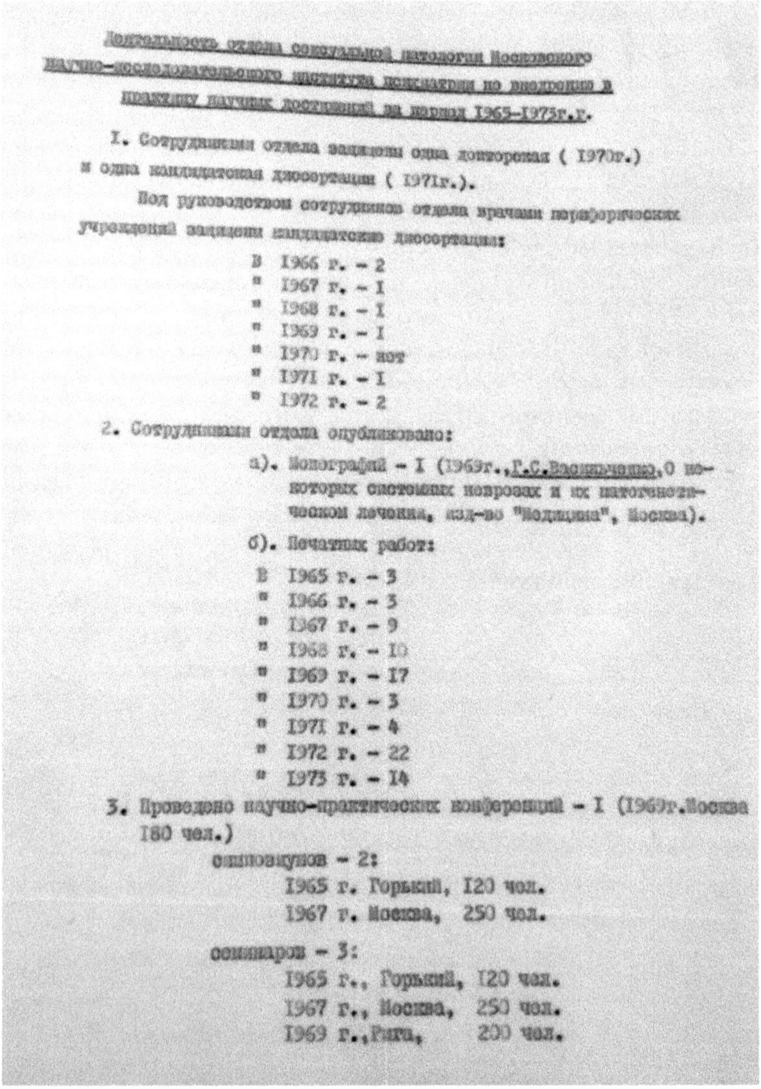

Деятельность отдела сексуальной патологии Московского научно-исследовательского института психиатрии по внедрению в практику научных достижений за период 1965-1973г.г.

I. Сотрудниками отдела защищены одна докторская (1970г.) и одна кандидатская диссертации (1971г.).

Под руководством сотрудников отдела врачами периферических учреждений защищены кандидатские диссертации:

в 1966 г. – 2
" 1967 г. – I
" 1968 г. – I
" 1969 г. – I
" 1970 г. – нет
" 1971 г. – I
" 1972 г. – 2

2. Сотрудниками отдела опубликовано:

а). Монографий – I (1969г., Г.С.Васильченко, О некоторых системных неврозах и их патогенетическом лечении, изд-во "Медицина", Москва).

б). Печатных работ:

в 1965 г. – 3
" 1966 г. – 3
" 1967 г. – 9
" 1968 г. – 10
" 1969 г. – 17
" 1970 г. – 3
" 1971 г. – 4
" 1972 г. – 22
" 1973 г. – 14

3. Проведено научно-практических конференций – I (1969г. Москва 180 чел.)

симпозиумов – 2:
1965 г. Горький, 120 чел.
1967 г. Москва, 250 чел.

семинаров – 3:
1965 г., Горький, 120 чел.
1967 г., Москва, 250 чел.
1969 г., Рига, 200 чел.

Figure 6 Undated report on the activities of the Department of Sexopathology, p. 1

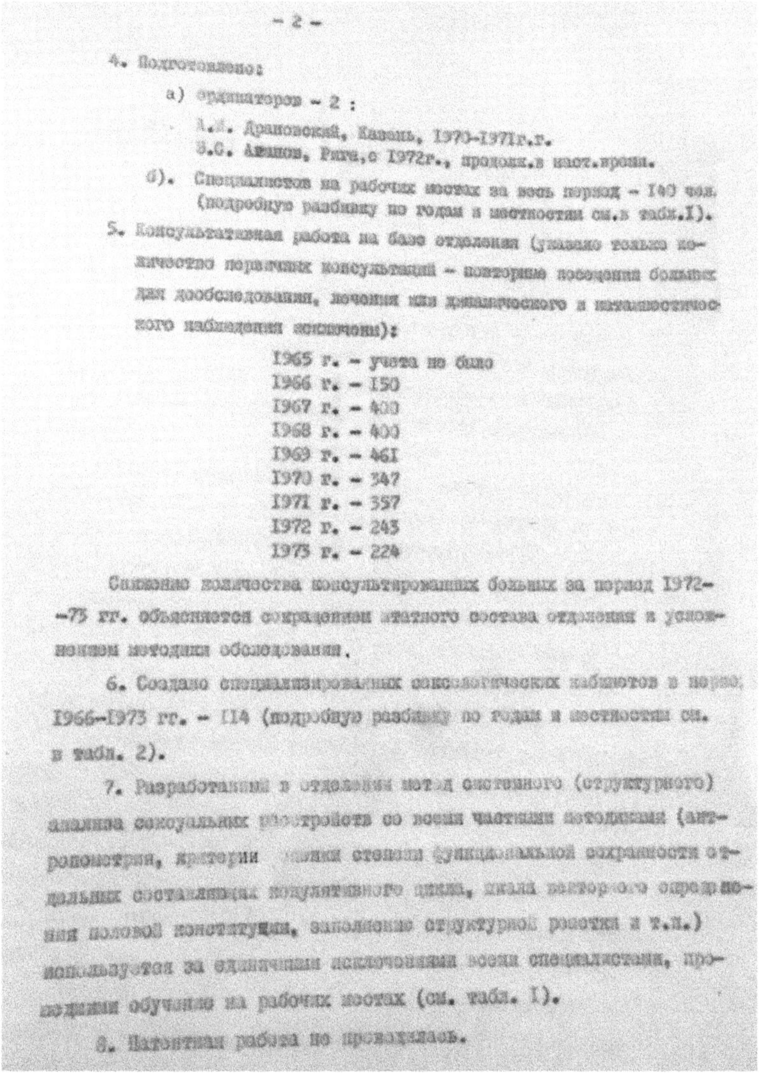

– 2 –

4. Подготовлено:

а) ординаторов – 2 :

А.М. Драповский, Казань, 1970-1971г.г.
В.С. Аминов, Рига, с 1972г., продолж.в наст.время.

б). Специалистов на рабочих местах за весь период – 140 чел.
(подробную разбивку по годам и местностям см.в табл.I).

5. Консультативная работа на базе отделения (указано только количество первичных консультаций – повторные посещения больных для дообследования, лечения или динамического и катамнестического наблюдения исключены):

1965 г. – учета не было
1966 г. – 150
1967 г. – 400
1968 г. – 400
1969 г. – 461
1970 г. – 347
1971 г. – 357
1972 г. – 243
1973 г. – 224

Снижение количества консультированных больных за период 1972–73 гг. объясняется сокращением штатного состава отделения и усложнением методики обследования.

6. Создано специализированных сексологических кабинетов в период 1966–1973 гг. – 114 (подробную разбивку по годам и местностям см. в табл. 2).

7. Разработанный в отделении метод системного (структурного) анализа сексуальных расстройств со всеми частными методиками (антропометрия, критерии оценки степени функциональной сохранности отдельных составляющих копулятивного цикла, шкала векторного определения половой конституции, заполнение структурной решетки и т.п.) используется за единичными исключениями всеми специалистами, прошедшими обучение на рабочих местах (см. табл. I).

8. Патентная работа не проводилась.

Figure 7 Undated report on the activities of the Department of Sexopathology, p. 2

Figure 8 Seminar on Sexology in Moscow (1967)

Figure 9 Seminar on Sexology in Moscow (1967)

Figure 10 Seminar on Sexology in Moscow (1967)

Figure 11 Medical Seminar on Psychotherapy and Sexology in Gorkii (1966)

Sexology elsewhere in the world

Unlike the Soviet Union, where understanding of homosexuality as a treatable disorder was only beginning to gain recognition among doctors, in some countries of the Eastern bloc the medicalisation of homosexuality had already taken place and even led to decriminalisation of sodomy statutes. One such country was Czechoslovakia, where, as Kateřina Lišková has shown, prominent sexologists started to decry the existing anti-homosexual legislation as early as 1953, promoting the view that homosexuality was a medical problem and had nothing to do with the police. Among them was sexologist Karel Nedoma, who argued in 1953 that a person's contribution to society in the form of his labour was more important than his homosexuality.[47] Another prominent Czechoslovak sexologist, Kurt Freund, argued likewise. In fact, the two co-authored a paper, *The Problem of Responsibility and Corrective Measures in Sexual Delinquents* in 1959, arguing that homosexuality was not dangerous to society.[48] The authorities heard their arguments and decriminalised consensual homosexuality between two adults in Czechoslovakia in 1961.[49]

Even after the decriminalisation of sodomy, Freund retained his scientific interest in homosexuality. Unlike his Soviet colleagues, he believed that homosexuality could not be cured, expressing this view in a report, 'On the Problem of Homosexuality in Males' (1965), in the journal *Czechoslovak Medical Review*.[50] In his article Freund questioned the usefulness of psychotherapy as far as homosexuality was concerned: 'Among doctors treating homosexual men, unfounded optimism is still prevalent. This is the case, mainly, with the proponents of psychoanalysis. In most cases, they still imagine that homosexual preference can be turned into heterosexual.'[51] Freund then argued that such conclusions stemmed from insufficient follow-up examinations of the patients after the treatment and unreliable testimonials from those patients who had problems with the law because of their homosexuality. Such patients, he claimed, simply wanted to secure a medical certificate attesting to their 'recovery'. Freund then concluded that 'psychotherapy of homosexuality in the vast majority of cases is not warranted (ne pokazana)', since even if the doctors managed to instil 'heterosexual adaptations' in their patients, their homosexual desire never ceased.[52]

Medicalisation of homosexuality and the corollary decriminalisation of sodomy laws were under way in Western countries as well. In the UK, for instance, changes towards medicalisation and the decriminalisation of consensual homosexual acts began after the Departmental Committee on Homosexual Offences and Prostitution, better known as the Wolfenden Committee, published a report on 4 September 1957 that recommended decriminalising homosexual sex between two consenting adults and encouraged further research into the aetiology and medical treatment of homosexuality.[53] This report's recommendations were greeted with enthusiasm by British psychiatrists who started trying various methods for the medical treatment of homosexuality, with aversion therapy believed to be the most efficacious treatment option.[54] Even so, there were still medical professionals in the UK who espoused views contrary to the mainstream perception of homosexuality as a fixable aberration. These doctors advised their patients to have psychoanalysis only if they felt out of accord with their homosexuality.[55] Although the Wolfenden Committee recommended decriminalising homosexuality between two consenting males as early as 1957, this recommendation became law only in 1967.[56]

Developments of another nature were taking place across the Atlantic, where as early as the late 1940s a new perspective on homosexuality emerged that framed it as a normal variant of human sexuality. This view was presented in a 1948 study called *Sexual Behavior in the Human Male* by American sexologist Alfred Kinsey.[57] Kinsey's work refuted the hitherto conventional binary view between 'normal and abnormal' sexuality and demonstrated that homosexual activity was far from a rare phenomenon. Most notably, his research revealed shocking statistics: 37 per cent of the male population examined by Kinsey had sexual contacts with other men. These findings led Kinsey to design a scale for rating the prevalence of homosexual behaviour in a male from zero to six, with zero standing for exclusive heterosexuality and six standing for exclusive homosexuality.[58] Kinsey's study was followed by a series of papers by an American psychologist Evelyn Hooker, who proved the heretofore untested link between maladjustment and homosexuality.[59]

The emergence of these ideas stood in marked contrast to the stepped-up homophobia of McCarthyism and still existing sodomy laws in the United States which, despite attacks by renowned American jurists and attorneys, remained in place.[60] Furthermore, there was no shortage of scientific studies that continued to relentlessly popularise the view of homosexuality as a sickness. One such study was *Homosexuality: A Psychoanalytic Study* (1962), written under the primary authorship of psychiatrist Irving Bieber.[61] Bieber believed that every homosexual could be cured of his 'disease' if he was sufficiently motivated.[62] These pathologising views of homosexuality came under attack from members of the homophile movement, which emerged in the 1950s and became more active in the 1960s in the US.[63] In 1973 the activism of the movement and later gay liberationists eventually led to the elimination of homosexuality from the list of psychiatric disorders.

The development of Soviet thinking on homosexuality was going in a different direction – towards the pathologisation and medicalisation of homosexuality. However, the emerging status of homosexuality as a disease did not have a similar effect in Russia – Soviet sexopathology was still too weak to launch a comprehensive campaign against the existing sodomy law or to claim homosexuality for the sexological and psychiatric professions. Soviet sexologists made very few attempts to suggest that homosexuality should be a matter of therapeutic, rather than legal, concern, and these attempts did not lead to the decriminalisation of sodomy.

Male and female homosexuality as a medical disorder in the 1960s: Elizaveta Derevinskaya and Nikolai Ivanov

Before the emergence of sexopathology, GULAG doctors of the 1950s made attempts to re-medicalise homosexuality, claiming their authority over the issue of lesbianism. As seen in Chapter 1, they contended that female homosexuality was a temporary phenomenon which would disappear on its own once the prisoner lesbian was released. Around this time, doctors in the 'free' society displayed interest in the issue of lesbianism, but from a more sophisticated perspective. These doctors viewed lesbianism as a pathological condition, treatable with psychotherapy and medication. One of them was Elizaveta Derevinskaya, a trainee psychiatrist, whose research was focused on the examination of ninety-six lesbians (most of whom came from the Karaganda corrective labour camp) over the period 1954 to 1964.[64] Derevinskaya presented her research in a dissertation, 'Materials on the Clinical Picture, Pathogenesis, Therapy of Female Homosexuality', which she defended on 4 June 1965 in the Karaganda State Medical Institute.[65]

Derevinskaya's dissertation is interesting in several ways. First, she started researching the topic of her dissertation as early as the 1950s, at a time when Soviet sexopathology was not yet established as an official science. Examining the content of the dissertation, Dan Healey argues that its appearance was seemingly due to the anxieties of GULAG officials regarding the possibility of a spread of camp perversions into wider society after their release.[66] Secondly, it appears that Abram Svyadoshch, a prominent psychiatrist and Derevinskaya's supervisor, did not actively participate in the formative seminars on sexopathology held in Gorkii; perhaps it was because at that time he was based in Karaganda or due to some other reason. Despite Derevinskaya's and Svyadoshch's remoteness from Moscow and Gorkii, where the practitioners of sexology were congregating in the 1960s, Derevinskaya's dissertation upheld the medicalising approaches to the homosexual body which the new science promoted. Citing the works of Soviet psychiatrists who framed homosexuality exclusively as a 'psychopathy', Derevinskaya argued that 'a wide range of sexual perversions can be observed outside psychopathy'.[67] In particular, she invoked the description of a 'typical' homosexual which Izmail Sluchevskii provided in his manual *Psychiatry* (1957), describing them as 'deceitful and immoral' and as individuals defying social norms. Derevinskaya noted that 'among homosexuals there can be found individuals who do not possess characteristics vividly described by I. F. Sluchevskii', thereby insisting on a more complex viewing of the problem of homosexuality.[68]

As part of her studies Derevinskaya came into close interaction with the objects of her research. Under her medical gaze, lesbians openly confessed and disclosed their past histories and desires. They recalled when they had first felt sexual attraction to members of the same sex, described the manifestations of gender non-conformity in childhood, frequency of masturbation, roles in homosexual intercourse and when they first had homosexual sex. Derevinskaya's subjects unabashedly described their love affairs with other women and shared the innermost thoughts about their sexuality along with the intimate details of their lives. For example:

> During a conversation with Professor A. M. Svyadoshch, the patient admitted that she now loves a doctor and misses her, that for two months after discharge from the hospital she did not receive letters from her [the female doctor]. Then she [patient] decided to go back to the hospital and see the doctor at all costs. To this end, she staged a suicide attempt: she claimed that she had drunk mercury from two thermometers and eventually was taken to a psychiatric hospital.[69]

Some women confessed that they were not comfortable with their sexuality and communicated their willingness to find a cure. Describing one such woman in a case study, Derevinskaya wrote:

> She has been intimately involved with women since she was twenty, playing the role of a woman. She claims she receives satisfaction during homosexual relationships. She says that it is disgusting, she considers herself to be a perished woman (pogibshei zhenshchinoi), she asserts that she wants to be like all women, but she cannot do it herself.[70]

Another woman confessed that she would like to come back to her husband, from whom she was divorced, but her homosexual liaisons were preventing this:

> At the age of nineteen, she met a young man whom she really liked, got married, but receiving no sexual satisfaction, she began to masturbate again. Five months later she left her husband, lived alone for a while, then met a girl, entered into a homosexual relationship with her. The husband asked her to return to him. She says that she is not able to leave her [female] partner, although she would like to do it and she understands that her relationship is unnatural. She asks her to get rid of this orientation (napravlennosti).[71]

Apart from carefully listening to the lesbian women, Derevinskaya subjected them to a barrage of medical tests, which ranged from measuring blood pressure to thorough gynaecological examinations.[72] Their confessions and the results of their medical examinations were then carefully typed up into individual case histories, some of which were presented in her dissertation. Both Derevinskaya and her subjects had a stake in the medicalisation of female homosexuality: while she was willing to expand medical jurisdiction over lesbianism, offering psychotherapy and neuroleptics, her subjects actively assisted her by sharing their stories, and some readily accepted the prospect of undergoing treatment. Far from being a study of former GULAG inmates, Derevinskaya's research extended beyond places of confinement, as some of the women she examined had been found by her in 'free' society. She documented the case of a cohabiting lesbian couple who considered themselves married. One, O. A., entered the psychiatric hospital of the Karaganda Medical Institute to treat several psychological disorders which afflicted her. During her stay at the hospital, O. A.'s wife paid her visits, which Derevinskaya documented in her dissertation:

> Soon the patient's [O. A.'s] 'wife' came to the clinic to see her. She refused to provide any information about herself. The patient [O. A.] hugs, kisses and caresses her 'wife'. After being discharged from hospital, the patient left with her partner ... We visited the patient at her home after discharge from hospital three years later. She claims that she is living happily with her 'wife' and works as a guard (okhrannikom). She is going to relocate to another city to the house of her wife's relatives. She has a good relationship with them.[73]

Derevinskaya's dissertation is rare evidence of the existence of scarcely explored medical practices of inquiring into the homosexual cohort in places of confinement and psychiatric clinics. Many more reports and dissertations on the issue of homosexuality are likely to be stored in Russian archives, regional psychiatric clinics and similar institutions. GULAG and prison infirmaries were likely to be the places where doctors examined the issue of homosexuality, but only those who harboured a special interest in the topic, like Derevinskaya and Svyadoshch, wanted to publish the results of their interactions. Most such works remained unpublished and, as I have shown, were only circulated among prison officials as manuscripts.

However, it was not only lesbians under medical scrutiny – some doctors now sought to impose medical interpretations on male homosexuality, offering psychotherapeutic treatments. One of them was Nikolai Ivanov, a former trainee of Igor Sumbaev and one of the pioneers of Soviet sexology in the 1960s. At the heart of Ivanov's psychotherapy for homosexuality lay an intimate conversation between him and the patient, in the course of which the former was expected to confess his desires and talk about them at length.

Ivanov described his model of treatment in a monograph, *Questions of Psychotherapy of Functional Sexual Disorders* (1966), which discussed impotence, female frigidity and sexual perversions.[74] That Ivanov put sexual perversions on a par with these ailments suggests that he viewed them as treatable conditions, rather than a criminal psychopathy, which, as we have seen, was the conventional framing of homosexuality in the books on psychiatry. Opening his discussion of sexual perversions (seksual'nye perversii), Ivanov argued that they stemmed from premature sexual experiences, thereby echoing the views of Soviet sex educators:

> Soviet clinicians have gathered convincing evidence that various forms of sexual perversions are due to unfavourable factors of upbringing, especially the conditions in which an adolescent or a young man prematurely experiences intense exciting feelings (intensivnye volnuyushchie vpechatleniya), being, for example, an onlooker of a sexual scene or being 'instructed' by his more experienced peers.[75]

Ivanov's view and those of sex educators concurred on yet another point: sexual perversions stemmed from excessive sexual desire, a 'pathological increase in sexual attraction', which he believed to be a 'halfway house' (perekhodnaya forma) between normal and perverse sexual life. In order to prevent this pathology and its undesirable consequences, Ivanov recommended elimination of all sexual stimuli from the patient's life. He also advised that patients with excessive sexual drive engage in physical labour and sports, which would make them oblivious to 'sexual fantasies' (seksual'no okrashennye predstavleniya). More radical measures for tackling excessive sexual desire included prescription of sedative and libido-quelling medications in large doses, mainly bromine and Aminazin.[76]

Among all sexual perversions, homosexuality, according to Ivanov, 'occupied a central place'.[77] Although he did not elaborate on how his view of homosexuality as a medical condition squared with the existing anti-sodomy law, he claimed that: 'Most perversions are to be situated within the competence of psychiatry (otnositsya k kompetentsii psikhiatorov), since the most important method for its treatment is psychotherapy.'[78] A cardinal feature of Ivanov's psychotherapeutic treatment of homosexuality was the assumption that a homosexual had to work hard on self-improvement: he was expected to rechannel his sexual desire to the opposite sex by commanding himself to stop thinking about men and by trying to increase his contact with women. Ivanov's treatment scheme therefore involved not only a psychological but a social dimension. Recovery was not only about reducing homosexual desire but about reintegrating the homosexual into society and the collective. This social dimension embedded in Ivanov's practice was a cornerstone of Soviet psychiatry.[79]

The concept of working on oneself to become a better Soviet citizen, which lay at the core of Ivanov's psychotherapy, was not unique. As Oleg Kharkhordin has shown, this concept was an important element of the educational system and ideology of the late Soviet era, with its goal of encouraging Soviet citizens to self-improve and so raise a generation of New Soviet Persons.[80] Examining Soviet literature on self-training, published during this period, Kharkhordin summarised the main practices central to the process of working on oneself. Generally, it comprised three stages: the first stage of 'self-cognition and self-evaluation', the second stage involving 'self-compulsion or self-stimulation, leading to self-training of will power', and the final stage of 'self-control or self-command'.[81] Most importantly, the process of working on oneself began with 'the realisation of certain personal deficiencies, revealed in the process of self-evaluation'.[82] Ivanov's treatment scheme appears to draw on a similar framework. He argued that for treatment to be successful, a prospective patient had to realise what a serious disadvantage his homosexuality was: 'In case of homosexuality one of the telling signs [of the patient's amenability to treatment] is the patient's attitude to his perversion, whether he has awareness of the inappropriateness of his desire (neadekvatnost' vlecheniya).'[83] Ivanov emphasised this point twice in his text: 'It should be noted once again that treatment is successful only in those cases when the patient, suffering, realises the inappropriateness (neadekvatnost') of his way of living, wants to get rid of his pathological desire and persistently, purposefully follows the doctor's corrective suggestions.'[84]

Conversely, patients who were not able to perceive their homosexuality as a serious disadvantage were not amenable to treatment:

> If the patient finds his state burdensome (tyagotitsya svoim sostoyaniem), then the conduct of psychotherapy is rational (ratsional'no). If the patient, as is often the case, has come to terms with his sexual

> perversion long ago, and does not find it burdensome (ne tyagotitsya im), but on the contrary, thinks of it as something that makes him superior or original, then the treatment should not be started.[85]

Apparently not all homosexuals perceived their desire as pathological – as this comment suggests, some of them, despite the social stigma, could have a strong homosexual identity and were comfortable with their sexuality. Ivanov's observation is consistent with our scant knowledge on self-awareness of Soviet homosexuals in the 1950s: we know that at this time urban homosexual subcultures existed in large cities such as Moscow, where homosexuals possessed self-awareness and had established cruising habits.[86]

The importance of self-evaluation as a prerequisite for successful treatment is evident in another comment by Ivanov: 'In the cases of patients actively leading a perverse sexual life, the possibility of a positive psychotherapeutic effect is high, if the patient came to the doctor in a state of acute emotional crisis (dushevnyi krizis) and with awareness that one cannot go on living like this.'[87] This realisation, Ivanov argued, could also be a result of unreciprocated or betrayed (obmanutaya) love:

> Such critical feeling (kriticheskoe perezhivanie) is especially evident in the cases of unreciprocated or 'misplaced' (obmanutoi) love. A torturous disappointment (muchitel'noe razocharovanie) and spiritual dejection (dushevnaya ugnetennost') arising from it provide a propitious moment for a psychotherapist to intervene, especially when such spiritual crisis is related to deep concerns (ostrye perezhivaniya) of an approaching danger and threat of social responsibility for his desire.[88]

These fears of some of Ivanov's patients were far from being unfounded, as in the late 1950s and during the 1960s policing of homosexual men intensified and the KGB occasionally participated.[89] The police monitored homosexuals in parks and public toilets and resorted to the help of informants, recruited from other homosexuals who were blackmailed and encouraged to incriminate others.[90] Starting from 1965, the USSR health ministry, concerned with the growing rates of STIs, stepped up surveillance and monitoring of homosexuals, resorting to the help of doctors working in STI clinics as well as the police.[91]

After the patient realised his deficiency and the danger of living with it, he was to embark on the long path towards recovery. With the help of self-control and self-command, the patient was 'to resist his pathological desire' with his own efforts.[92] He was to do so with the help of 'autogenic training', a complex form of self-hypnosis, which Ivanov borrowed from German psychiatrist Johannes Heinrich Schultz, who developed it in 1932.[93] This self-hypnosis aimed to help the patient subdue any exciting images (budorazhashchee predstavlenie) and make him devise an individual formula of resistance (formula soprotivleniya) against his homosexual urges.[94] The patient was constantly to repeat to himself one of the phrases offered to him by his doctor, such as 'I am now free of my previous desires, I am indifferent to anything that used to excite me.'[95] Other patients, Ivanov noted, also pledged that they would not succumb to 'anything tempting'.[96]

As the treatment proceeded, the patient was to get into a special state of mind, the so-called 'sexual-psychological vacuum' (seksual'no-psikhologicheskii vakuum). This state was characterised by the disappearance of homosexual urges on the part of the patient.[97] Once the patient reached this state, it was time for the doctor to help the patient to 'activate social communication with persons of the opposite sex'.[98] Here again the patient was expected to summon his concentration to achieve this task. Ivanov recommended that 'at this stage, the patient is strongly recommended to concentrate all his attention on the positive qualities of personality [of a woman] as a whole'.[99] The patient was responsible for creating conditions under which he could successfully obtain heterosexual desire, which would 'burst into a luminous flame' (vspykhnut' iarkim plamenem), once the patient organised his way of life 'in such a way that friendly relationships with the individuals of the opposite sex could facilitate the creation of conditions for the emergence of such feelings'.[100] Importantly, Ivanov assigned little importance to the use of medication in the treatment of homosexuality, stating that 'medical therapy of sexual perversions does not have any substantial importance'.[101] However, if the patient insisted on medical intervention, then the doctor could prescribe such medicine to alleviate the patient's sexual urges.[102]

Ivanov's emphasis on the importance of a conscious decision to undertake psychotherapeutic treatment on the part of the homosexual patient suggests that Ivanov was against coercive techniques and did not seek to force psychotherapy on his patients, unlike other

Soviet psychiatrists whom I will discuss later. In some cases, he actively tried to dissuade his patients from undergoing psychotherapy for homosexuality. One of Ivanov's former patients, Leonid, who turned up in Ivanov's consultation room in 1965, recalled:

> I realised that I had an anomaly (anomaliya). I was attracted to men. I made numerous attempts to date girls. Through my acquaintances I came to Ivanov. After reassuring me that our conversation would not go beyond the walls of his office, he asked me: 'Is it worth breaking nature (lomat' prirody)?' And after I told him that I had had contacts with women, he said that we could try.[103]

Ivanov's reassurance of the patient that their conversation would not go beyond the walls of the consultation room, as well as the fact that Leonid was offered treatment for homosexuality, may be construed as a sign of what Vladimir Shlapentokh has called 'privatisation', a process that had been under way in Soviet society since the mid-1950s.[104] One of the main features of this process was a growing 'unofficial public life' and Ivanov's medical practice certainly was an expression of such – according to the official views of the state, male homosexuality was still a punishable crime. Yet Ivanov not only believed that homosexuality could be natural in some cases, he also offered medical treatment for it, which at that time was not acknowledged by official Soviet medicine. His consultation room offered some degree of privacy for his patients and it was also a place where official views on homosexuality were challenged while alternative, unofficial approaches to this phenomenon were undertaken.

Drawing on Leonid's terse summary, it is difficult to reflect further on the extent of unofficial and private interactions between the patient and the doctor and their implications for the medical treatment of homosexuality during that period. The existing accounts of Soviet psychiatric practice of this time, however, suggest that, although a Soviet psychiatrist was no private entrepreneur and was usually attached to a public hospital, his relationship with the patient often took on unofficial and informal undertones. For instance, there were no standard psychotherapeutic hours – a session could vary from half an hour to two hours and more; a patient or former patient could see his therapist without an advance appointment. Psychiatrists were eager to meet their patients any time, since they believed that 'the patient should know that the doctor is available to him whenever he needs him'.[105] The informality of such interactions, and the potential rapport arising with it, could have certainly facilitated the trust between the two in some cases and could have led some homosexuals to open up to their therapists.

Ivanov started administering psychotherapy to Leonid, but soon had to discontinue the treatment – Ivanov suffered a stroke in 1966 and was no longer able to work with his patients.[106] Focused on his own health, Ivanov then handed his patients over to his ambitious young protégé, a psychiatrist from Gorkii – Yan Genrikhovich Goland, who had been his dedicated trainee since the late 1950s.[107] Following on from the practice of his mentor, Goland further developed the medical treatment of homosexuality.

Confessions in Yan Goland's consultation room

Like his mentor, Goland promoted the view that male homosexuality was a treatable medical condition, which the patient could eliminate with his own efforts under a psychiatrist's careful supervision. Underlying Goland's model of treatment were the same conceptions, revolving around the idea that the patient was to become a heterosexual person through control, concentration and work on himself. A new element in Goland's scheme was emphasis on the education of the patient on how to 'adapt' himself to the individuals of the opposite sex and on how to appreciate their beauty. Goland reported positive outcomes of the treatment of former Ivanov's patients in a report 'On the Question of Psychotherapy of Homosexuality', presented at a conference on psychiatry in Kharkov in 1968.[108] In his report, Goland described a more elaborate model of medical treatment for homosexuality which consisted of three stages. The aim of the first stage was to 'establish a sexual-psychological vacuum', a special state characterised by disappearance of homosexual desire; the second stage was aimed at teaching the patient how to appreciate women's beauty and establish social contacts with them; the third stage was to help the patient further develop his 'heteroerotic' desire towards women.[109]

During the first stage, the patient was given hypnotic suggestions to develop a 'calm, cold and indifferent attitude to men'.[110] The patient was to use auto-training, which would help him distract himself from his 'fixations' on men.[111] Obtaining patients' feedback after this stage was completed, Goland noted that they reported 'a feeling of liberation and joy of victory over oneself', 'indifference and tranquillity' and 'freedom from dangerous desire'.[112] Here Goland placed special emphasis on the fact that on completion of this stage of the treatment the patient was able to 'rationally' (ratsional'no) and 'positively' (pozitivno) assess his new state, guided by his intellect, rather than feelings. During the second stage, hypnotic suggestions were accompanied with pictures of women shown to the patient. Here, a special emphasis was placed on educating (vospitanie) the patient on how to develop an 'aesthetic interest' towards women and to gain skills of 'adaptation among women'.[113] The patient was taught to 'develop his communicative skills' with women by following the doctor's instructions and fulfilling the assigned homework.[114] Any unwanted sexual feelings towards men were to be controlled by the patient's will and 'rechannelled' towards women.[115] Finally, during the third stage, the patient was shown more sexually explicit images of women. The outcomes reported by the patients were the following: 'jealousy towards women' (chuvstvo revnosti k zhenshchine), 'erection from strong heterosexual stimuli', 'erection after touching a woman', 'intensification of erotic feelings during intimate contacts with women' and 'the appearance of a vivid stable heterosexual desire'.[116] Summarising the techniques and the patients' reactions, Goland concluded that he managed to 'rechannel' the patients to 'completely heterosexual activities'. Yet he added that this treatment scheme could be effective only if patients displayed an 'eagerness to be treated' and if they considered their homosexual desire to be 'an anomaly, preventing them from having a fulfilling social life'.[117]

Goland's unpublished manuscripts give us a new perspective on his therapeutic approach to homosexuality and a glimpse of what was actually happening in his consultation room. Particularly illuminating are the questionnaires that Goland designed to evaluate his patients' progress in transitioning from homosexual orientation to heterosexual, in which the patient was offered statements to choose from that best described his state. The questionnaire contained the following:

Have any of the following changes taken place:

I. Fixations of attention (fiksatsiya vnimaniya) on persons of the same sex have become:

   (a) extremely rare
   (b) episodic and do not contain any stirring (volnuyushchii) erotic component.
   (c) communication with persons of the same sex is smooth and calm.

II. The disappearance of homosexual dreams (gomoseksual'nykh snovidenii). Even if persons of the same sex appear in the dream, it happens without erotic emotions (eroticheskoe perezhivanie).

III. Even when slightly inebriated, there is no display of homosexual tendencies, while previously inebriation used to trigger their realisation.[118]

The questionnaire also asked patients to describe their emotional state. The available multiple-choice responses included: 'feeling of liberation, joy, victory over oneself', 'indifference, tranquillity', 'a sense of ill-being' (chuvstvo neblagopoluchiya) with 'elements of confusion', 'fear of losing erotic emotions', 'uncertainty about acquiring heterosexual feelings', 'comfortable, calm'. These statements were used by Goland in his reports on the success of his enterprise.[119] Even though, as we can see, Goland expected to hear answers that reflected the unsatisfactory state of his patients, he was still convinced that these were initial reactions that would soon go away. The questions given at the end of the questionnaire attest to that: 'When did you overcome (pereboleli) the feelings of your new state, get accustomed to it, accept [it] as normal in the course of treatment? When did you start welcoming (privetstvovat') this state and wait for a new treatment stage?'[120]

Prior to the second stage of psychotherapy, aimed at helping the patient 'rechannel' his sexual interest towards women, the patient was to tell the doctor how he felt about women in another questionnaire, which featured the following questions: 'Have you had a perverse attitude (prevratnyi vzglyad) to the persons of the opposite sex?' 'What is your aesthetic perception (esteticheskoe vospriyatie) of the woman before treatment?' 'Was there a total absence of aesthetic perception of the woman?' The patient was also provided with a set of statements to choose from to describe the nature of his relations with women: 'calm, just business-like (chisto delovye)', 'tentative (nereshchitel'nyi), shackled (skovannyi), timid (boiazlivye) relations, prevalence of a desire to avoid female society', 'suspicions that the woman can reveal (razoblachit') your vice' and 'a feeling of dislike, an urge to minimise communication'.[121]

Once the second stage was completed, the patient was to document his feelings and impressions in his answers to a new set of questions. These included:

> Have you acquired skills of communication with women? Are you able to see the fineness of the woman's physique (izyashchestvo form), spirituality (odukhotvorennost') and tenderness (nezhnost')? Was there a necessity to talk with women? Have you acquired or strengthened communication skills with women? Have you started having dreams where you have situations of non-sexual and sexual communication with women?

Other questions were: 'Have you come up with a paragon of a beautiful female face? Have you got an idea of a beautiful female face? Does seeing a female image fill you with positive emotions (svetlye emotsii)?'[122] Goland's belief that the patient's start of intimate relations with women was an indicator of the treatment's success apparently stemmed from his belief that underlying his patient's homosexuality was a phobia of women. Such belief was also characteristic of some psychiatrists trying to cure homosexuality in the US at that time.[123]

Apart from the questionnaires, Goland encouraged his patients to produce a written account of their feelings and attempts at dating women, which was part of the therapy. In an unpublished draft for a conference paper, Goland cited the excerpts from his patients' diaries, presenting them as evidence of the success of his therapy. One of his patients wrote on 13 February 1968: 'I am in a good mood. I still have full confidence in a positive outcome, but I wish that it all could be happening faster.'[124] Goland then went on to describe his patient's romantic rendezvous with a woman:

> I went out with N. for the second time and we went to the circus. Male and female athletes were performing there, yet I had no curiosity whatsoever in their musculature (muskulatura) or anything else. Somehow, I forgot about it, I was delighted by the performance.

> Fixations on the lads (khloptsy) are very weak, sometimes I don't think about them at all. I still find attractive facial features and haircuts of the girls I see on the street.[125]

Several days later, the patient reported a new breakthrough – the appearance of sexual arousal at a woman. Goland provided the patient's diary entry dated from 29 February 1968, in which the patient described his first sexual emotions, experienced at his friends' flat, where he saw a girl sitting on bed: 'One of the girls was sitting on bed in such a way that her legs were showing above the knees. Looking at that, I felt a slight arousal (nebol'shoe vozbuzhdenie).' Goland's report ended with this observation and did not provide any comments.

It was not only Goland's patients who reported their 'progress' towards acquiring heterosexuality. Wives who brought their husbands to Goland for treatment of homosexuality also noticed positive changes in the behaviour of their spouses. Nadezhda, who brought her husband Andrei to Goland in 1967, was very content with the treatment outcomes, reporting: 'He started helping me about the house, beating carpets, doing the shopping (skhodit v magazine). Now he never leaves me alone, he is always with me everywhere. He flirts with me, whenever we are alone. He started thinking about having a baby.'[126] According to Nadezhda, Andrei became more attentive to her: 'Previously, he never paid attention to the way I dressed or my hair. Now he buys me fashion magazines and gives me presents.'[127] But the most important improvement was that Andrei resumed having sexual relations with Nadezhda:

> He started sexual relations with me very unexpectedly for me. It was after the 1968 new year ... After the first time he started showing more affection and day after day I could feel his growing desire. The intervals between intimacies (sblizhenie) at first lasted three weeks, then two, now one.[128]

The renewed ambitions of the Khrushchev-era leaders to mould a New Soviet Person led them to pay more attention to Soviet families, where such a person would be raised. Various collectives were mobilised to 'help' spouses whose marriages were on the brink of collapse, by pressuring them into improving and retaining their relationships.[129] Local party organs, trade-union organisations and voluntary groups also intervened in family life by advising spouses on how to properly raise their children.[130] Goland's unofficial practice of medical treatment of homosexuality, which started to get off the ground in the first years under Brezhnev, essentially complemented these efforts, despite not being officially authorised. It addressed homosexuality, a problem that, just like male impotence, had far-reaching implications for marriage and its stability. What's more, Goland's psychotherapy not only set out to eliminate perverse sexual desire, it also sought to mould a homosexual into an active contributor to the society, a loving husband and father. Achieving the latter was equally important – after the treatment of her husband was over, Nadezhda noted that her husband started finally participating in their family life.[131]

Performing medical treatment of homosexuality unofficially, Goland attempted to institutionalise his practice and thereby claim his medical authority over the issue. In 1969 he wrote a letter to Pavel Posvyanskii, the head of the Moscow Department of Sexopathology, in which he deplored an unsatisfactory provision of sexological help in the city of Gorkii.[132] Goland lamented that the Gorkii psychiatric clinic, operating under the Gorkii Medical Institute, was failing to provide adequate sexological help to patients with sexual disorders, due to their increasing numbers. As an example, he noted that in 1968 the clinic's sexologists treated 371 people and those wanting to arrange an appointment with the doctor had to wait an average of six months. To resolve this problem, Goland suggested opening a 'sexological method centre' staffed with qualified sexologists and providing sexological help for a range of problems.[133]

Apart from providing neuropathologists, urologists and psychiatrists with special sexological training and offering treatment for a wide range of sexual disorders, the sexological centre would be a place where homosexuals could come for medical help. According to Goland's plan, the centre would provide homosexuals with 'special psychotherapy', which, as he stressed, was 'a type of medical aid absent in the clinics of the country'.[134] Goland's request was welcomed by Posvyanskii, who requested additional information from Goland in order to raise this question with the Ministry of Health, which would have the ultimate right to endorse such initiatives.[135] Yet, unfortunately for Goland, his plan never materialised and the idea never became reality – as he explained to me later, the reason lay in the lack of funding. Whether it was genuine lack of funding or whether the Ministry of Health was wilfully reluctant to endorse a centre whose activities, primarily medical treatment of homosexuality, would conflict with the official standing of homosexuality as a crime remains unclear. However, if such a centre had been opened it would have furthered the perception of homosexuality not as a crime, but as a disease. This would have given doctors more leverage to argue for the decriminalisation of sodomy.

Kosarev's article: attempts to frame homosexuality as a disease (1967)

The re-emergence of serious discussions on male homosexuality in Soviet medical books inevitably invited the question: how could the medical status of male homosexuality square with the existing sodomy law? Although the doctors, as discussed above, implicitly claimed homosexuality for the medical profession, none of them shed light on this seeming inconsistency. One of the first sexologists to raise the issue was V. K. Kosarev, a psychiatrist from the Serbskii Central Research Institute of Forensic Psychiatry, about whom we know almost nothing. In 1967 he published an article, 'On the Question of the Forensic and Psychiatric Importance of Homosexuality', in an edited volume, *Problems of Sexopathology*, in which he proposed to subject homosexuals to medical treatment rather than punish them in prisons.[136]

Kosarev opened his article by briefly discussing how other countries tackled the issue of homosexuality, reminding the reader that in East Germany consensual sodomy between two male persons had already been decriminalised: 'It should be noted that in the GDR, as well as in other socialist and capitalist countries, homosexuality (except for the cases where it is forcible and conducted in relation to children) is not punishable by law.'[137] According to Kosarev, the same was the case in Czechoslovakia: 'Czechoslovakian psychiatrist Bouchal notes that since the adoption of the new legislation in Czechoslovakia (since 1962) on the repeal of punishment for homosexuality, there ostensibly has been no increase in the number of homosexuals or any change in their behaviour.'[138] Kosarev paid particular attention to the arguments of Czechoslovakian sexologists

Kurt Freund and Karel Nedoma, who contended that homosexuals should be viewed as individuals with 'diminished responsibility':

> Psychiatrists Nedoma and Freund (Czechoslovakia) in their paper 'The Problem of Responsibility and Corrective Measures in Sexual Delinquents' (1959) posit that in the cases of sex crimes one may always bear in mind the abnormal mental or sexual state that restricts the freedom of an individual to make a decision. Some of these crimes fall under the category of 'diminished responsibility' (umen'shennaya vmenyaemost'), adopted in the legislation of some countries. The authors believe that the punishment of such individuals is ineffective, thus, according to the authors, individuals with sexual perversions, dangerous to society, should be treated in a closed medical institution with a specific medical focus.[139]

It is interesting that in their original article, which paved the way for decriminalisation of consensual sodomy in Czechoslovakia, Nedoma and Freund actually argued that it was paedophiles and sadists who fell under the category of 'diminished responsibility', not homosexuals. On the contrary, Nedoma and Freud believed that homosexuality was not 'dangerous for society' and therefore should not be considered a crime. They also stated that 'an exclusively homoerotic person could not be attuned to heterosexuality' and that doctors could not cure such an individual 'by prescribing him to get married'.[140] Yet, for some reasons, Kosarev chose to avoid mentioning these important points in his article. Justifying the importance of applying the framework of 'diminished responsibility' to homosexuals, he wrote: 'On the one hand, it allows us to appreciate the role of social and organic factors in the formation of homosexuality and on the other hand it underlines the necessity to employ a differentiated approach to the forensic and psychiatric examination of individuals suffering from sexual perversions.'[141] Apparently, it was not Kosarev's intention to suggest that Soviet homosexuals should be viewed as persons with 'diminished responsibility' – Soviet law did not permit such determination and recognised only 'imputability' or 'non-imputability'.[142] What seems to lie behind his evocation of Nedoma and Freund's article was a simple suggestion that Soviet homosexuals tried in the courts for sodomy should be carefully examined to see if their imputability could be established and their sentence mitigated.

The protagonist of Kosarev's case study, 24-year-old man M., was accused of not only sodomy but depraved acts against minors, and so technically he fell under the category of individuals dangerous to society. While working in a boarding school (shkola internat), the convicted M. on numerous occasions invited the school's children (vospitanniki internata) to his room, where he indulged in mutual masturbation with them. Furthermore, M. indulged in sodomy with one of the school's teachers, performing a 'passive' role.[143] The combination of these offences led M. to being sentenced to five years in prison (Kosarev did not specify the type of the sentence).[144]

The prison, however, failed to correct M., because his homosexuality appeared to be more than a criminal act – it seemed to be an unflagging pathological desire that M. wished to rid himself of. Kosarev wrote:

> It was extremely distressing for M. to live among men in penitentiary facilities as the sight of the men always caused him to feel sexual arousal ... From prison, on numerous occasions, he wrote letters to the editors of *Zdorov'e* journal, the Health Ministry and to the chief specialist in forensic psychiatry with a request 'to investigate his disease and bring back his male happiness (muzhskoe schast'e)'.[145]

M.'s request was finally responded to and in 1966, two years into his gaol term, he was sent to the Serbskii Central Research Institute of Forensic Psychiatry, where psychiatrists scrutinised him. Psychiatrists established that M. had displayed homosexual tendencies from early childhood. Presenting facts from M.'s medical history, Kosarev noted that 'since his pre-school age M. preferred the society of his female peers', 'he liked to put on women's clothes' and at these moments he 'forgot that he was a boy'.[146] A significant milestone in M.'s development as a homosexual was the moment when he started masturbating. I have already noted in Chapter 2 that Soviet sex educators carefully sought to prevent young people from acquiring this habit, believing that it could put children on a slippery slide towards homosexuality. This appeared to be the case with M.: 'At the age of twelve or thirteen he started masturbating – every time he was fantasising about the boy he liked. That was also when he started to incline his male peers (mal'chikov-sverstnikov) towards mutual masturbation.'[147] Kosarev also emphasised M.'s feminine habits which had been evident throughout his early years: 'until the age of sixteen, M. continued to play with dolls, enjoyed singing and dancing ... When he was living at his sister's place, in her absence, he often tried on her dresses, shoes, put on lipstick, painted his brows.'[148] Kosarev especially noted that M. had always been saddened by the fact he was not born a woman.[149]

Although some of these descriptions are congruent with the Stalin- and Khrushchev-era psychiatric understandings of a typical homosexual as an effeminate individual, Kosarev presented M. as an individual who was genuinely suffering from his perversion and could not do anything about it. Likewise, Kosarev's attitude to M.'s homosexuality appears to be sympathetic, when we consider some other details drawn from M.'s medical history: 'He often confessed to the doctor that it was difficult for him to be in the society of men, because the sight of undressing men caused him sexual arousal. At these moments, he becomes as if drunk (slovno pyanyi).'[150] Kosarev depicted M. as an unhappy and profoundly dejected person, who found little understanding from the people surrounding him:

> During his stay in the institute (Serbskii Institute), M. had displayed an increased sexual interest towards other young patients in his ward. He attempted to sit on the bed of his 'chosen one' (izbrannik), talking about something with him ingratiatingly for a long time, tried to put his arms around him (obnimat'). He was in despair if 'the chosen one' did not understand his 'warm feeling (teploe otnoshenie) coming from the soul'. At these moments he was crying in his bed, declaring that he did not want to live.[151]

Kosarev emphasised the fact that M. was not a psychopath, but a person who was struggling with his desire, who would sacrifice a lot to get rid of his homosexuality:

> On numerous occasions he [M.] asked doctors to help him 'regain man's happiness' and help him 'become a full-fledged (polnotsennyi) man'. In our conversations with him, it became clear that his desire 'to become a full-fledged man' appeared in places of confinement, where he realised that the continuation of his previous behaviour would inevitably lead him to run against the law. Somewhat demonstratively, he declares that 'he would agree to rid himself of his sexual feeling (polovoe chuvstvo)' in order to 'resign himself fully to labour' and 'profit the people with his labour'.[152]

Kosarev added that M. 'possessed a store of knowledge', that his speech was 'well-bred' (gramotnaya) and with a 'good vocabulary' (khoroshii zapas slov); he also noted that M. was 'well versed in social affairs' (obshchestvennye sobytiya) and was able 'to critically assess the unfavourable situation he was in'.[153] Perhaps these observations led Kosarev to hope that M. could still be reclaimable for the Soviet project and society more broadly. Indeed, M. not only expressed his desire to labour 'somewhat demonstratively', he also displayed a certain measure of cultured behaviour or 'culturedness' (kul'turnost'). This was an important instrument in moulding the New Soviet Person and Soviet leaders struggled to inculcate it in people from the very onset of the Soviet regime.[154] 'Culturedness' implied having wide erudition in classical literature and art, as well as knowledge of social etiquette; a 'cultured' person was to have a range of personal qualities contrary to vulgarity, cruelty and evil.[155] One of a whole range of methods by which Soviet leaders instilled 'culturedness' in their people was popular advice literature with instructions on how to be a cultured person; during the 1960s, as Catriona Kelly has shown, this literature accorded ample attention to the subject of 'kul'tura rechi' (culture of speech) and to the task of forming linguistic etiquette in Soviet people.[156] It was the desirable qualities of a 'cultured' Soviet person, primarily erudition and good speech, that Kosarev apparently discerned in his patient, and these very qualities possibly led him and other doctors to conclude that M.'s homosexuality was not a vice, but an unfortunate affliction.

After subjecting M. to a battery of medical tests, a commission of psychiatrists came to the conclusion that M. was sick, as he had demonstrated an inclination to sexual perversions in early childhood. The type of sentence that had originally been handed down to him was modified accordingly: his offence was requalified under Article 362 of the RSFSR Criminal Code, which allowed for relief from punishment due to chronic psychiatric illness.[157] Kosarev summarised the psychiatric commission's decision:

> Taking into consideration M.'s organic predisposition and increased sexual arousal (vozbudimost'), which manifested itself quite early and which turned into a syndrome of sexual perversions under the corresponding external circumstances ... the commission deemed it possible to interpret M.'s actions under Article 362 of the RSFSR Criminal Code and send him for treatment to a minimum-security psychiatric hospital (obshchego rezhima).[158]

Despite Kosarev's proposal to regard homosexuality as a pathological condition and thus to free homosexuals of a prison term, he did not lay out his ideas in more detail. He did not specify whether it was the homosexual himself who had to bring his 'illness' to the attention of the court or if it was the court that had to decide whether the homosexual in question had to be sent for medical examination. Other experts in the field who acknowledged the importance of taking into account the defendant's psychiatric health in sodomy cases were no less ambiguous. A prominent Soviet forensic expert, for example, Mikhail I. Avdeev, wrote in *Forensic Examination of Living Individuals* (1968), a manual for forensic experts, that homosexual proclivities of a sodomy offender could have a psychopathological nature: 'When investigating the cases of sodomy psychiatric examination may be required, because in some cases sodomy may be a display of psychopathological peculiarities of the subject.' Although this represented a significant shift from his previous framing of homosexuality as a vice that required no psychiatric scrutiny, he did not provide further instructions in which cases such examination was required and what investigators were to do if the perpetrator's crime indeed was a result of 'psychopathological peculiarity'.[159]

Another key issue omitted by Kosarev was whether those charged with sodomy could choose either treatment or a prison sentence, as they could at that time in England.[160] In Czechoslovakia, prior to the decriminalisation of consensual homosexuality, medical treatment of homosexuality was also seen by authorities as an alternative to legal punishment.[161] Was this also the case in the Soviet Union? Scholars have demonstrated that some Soviet homosexual men could consent to undergoing medical treatment in hospitals, considering it a better alternative to incarceration, yet more evidence is needed to establish how widespread such incidents were.[162]

Soviet sexopathology and Alfred Kinsey

Apart from relying on sexology from socialist countries, Soviet doctors actively engaged with the findings of Western specialists, especially those of Alfred Kinsey, who argued that homosexuality was a natural variant of human sexuality and far more widespread than conventional wisdom dictated. Although recent historiography has questioned Kinsey's methods and findings, at the time of their production they were revolutionary, and Western liberation movements owed a lot to Kinsey.[163] Soviet sexologists were certainly aware of Kinsey's studies and some of them willingly incorporated them in their work. Elizaveta Derevinskaya's dissertation on lesbians cited Kinsey and had a lively awareness of Western sexology. Others, inspired by his work, attempted to undertake similar research which would examine the sexual behaviour of the Soviet people. Igor Kon tells us about his student Sergei Golod, who in the early 1960s 'expressed a desire to study the sexual behaviour of contemporary Soviet young people under the influence of Kinsey's book'.[164] Despite Kon's admonition that the subject would be 'non-dissertationable', Golod decided to proceed with his idea. The project was fraught with numerous obstacles: the Party regional committee was reluctant to approve the questionnaires, and potential participants were afraid to answer even the most innocuous questions.[165] Eventually the Party officials branded Golod's dissertation 'an ideological diversion against Soviet youth' and the defence of the dissertation was suspended indefinitely.[166]

In fact, some Soviet medical professionals had more luck with their studies of sexual behaviour of Soviet people. One of them was Il'ya Popov, a trainee psychiatrist, who defended his dissertation 'Materials on the Sex Life of Male Workers of an Industrial City of Central Kazakhstan' at the Karaganda State Medical Institute in 1968 (Figure 12).[167] He conducted his research under the supervision of Abram Svyadoshch, the psychiatrist who supervised Elizaveta Derevinskaya's dissertation. Despite its significance, Popov's dissertation was never published. In his study he examined the prevalence of homosexual behaviour among Soviet men, comparing his findings to those produced by Alfred Kinsey.

Popov examined a sample of 500 men drawn from the city of Timer-Tau in the Kazakhstan Republic. Although he did not specify exactly how he chose the subjects for his study, he noted that all of them were workers and all of them willingly took part in his research. Between 1965 and 1967 each man underwent physical examination and was interviewed by Popov. At the interview each man was offered twelve pages of questions concerning various aspects of his sex life.[168] Each was asked questions about the most intimate aspects of his life: whether he had engaged in sexual play when he was a child, and if so whether he did so with boys or girls; when he first started masturbating and what his attitude to it was; whether he

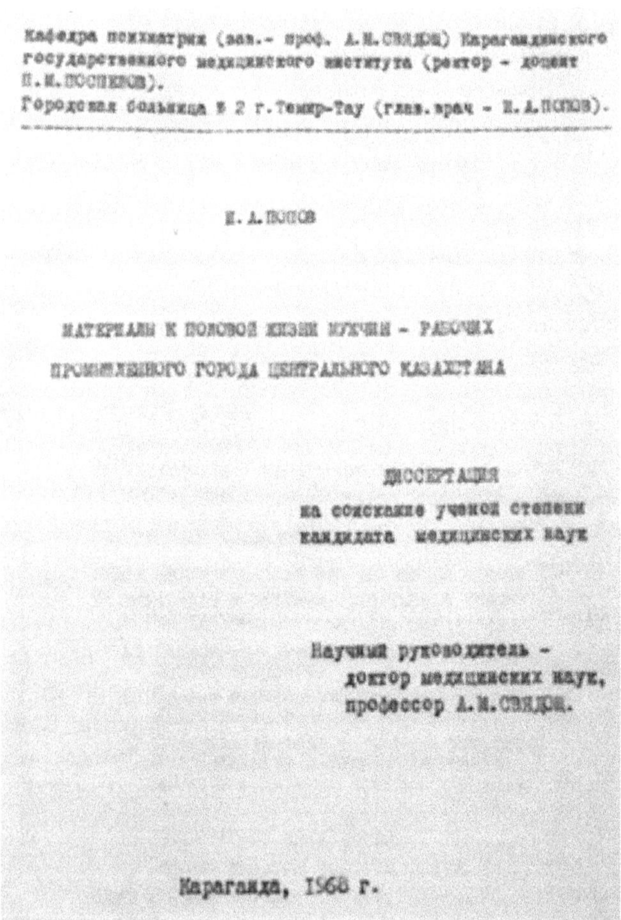

Кафедра психиатрии (зав.- проф. А.М.СВЯДОЩ) Карагандинского государственного медицинского института (ректор - доцент П.М.ПОСПЕЛОВ).
Городская больница № 2 г.Темир-Тау (глав.врач - И.А.ПОПОВ).

И.А.ПОПОВ

МАТЕРИАЛЫ К ПОЛОВОЙ ЖИЗНИ МУЖЧИН - РАБОЧИХ
ПРОМЫШЛЕННОГО ГОРОДА ЦЕНТРАЛЬНОГО КАЗАХСТАНА

ДИССЕРТАЦИЯ
на соискание ученой степени
кандидата медицинских наук

Научный руководитель -
доктор медицинских наук,
профессор А.М.СВЯДОЩ.

Караганда, 1968 г.

Figure 12 ‘Materials on the Sex Life of Male Workers of an Industrial City of Central Kazakhstan’ (1968)

had extramarital sex and if so at what age did the first such instance occur. The participants were also asked whether or not they had engaged in homosexual relations.[169] Aware that participants might not understand some of the terms of the questionnaire, Popov first organised a lecture detailing specificities of male sexual development and male sexual life, as well as the objectives of his study.[170] Following the lecture and before the interview, each study subject was told the importance of being honest and giving precise answers to the questions provided.[171]

The participants of the study were asked about the objects of their sexual play during childhood, whether these were boys or girls.[172] Before providing his own data, Popov evoked Kinsey's findings: 'According to Kinsey and his associates (1948), sexual play among children was homosexual in 60 per cent of cases and heterosexual in 40 per cent of cases.'[173] Popov's findings in the Soviet context suggested the contrary. Out of 500 only 428 men remembered their early childhood experiences:[174] 353 men stated that their sexual play was with girls, 27 men acknowledged having sexual play with boys, 12 men said they had sexual play with adults and 36 men said they played with both boys and girls.[175] Summarising his findings, Popov concluded: 'the data on childhood sexual play derived from the examined men has demonstrated that in most cases they are heterosexual in their essence'.[176]

Another question was whether they had ever indulged in homosexuality. Again, before providing his own data, Popov cited Kinsey's findings regarding the prevalence of homosexuality among American people: 'A. Kinsey believes that 37 per cent of the male and 24 per cent of the female population have a homosexual experience in the period between the beginning of sexual maturation and adulthood (starshii vozrast).'[177] By contrast, Popov's findings demonstrated that the rates of homosexuality among the examined men were minuscule: 'out of 500 men, only 6 state that they had homosexual relations at some points in their lives'.[178] Commenting on his findings, Popov noted:

> All respondents believed their homosexual liaisons to be a vice and attributed them to a period in their life when they could not be in the society of women (places of confinement, war years, prolonged expeditions). All respondents denied having homosexual liaisons at the time of examination. All six respondents who had such liaisons are now married.[179]

Popov's minuscule findings of homosexual activity among men could have also been a result of the methodology he employed – a public lecture on homosexuality delivered to his prospective informants could have encouraged them to underreport their own homosexual proclivities.

Although Popov suggested that his views on sexuality were progressive and ground-breaking, his work demonstrated a strong expectation that the prevalence of homosexuality in a socialist country like the Soviet Union was low compared to the US. Such expectation was not exclusively confined to Popov's study. Dagmar Herzog has shown that in the early 1960s East German scientists, examining the sexual life of the county's young people, were keen to demonstrate that the rates of homosexuality were low. He explains that East Germany's ruling party at that time 'was always apprehensive and anxious to keep from international attention any empirical data that could possibly be used against socialism by its "enemies"; it was no surprise that research that was able to demonstrate an especially low incidence of youth homosexual activity in the GDR was published'.[180] Herzog tells us about an East German medical professor who, after conducting a study of sexual behaviour of young GDR citizens in the early 1960s, concluded, 'disguising his sense of pride', that the incidence of homosexual activity was low among them.[181] Such stress on low rates of homosexuality in the GDR, in Herzog's view, was consistent with the regime's preoccupation with normality.[182]

Other Soviet sexopathologists also wrestled with the issues of normal sexuality and sexual perversions in light of Kinsey's findings. Pavel Posvyanskii, the head of the Department of Sexopathology of the Moscow Research Institute of Psychiatry, was one of them. In his article 'Sexual Perversions: Definition of the Phenomenon, Experience of Classification', Posvyanskii theorised on which aspects of one's sex life could be regarded as perverted.[183] He defined 'sexual perversions' (seksual'nye perversii) as 'pathological perversions of sexual desire', which were 'different from the physiological (normal) way of sexual intercourse'. Yet he pointed out that in real life this assumption was far from being cut and dried: the phenomenon of sexual perversions was rather complex and it was difficult to tell the normal from the pathological: 'However, the borders here between the norm and pathology are rather blurred and ill-defined to a greater degree than in other areas of medicine.'[184] Posvyanskii wrote: 'Numerous authors (including Kinsey's report) stress the difficulty in differentiating sexual perversions as morbid states from "perverse" (perverznyi) acts in normal sex life. Some authors ... go as far as to erase the border between the norm and pathology. Such a stance is not correct.'[185]

Here apparently Posvyanskii implied Kinsey's premise that homosexuality was a normal variant of human behaviour and expressed disagreement with it. The only point that Posvyanskii could agree on with his Western counterparts was that sexual practices other than traditional vaginal intercourse could be admissible: 'in customary sexual intercourse, during love play (lyubovnaya igra), often those forms of sexual intercourse, going outside the limits of normalcy, can be admissible (dopuskayutsya). Yet, under no circumstances can they be considered as perverse (perverznymi).'[186]

This statement brought clarity to one of the common misconceptions about sex in the Soviet Union that afflicted almost anyone – that normal sex could not be anything but vaginal intercourse. Such practices as oral or, even more so, anal sex between individuals of the opposite sex were believed to be a sign of debauchery. Mikhail Stern, a Soviet sexologist, attested to that fact, arguing that 'if a husband suggested such a thing, his wife would immediately begin to suspect that he had been leading a life of secret debauchery'.[187] Some criminologists also suggested that if a wife noticed that her husband inclined her to 'perverse forms of satisfaction of sexual desire' then it might be a sign of his latent homosexuality.[188] Finally, as I will show in Chapter 4, some Soviet legislators equated oral and anal sex to sexual perversions and believed that they were no less dangerous than sodomy between two men. Posvyanskii dispelled these beliefs, thereby partially acknowledging the validity of Kinsey's findings regarding the variations of human sexual behaviour. Yet, according to Posvyanskii, these variations were admissible only between men and women; sexual practices between individuals of the same sex apparently fell under the category of perverse sexual practices.

Conclusion

In a report presented at a scientific conference on sexopathology in Moscow in 1969, a doctor from Kiev, Y. Borisenko, stated: 'Sexology and sexopathology have great social importance, since they directly concern the issues of marriage, family and education of youth. Increasingly more attention has been paid lately to the theoretical and practical problems of sexopathology on the part of the medical community (meditsinskaya obshchestvennost').'[189] At the same conference, a doctor from Riga, Z. G. Russinova, mentioned an issue that Borisenko had not apparently deemed to be very pressing. This issue was homosexuality and the importance of lifting criminal sanctions for it so that Soviet homosexuals could seek medical help without fear of being apprehended: 'The question of sexual pathology should be viewed and resolved not only in medical but in social aspects. In particular, the time has come to raise the question of revising the existing legislation regarding male homosexuality, since the law deprives these individuals of the possibility to consult specialists for medical help.'[190]

Russinova's pronouncement represented a significant shift in the medical discussion of homosexuality, which intensified due to the emergence of a new branch of psychiatric science in the 1960s – sexopathology. First and foremost, it fostered a new 'scientific' perception of homosexuality, which was different from the hitherto simplistic 'police' understandings of it as a criminal psychopathy. In their texts, Soviet sexopathologists presented homosexuals as individuals who realised their deficient sexuality and sought a cure for it. Other homosexuals were depicted as educated individuals with the ability to consider and reflect on their state, which apparently made them reclaimable for Soviet society. The ability of homosexuals to reflect on their state was also an important sign that they were amenable to psychotherapeutic treatment, which taught them how to control their desire and educated them on how to communicate with individuals of the opposite sex. The latter two were consistent with the existing educational and ideological narratives of that time and, therefore, can be viewed as yet one more ramification of the Soviet intent to create a New Soviet Person.

In essence, Soviet medical practices around homosexuality in the 1960s were Foucauldian in nature – patients confessed their desires, while doctors carefully listened to them, subjected them to medical examinations and typed up their findings in articles and reports. Yan Goland, for example, didn't merely encourage his patients to describe the sexual acts they had engaged in, but asked them to 'reconstruct, in and around the act, the thoughts that recapitulated it, the obsessions that accompanied it, the images, desires, modulations and quality of the pleasure that animated it'.[191] In their diaries, letters and questionnaires Goland's patients described the objects of their desire, their fantasies and feelings unabashedly and without restraint. They confessed their obsessions with the male penis, their love of 'slim and athletic [male] bodies', their feelings of love and sexual attraction towards their unsuspecting male friends, as well as attempts to persuade them into mutual masturbation. They even told Goland about their techniques of self-pleasuring.

Sexopathologists also raised important questions of the legal status of male homosexuality in their works. Unlike psychiatric texts on homosexuality published in the period from 1930 to 1960, which simply stated that male homosexuality was a punishable offence, sexopathologists of the 1960s discussed whether homosexuals could be spared criminal punishment, considering their 'disease'. In doing so, they were drawing on the writings of Czechoslovakian and East German sexologists who had previously moved forward with similar arguments. However, when it came to the findings of the American sociologist Alfred Kinsey, who argued that homosexuality was a normal variant of human sexuality, Soviet sexopathologists disagreed and even tried to scientifically prove that the rates of homosexuality in the USSR were lower than in capitalist countries; such a stance was shared with scientists working in other socialist states.

Notes

1 To preserve the anonymity of the protagonists of the cases explored in this chapter, each one was assigned a pseudonym.

2 Typewritten feedback of a wife of Goland's former patient (hereinafter 'Nadezhda's feedback'), which she provided in September 1968 after her husband had completed a psychotherapy course for homosexuality. Yan Goland's personal collection, 2.

3 Nadezhda's feedback, 2.

4 Ibid, 3.

5 Frances Lee Bernstein, Christopher Burton and Dan Healey, 'Introduction: Experts, Expertise, and New Histories of Soviet Medicine', in *Soviet Medicine: Culture, Practice, and Science*, ed. Frances L. Bernstein, Christopher Burton and Dan Healey (DeKalb: Northern Illinois University Press, 2010).

6 Bernstein, *Dictatorship of Sex*, pp. 60–1.

7 Dan Healey, 'Unruly Identities: Soviet Psychiatry Confronts the "Female Homosexual" of the 1920s', in *Gender in Russian History and Culture*, ed. Linda Edmondson (Basingstoke, Palgrave Macmillan, 2001), pp. 116–38. See also: Healey, 'Homosexual Existence': 355.

8 Healey, *Homosexual Desire*, p. 139.

9 Ibid., p. 148.
10 Kon, *Sexual Revolution in Russia*, p. 242.
11 Yevgenii A. Popov, 'O klassifikatsii polovykh izvrashchenii', in *Problemy psikhiatrii i psikhopatologii*, ed. S. N. Davidenkov (Moscow: Biomedgiz, 1935), pp. 526–31.
12 Igor S. Sumbaev, 'K psikhoterapii gomoseksualizma', *Sovetskaya Psikhonevrologiya*, no. 3 (1936): 59–68.
13 Ibid., 60–5.
14 Aron I. Belkin, *Tretii pol: Sud'ba pasynkov prirody* (Moscow: Olimp, 2006), pp. 65–7.
15 Ibid., p. 266.
16 Ibid., p. 267.
17 P. Manenkov, 'Sluchai neobychnogo sozhitel'stva dvukh zhenshchin', in *Yubileinyi sbornik Posvyashchennyi Professoru N. I. Gorizontovu* (Novosibirsk: Novosib. gos. institut dlya usovershenstvovaniya vrachei i medinstituta, 1939), p. 102.
18 Mikhail O. Gurevich, *Psikhiatriya: Uchebnik dlya meditsinskikh institutov* (Moscow: Medgiz, 1949), p. 471.
19 Ibid.
20 Ibid.
21 Ibid.
22 Ibid.
23 Izmail F. Sluchevskii, *Psikhiatriya* (Leningrad: Medgiz, 1957), p. 343.
24 Ibid., p. 342.
25 Popov, 'Polovye izvrashcheniya', pp. 942–51.
26 Ibid., p. 951.
27 Ibid.
28 Kon, *Sexual Revolution in Russia,* p. 95.
29 Il'ya M. Porudominskii, 'Kto zhe lechit polovye rasstroistva?', *Meditsinskaya gazeta*, no. 96 (29 November 1963): 3.
30 Ibid.
31 Ibid.
32 Foucault, *History of Sexuality*, p. 26.
33 Peter H. Juviler, 'Cell Mutation in Soviet Society: The Family', in *Soviet Society and Culture: Essays in Honor of Vera S. Dunham*, ed. Terry L. Thompson and Richard Sheldon (Boulder and London: Westview, 1988), p. 42.
34 Field, *Private Life and Communist Morality*, p. 68.
35 Porudominskii, 'Kto zhe lechit polovye rasstroistva?', 3.
36 Pavel B. Posvyanskii, 'Sovremennye problemy seksopatologii', in *Aktual'nye voprosy seksopatologii: Sbornik statei,* ed. Dmitrii D. Fedotov (Moscow: Moskovskii nauchno-issledovatel'skii institut psikhiatrii, 1967), p. 17.

37 Ibid.
38 GARF, f. A-482, op. 48, delo 4039, l. 37.
39 Interview with Yan Goland, 1 April 2017, Nizhnii Novgorod.
40 Seminar vrachei po psikhoterapii i seksologii (1964), g. Gorkii. A photo from Yan Goland's personal archive. Popov was a trainee psychiatrist under Svyadoshch, who for some reason did not attend any of the seminars on sexology.
41 Nikolai Kibrik, '50 let otechestvennoi meditsinskoi seksologii', Rossiiskoe nauchnoe seksologicheskoe obshchestvo, http://1sexology.ru/4-50-let-otechestvennoj-medicinskoj-seksologii/ (accessed 16 November 2017). The Moscow Research Institute of Psychiatry was founded on 30 March 1920 and since then had been playing a key role in the establishment of the USSR psychiatric service. Various prominent psychiatrists had been working there, for instance Mark I. Sereiskii, the author of the entry on homosexuality in the first volume of the *Great Soviet Encyclopaedia*. Before becoming head of the Department of Sexopathology, Posvyanskii headed the Moscow Research Institute of Psychiatry himself. See: Anonymous, 'Istoriya Instituta', http://mniip.serbsky.ru/home-page/istoriya-instituta/ (accessed 10 March 2018). On the history of the institute, see also: Vladimir V. Kovalev, 'Vklad Moskovskogo nauchno-issledovetel'skogo instituta psikhiatrii MZ RSFSR v psikhiatricheskuyu nauku i praktiku za 60 let i perspektivnye zadachi', in *Tezisy dokladov, posvyashchennykh 60-letiyu Moskovskogo nauchno-issledovatel'skogo instituta psikhiatrii MZ RSFSR i 50-letiyu Moskovskoi gorodskoi klinicheskoi psikhiatricheskoi bol'nitsy № 4 im. P. B. Gannushkina: Konferentsiya, Moscow okt. 1981* (Moscow: Moskovskii NII psikhiatrii, 1981), pp. 3–6.
42 Anonymous, 'Otdelenie seksologii i terapii seksual'nykh disfunktsii', Moskovskii NII psikhiatrii, http://mniip.serbsky.ru/nauka/nauchnye-podrazdeleniya-instituta/otdelenie-seksologii-i-terapii-seksualnyx-disfunkcij/ (accessed 16 November 2017).
43 Anonymous, 'Deyatel'nost' otdela seksual'noi patologii Moskovskogo nauchno-issledovatel'skogo instituta psikhiatrii po vnedreniyu v praktiku nauchnykh dostizhenii za period 1965–1973 g.g.', undated report, Archive of the Department of Sexopathology.
44 Seminar vrachei po psikhoterapii i seksologii (1966), g. Gorkii. A photo from Yan Goland's personal archive.
45 Anonymous, 'Deyatel'nost' otdela seksual'noi patologii', 2.
46 Ibid., 1.
47 Kateřina Lišková, 'Now You See Them, Now You Don't: Sexual Deviants and Sexological Expertise in Communist Czechoslovakia', *History of the Human Sciences* 29, no. 1 (February 2016): 54.
48 Ibid.

49 Ibid.
50 Kurt Freund, 'K problematike gomoseksualizma u muzhchin', *Chekhoslovatskoe meditsinskoe obozrenie* 6, no.1 (1965).
51 Ibid., 21.
52 Ibid.
53 Tommy Dickinson, *Curing Queers: Mental Nurses and Their Patients, 1935–74* (Manchester: Manchester University Press, 2015), pp. 57–61.
54 Ibid., pp. 61–76.
55 Alkarim Jivani, *It's Not Unusual: A History of Lesbian and Gay Britain in the Twentieth Century* (Bloomington and Indianapolis: Indiana University Press, 1997), p. 122.
56 Dickinson, *Curing Queers*, p. 200.
57 Ronald Bayer, *Homosexuality and American Psychiatry: The Politics of Diagnosis* (New York: Basic Books, 1981), p. 43.
58 Ibid.
59 Henry L. Milton, *Departing from Deviance: A History of Homosexual Rights and Emancipatory Science in America* (Chicago and London: University of Chicago Press, 2014), pp. 219–42.
60 On the homophobia of the McCarthy era and its implications, see Johnson, *Lavender Scare*; D'Emilio, *Sexual Politics*, p. 144.
61 Jack Drescher and Joseph P. Merlino, eds, *American Psychiatry and Homosexuality: An Oral History* (New York and London: Harrington Park, 2007), p. xvi. On other psychiatrists promoting the psychopathological status of homosexuality during this period: Bayer, *Homosexuality and American Psychiatry*, pp. 28–38. For the book: Irving Bieber, ed., *Homosexuality: A Psychoanalytic Study* (New York: Random House, 1962).
62 Bayer, *Homosexuality and American Psychiatry*, p. 33.
63 For instance, in December 1964 four gay protesters showed up at a public lecture, 'Homosexuality: A Disease', given by one of the psychoanalysts who participated in Bieber's studies. They demanded an opportunity to rebut the speaker and were eventually allowed to do so inside ten minutes. For a more nuanced account of the emerging homophile movement in the US: Bayer, *Homosexuality and American Psychiatry*, pp. 67–100.
64 Elizaveta M. Derevinskaya, 'Materialy k klinike, patogenezu, terapii zhenskogo gomoseksualizma' (Dissertatsiya na soiskanie uchenoi stepeni kandidata meditsinskikh nauk, Karaganda State Medical Institute, 1965), 39. I was first alerted to this dissertation by Dan Healey.
65 Ibid.
66 Healey, *Homosexual Desire*, p. 241.
67 Derevinskaya, 'Materialy k klinike', 28.

68 Ibid., 29.
69 Ibid., 122.
70 Ibid., 211.
71 Ibid., 220.
72 Ibid., 118.
73 Ibid., 119.
74 Nikolai V. Ivanov, *Voprosy psikhoterapii funktsional'nykh seksual'nykh rasstroistv* (Moscow: Meditsina, 1966).
75 Ibid., pp. 128–9.
76 Ivanov, *Voprosy psikhoterapii*, p. 130; Alexander Podrabinek, *Punitive Medicine* (Ann Arbor: Karoma, 1980), p. 132.
77 Ivanov, *Voprosy psikhoterapii*, p. 132.
78 Ibid., pp. 133–4.
79 Sidney Bloch and Peter Reddaway, *Russia's Political Hospitals: The Abuse of Psychiatry in the Soviet Union* (London: Victor Gollancz, 1977), pp. 42–3.
80 Kharkhordin, *Collective and the Individual*, pp. 231–78.
81 Ibid., p. 242.
82 Ibid.
83 Ivanov, *Voprosy psikhoterapii,* p. 134.
84 Ibid., p. 139.
85 Ibid., p. 134.
86 Perhaps Ivanov referred to homosexual men working in the world of art. Dan Healey argued that this world of art offered Soviet homosexuals 'the hope of respectability and even prestige'. Healey wrote that 'homosexuals believed with some justification that they were tolerated there, and they gravitated towards music, drama, dance, the visual arts and allied professions'. Apparently, some homosexual men from these milieus could believe that their homosexuality was the cornerstone of their talent, and this was Ivanov's main point here. On homosexual men in the Soviet cultural world, see: Dan Healey, 'Moscow', in *Queer Sites: Gay Urban Histories since 1600*, ed. David Higgs (London: Routledge, 1999), pp. 55–6.
87 Ivanov, *Voprosy psikhoterapii*, p. 135.
88 Ibid.
89 Healey, *Russian Homophobia*, p. 171. Ben de Jong also tells us that it was not uncommon for the police to resort to the help of young boys, who were instructed to entice homosexuals and subsequently bring them to the attention of militia; see: Ben de Jong, '"An Intolerable Kind of Moral Degeneration": Homosexuality in the Soviet Union', *Review of Socialist Law* 4 (1982): 346.
90 Healey, *Russian Homophobia*, p. 171.

91 Ibid., p. 172.
92 Ivanov, *Voprosy psikhoterapii*, p. 137.
93 This technique was widely practised in Europe, Russia and Japan, but was far less popular in North America. On its history and essence, see: Wolfgang Linden, 'The Autogenic Training Method of J. H. Schultz', in *Principles and Practice of Stress Management*, 3rd edn, ed. Paul M. Lehrer, Robert L. Woolfolk and Wesley E. Sime (New York: Guilford, 2007), pp. 151–71. Schultz believed that homosexuality was a result of childhood trauma or seduction during adolescence and that it could be cured by psychotherapy – he advanced these claims in his sex education book, published in 1941. Schultz's view resonated with a great number of his colleagues and even high-ranking Nazis. See: Harry Oosterhuis, 'Medicine, Male Bonding and Homosexuality in Nazi Germany', *Journal of Contemporary History* 32, no. 2 (April 1997): 193.
94 Ivanov, *Voprosy psikhoterapii,* p. 138.
95 Ibid.
96 Ibid.
97 Ibid., p. 136.
98 Ibid.
99 Ibid., p. 137.
100 Ibid.
101 Ibid., p. 138.
102 Ibid., p. 139
103 A videotaped undated interview with Leonid, conducted by Yan Goland in the early 1990s, in the course of which both discussed how they first met each other through Nikolai Ivanov.
104 Shlapentokh, *Public and Private Life*, pp. 153–4.
105 Isidore Ziferstein, 'The Soviet Psychiatrist: His Relationship to His Patients and to His Society', *American Journal of Psychiatry* 123, no. 4 (1966): 442.
106 Interview with Goland, 1 April 2017.
107 Ibid.
108 Yan G. Goland, 'K voprosu psikhoterapii gomoseksualizma', in *Voprosy psikhoterapii v obshchei meditsine i psikhonevrologii: Tezisy i avtoreferaty konferentsii 23–27 dekabrya 1968 g.* (Kharkov: Ukrainskii institut usovershenstvovaniya vrachei, 1968), pp. 434–6.
109 Ibid., p. 434.
110 Ibid., p. 435.
111 Ibid.
112 Ibid.
113 Ibid.
114 Ibid., p. 436.

115 Ibid.
116 Ibid.
117 Ibid.
118 An undated typewritten document describing the first stage of psychotherapy for homosexuality – 'sexual-psychological vacuum' (hereinafter 'Sexual-Psychological Vacuum'). It also contains a questionnaire for patients, evaluating the progress of their treatment. Yan Goland's personal archive.
119 Ibid.
120 An undated typewritten document describing the second stage of psychotherapy for homosexuality, aimed at rechannelling the patient's sexual interest from men to women (hereinafter, 'Second Stage of Psychotherapy for Homosexuality'). This document contains questions for patients, evaluating their progress and their suitability for further treatment. Yan Goland's personal archive.
121 Ibid.
122 Ibid.
123 Bayer, *Homosexuality and American Psychiatry*, p. 29.
124 Yan Goland, untitled and unpublished paper on psychotherapy of homosexuality, 1968 (hereinafter, 'Goland's 1968 paper'). Here Goland discusses the process of his patient's getting accustomed to talking to women. Goland cites the diary of an identified patient who underwent psychotherapy for homosexuality treatment in 1968. Yan Goland's personal archive, 2.
125 Ibid., 2.
126 Ibid., 3.
127 Ibid.
128 Ibid., 4.
129 Edward Cohn, *The High Title of a Communist: Postwar Party Discipline and the Values of the Soviet Regime* (Dekalb, IL: Northern Illinois University Press, 2015), pp. 142–65.
130 Field, *Private Life and Communist Morality*, p. 89.
131 Scholars have recently shed new light on the notions of the 'ideal father' during the Khrushchev era: he was expected not only to provide financial support for the family and participate in disciplining his children, but to be more emotionally engaged in the family life on a day-to-day basis. The issue of whether the Soviet man was supposed to play a crucial role in the maintenance of the family home was still ambiguous: Claire E. McCallum, 'Man about the House: Male Domesticity and Fatherhood in Soviet Visual Satire under Khrushchev', in *The Palgrave Handbook of Women and Gender in Twentieth-Century Russia and the Soviet Union*, ed. Melanie Ilič (London: Palgrave Macmillan, 2018), p. 343.

132 Yan Goland, typewritten letter to Pavel Posvyanskii, 1969. Yan Goland's personal archive.

133 Ibid., 4.

134 Ibid.

135 Pavel B. Posvyanskii, typewritten letter in response to Goland, July 1969. Yan Goland's personal archive.

136 V. K. Kosarev, 'K voprosy o sudebno-psikhiatricheskom znachenii gomoseksualizma', in *Aktual'nye voprosy seksopatologii: Sbornik statei,* ed. Dmitrii D. Fedotov (Moscow: Moskovskii nauchno-issledovatel'skii institut psikhiatrii, 1967), pp. 292–300.

137 Ibid., p. 292.

138 Ibid.

139 Ibid., p. 293. Karel Nedoma and Kurt Freund, 'Otazka Pricetnosti a napravnych opatreni u sexualnich delikventu', *Ceskoslovenska Psychiatrie* 4, no. 9 (1959): 264–9. Although the article is in Czech, it was supplemented with a summary in Russian, which Kosarev appears to have reproduced in his paper.

140 Lišková, 'Now You See Them, Now You Don't', 54.

141 Kosarev, 'K voprosy o znachenii gomoseksualizma', p. 294.

142 Dan Healey, 'Russian and Soviet Forensic Psychiatry: Troubled and Troubling', *International Journal of Law and Psychiatry* 37 (2014): 76.

143 Kosarev, 'K voprosy o znachenii gomoseksualizma', p. 294.

144 Ibid.

145 Ibid., p. 295.

146 Ibid., p. 293.

147 Ibid., p. 294.

148 Ibid., p. 294.

149 Ibid.

150 Ibid., p. 295.

151 Ibid., p. 296.

152 Ibid.

153 Ibid.

154 Catriona Kelly, *Refining Russia: Advice Literature, Polite Culture, and Gender from Catherine to Yeltsin* (Oxford: Oxford University Press, 2001), pp. 230–393.

155 Michele Rivkin-Fish, *Women's Health in Post-Soviet Russia: The Politics of Intervention* (Bloomington and Indiana: Indiana University Press, 2005), p. 12.

156 Kelly, *Refining Russia,* p. 334. On the concept of 'culturedness', see also: Catriona Kelly, 'Kul'turnost' in the Soviet Union: Ideal and Reality', in *Reinterpreting Russia*, ed. Geoffrey Hosking and Robert Service (London and Sydney: Arnold, 1999), pp. 199–213. On the promotion

of kul'turnost' in the Khrushchev-era sex education manuals, see: Field, *Private Life and Communist Morality*, pp. 89–97.

157 Normally such individuals would be sent for forced treatment or for treatment in conventional psychiatric clinics. See for example: Nina I. Felinskaya, *Reaktivnye sostoyaniya v sudebno-psikhiatricheskoi klinike* (Moscow: Meditsina, 1968), p. 264.

158 Ibid., p. 300.

159 See: Mikhail I. Avdeev, *Sudebno-meditsinskaya ekspertisa zhivykh lits* (Moscow: Meditsina, 1968), p. 323. For Avdeev's earlier texts, see: Mikhail I. Avdeev, *Sudebnaya meditsina* (Moscow: Gosudarstvennoie izdatel'stvo yuridicheskoi literatury, 1951), pp. 375–6; Mikhail I. Avdeev, *Sudebnaya meditsina* (Moscow: Gosudarstvennoie izdatel'stvo yuridicheskoi literatury, 1953), pp. 451–3.

160 Dickinson, *Curing Queers*, p. 1.

161 Nathan Ha, 'Detecting and Teaching Desire: Phallometry, Freund, and Behaviorist Sexology', *Osiris* 30, no. 1 (2015): 210.

162 Franeta, *My Pink Road to Russia*, pp. 203–31.

163 See: Jonathan Gathorne-Hardy, *Alfred Kinsey: Sex the Measure of All Things, a Biography* (London: Chatto & Windus, 1998); James H. Jones, *Alfred Kinsey: A Public/Private Life* (London: W. W. Norton, 1997); Ron Jackson Suresha, *Bisexual Perspectives on the Life and Work of Alfred C. Kinsey* (London: Routledge, 2010). On the influence of Kinsey's studies on the Western gay liberation movement, see: Bayer, *Homosexuality and American Psychiatry*, p. 42–6.

164 Kon, *Sexual Revolution in Russia*, p. 86

165 Ibid., p. 87.

166 Ibid., pp. 86–7.

167 I. A. Popov, 'Materialy k polovoi zhizni muzhchin-rabochikh promyshlennogo goroda tsentral'nogo Kazakhstana (Dissertatsiya na soiskanie uchenoi stepeni kandidata meditsinskikh nauk, Karaganda State Medical Institute, 1968).

168 Ibid., 57–71.

169 Ibid., 67.

170 Ibid., 57.

171 Ibid.

172 Ibid., 94.

173 Ibid.

174 Ibid.

175 Ibid. Popov clarified that that those twelve men who reported having sexual play with adults during their childhood stated that these games were often initiated by women and that these instances occurred during the war. Ibid., 95.

176 Ibid.
177 Ibid., 171.
178 Ibid.
179 Ibid., 172.
180 Herzog, *Sex After Fascism*, p. 198.
181 Ibid., p. 328.
182 Ibid.
183 Pavel Posvyanskii, 'Seksual'nye perversii: Opredelenie ponyatiya, opyt klassifikatsii', in *Voprosy seksopatologii: Materialy nauchnoi konferentsii* (Moscow: Moskovskii nauchno-issledovatel'skii institut psikhiatrii, 1969), p. 144.
184 Ibid.
185 Ibid., p. 145.
186 Ibid.
187 Mikhail Stern and August Stern, *Sex in the USSR*: (New York: Times Books), p. 73.
188 Mikhail N. Khlyntsov, *Rassledovanie polovykh prestuplenii* (Saratov: Privolzhskoe knizhnoe izdatel'stvo, 1965), p. 152.
189 Y. A. Borisenko, 'Voprosy seksologicheskoi pomoshchi, podgotovka kadrov, opyt prepodavaniia kursa seksopatologii v vysshikh meditsinskikh zavedeniiakh Kieva', in *Voprosy seksopatologii: Materily nauchnoi konferentsii* (Moscow: Moskovskii nauchno-issledovatel'skii institut psikhiatrii, 1969), p. 7.
190 Z. G. Russinova, 'K voprosy organisatsii seksologicheskoi pomoshchi naseleniyu', in *Voprosy Seksopatologii: Materialy nauchno-prakticheskoi konferentsii* (Moscow: Moskovskii nauchno-issledovatel'skii institut psikhiatrii, 1969), pp. 12–14, p. 13.
191 Foucault, *History of Sexuality*, p. 63.

4

Soviet legal and criminological debates on the decriminalisation of homosexuality (1959–75)

Those few historians who have attempted to write the history of Soviet sexuality concur that, from the 1930s through to the Soviet collapse, Soviet society and especially the Soviet state were deeply hostile to anything that deviated from 'traditional' sex in the bedroom.[1] Sex was generally deemed a topic unfit for public discussion, and any deviations from 'normal' sexuality were condemned and criminalised by Soviet law.[2] And yet, despite these long-standing and institutionalised prudish attitudes towards sex and hostility towards homosexuality, during the late Soviet period a group of legal scholars spoke out in favour of decriminalising consensual sodomy. This is in sharp contrast to the conventional view of the Brezhnev period as a time of stagnation and sexual conservatism and offers a window onto a very different dimension of that period – and yet we know very little about it. The fact that these debates took place has been noted by pioneering scholars of Soviet sexuality Igor Kon and, more recently, Dan Healey, yet neither has discussed them in much detail.[3]

The emerging scholarship on the Brezhnev era offers a more nuanced account of this period, challenging its characterisation as a time of mere stagnation. Mark Sandle has argued that although scholars customarily view the Brezhnev years as 'an era dominated by the orthodox platitudes of the official ideology', intellectual life during this time was characterised by 'struggle, conflict and creativity'.[4] More recent studies have also emphasised that the Brezhnev era was accompanied by 'the liberalisation of social, economic, and political life' and 'a dialogue among different socialist publics as well as state authorities'.[5] This chapter will add to this perspective, showing that similar trends were evident among legal scholars who discussed and challenged the criminal status of homosexuality in their manuals, textbooks and dissertations on sex crimes in the period from 1959 to 1975.

Proponents of decriminalisation of consensual sodomy based their arguments on the nascent expertise of Soviet sexology, positing that the regulation of same-sex desire should be assigned to the realm of medicine rather than law. Some of these scholars went so far as to argue that homosexuality was not a medical issue at all, but a natural variant of human sexuality and hence did not require medical intervention. These arguments invited sharp criticism from conservative scholars, who asserted that homosexuality violated socialist morality and therefore should be punishable by law (some of them even insisted on criminalising lesbianism). In this chapter I will argue that the positions of these two groups of scholars regarding the anti-sodomy statute and criminal status of lesbianism were becoming more pronounced and elaborate under Brezhnev. While proponents of criminalising homosexuality demonstrated increasing hostility towards the idea of relegating the issue of same sex to medicine, strongly opposing any push for decriminalisation, their opponents fiercely argued the opposite, denying that consensual sodomy was a threat to Soviet society.

By examining the debates over the criminal status of homosexuality from the late 1950s up to the mid-1970s, this chapter first contributes to our understanding of the interplay between the broader European movement towards decriminalisation of sodomy and related debates in the Soviet Union. Second, it sheds light on the extent to which Soviet jurists were willing to accept medical knowledge as another form of control over the homosexual body, apart from legal oppression. Third, it challenges the existing scholarly consensus whereby lesbianism was a completely taboo topic in professional and academic circles under Khrushchev and Brezhnev, demonstrating instead that, like male homosexuality, it was a highly debated topic.[6] Finally, it lends fresh insight into the events which preceded the Russian Federation's eventual decriminalisation of sodomy in 1993, showing that calls for decriminalisation had in fact been present for decades in Soviet juridical discourse.

In this chapter I seek answers to the following questions. Did the arguments about decriminalisation of consensual sodomy, which liberal scholars promoted, constitute calls for a genuine liberation, or merely a reassignment of the issue to the realm of medical controls? How did Soviet jurists conceptualise female homosexuality in legal terms and what was their understanding of it? How strongly did a medical view of homosexuality influence legal opinions and shape legal discussions? Why had these debates resulted in decriminalisation of homosexual activity elsewhere in the communist bloc but not in the Soviet Union? I will begin this chapter by looking at the brief discussions of the law on sodomy that took place in the late 1950s in the RSFSR and in the early 1960s in the Latvian SSR during the drafting of new criminal codes in these republics. I then examine the discussion between civilian and MVD scholars of the criminal status of homosexuality in the USSR in the period from 1965 to 1975. The chapter concludes by reflecting on the implications of the discussion and the possible reasons why it did not result in the decriminalisation of consensual sodomy in the Soviet period.

'The article stays, then': Soviet jurists and Stalinist sodomy law (1959)

In 1956, three years after Stalin's death, Khrushchev launched his de-Stalinisation campaign, highlighting the necessity to restore 'socialist legality'. The terror of the Stalin era was now curbed, and as part of this process, scholars and officials were encouraged to contribute to the liberalisation of Soviet criminal law.[7] The study of criminology, which had been effectively proscribed under Stalin, was now gradually reviving, allowing for fresh criminological empirical research to emerge within the MVD as early as 1955.[8] This period also witnessed the preparation of new republican criminal codes, as legislative commissions including top Soviet specialists in crime and law were set up and entrusted with the task of reviewing the Stalin-era laws to decide which should remain in force.[9] As we shall see, the members of these commissions also discussed the law on sodomy at their meetings; in fact, it seems that there were attempts to moderate the penalty for consensual sodomy, by reducing the maximum sentence prescribed by Article 154a-I from five to three years. Most importantly, at this time there was a possibility that the article criminalising consensual homosexual acts between men could have been abolished, at least in the RSFSR.

References to possible liberalisation of the law first appear in the minutes of a meeting of a subcommittee of the RSFSR Legislative Commission held on 23 July 1959. This subcommittee comprised seven distinguished jurists and legal scholars, and was chaired by Boris Sergeevich Nikiforov.[10] As a recommendatory body responsible for proposing changes to the law, the subcommittee put forward a list of reforms of the existing Stalin-era laws, including the law on sodomy.[11] The new version of the law, which the Nikiforov commission proposed, read as follows:

> Article 100.
>
> In the first part of article 100 to introduce sanction [ustanovit' sanktsiyu] – deprivation of liberty for the term of up to three years or exile for the same term.
>
> For the second part of article 100 the draft as formulated is as follows:
>
> 'Sodomy committed with means of violence or in relation to a minor or with the use of dependent position is punishable by deprivation of liberty for the term from three to eight years with exile or without.'[12]

This new version of the law would have reduced the maximum sentence for consensual sodomy from five to three years with no minimum sentence. The proposed amendment to the second article of the law, which penalised aggravated sodomy, would have retained the maximum sentence of eight years but reduced the minimum from five to three years.

One month later, on 27 August 1959, a Commission of Legislative Propositions (Komissiya zakonodatel'nykh predpolozhenii), consisting of fourteen distinguished jurists and criminologists of the RSFSR, chaired by Aleksei Gertsenzon, gathered to approve the draft prepared by the Nikiforov commission.[13] The archival transcript of this discussion reveals that at this stage a proposal emerged to abolish the law on consensual sodomy altogether, despite the reduced maximum sentence for consensual sodomy already proposed by the Nikiforov commission:

> GERTSENZON – [...] Article 100 – sodomy.
>
> Any suggestions regarding the first part [on voluntary sodomy]?

NIKIFOROV – The first part of the law is totally incomprehensible.

STEPICHEV – The first part can be abolished.

GERTSENZON – There are suggestions to abolish the first part. I am opening this up to a vote. Does anyone support the abolition of the first part?

KOROTKOV – We can't abolish this norm. On what grounds do you want to do that?

GERTSENZON – Are we going to open up a discussion or not? Who is in favour of opening discussion of the article? (2)[14] We are not going to discuss it, then. The article stays, then. What are the suggestions regarding the essence of the Article? Here the punishment (repressiya) is to be reduced compared to the previous penalty. Deprivation of liberty for up to three years or exile for up to three years. So, comrades, are we approving the first part of the Article? We're approving it.

The second part: Any suggestions? No.

The whole article is approved.[15]

The brevity of the minutes leaves the participants' motives largely opaque and it is difficult to say whether other members, apart from Nikiforov and Stepichev, who expressed support for decriminalisation, were of a similar opinion, since almost none of them had previously spoken out on this issue. Nikiforov's role as chair of the subcommittee which proposed reducing the severity of the law and his comment that the law was 'totally incomprehensible' would appear to indicate that he was a strong proponent of abolishing the law entirely.

Judging by the reticence of other participants in the discussion of the sodomy law, compared to their extensive contributions on other articles of the Criminal Code, we might speculate that most of the scholars present found detailed discussions uncomfortable. As legal experts they would most likely have been inadequately prepared to objectively examine the issue. As Igor Kon has noted, the 'suppression of sexual culture' and absence of 'adequate understanding of sexuality in the public consciousness', peculiar to the Stalin era and certainly still prevalent during the early years of Khrushchev's rule, would have inhibited open discussion.[16]

Interestingly, despite the Gertsenzon commission approving Nikiforov's recommended version of the sodomy law, which reduced sentences for both consensual and aggravated sodomy, the proposed changes never became law. The archival sources are silent on the fate of the proposed reforms, which may either have been further reviewed and rejected or quashed by intervention of a higher-level authority. Yet the final version of the law, adopted by the Supreme Soviet of the RSFSR in 1960, differed from the version first proposed by the Nikiforov commission and later approved by the Gertsenzon commission. It read:

> Article 121. Sodomy
>
> Sexual intercourse between a male and a male (sodomy) is punishable by deprivation of freedom for a term of up to five years.
>
> Sodomy committed with the use of physical violence, threats or in relation to a minor, or with the use of the dependent position of the victim, is punishable by deprivation of freedom for a term of up to eight years.[17]

While minimum sentences both for consensual and aggravated sodomy were eliminated altogether, the maximum penalty for consensual sodomy was increased from three years (as the version approved by the Gertsenzon commission had proposed) to five years.

The Latvian case: attempts to criminalise lesbian sexual activity

New sources suggest that the process of revising the sodomy laws of the Stalinist Criminal Code in each of the Soviet republics varied. For instance, in Latvia, discussions about revising the legal treatment of homosexuality had a very different focus. On 24 March 1960, during drafting of the Criminal Code of the Latvian SSR, the head of the Latvian SSR's law commission considered a proposal from the Riga city directorate of the militia to extend the legal definition of sodomy and to criminalise female same-sex relations. The proposal noted that 'in practice one may encounter cases of satisfaction of sexual desire between persons of the same sex which do not fall under the definition of "sodomy", yet these activities also pose a danger to society'.[18]

The commission reconvened on 14 October 1960, but the minutes of this meeting make no reference to the militia's proposal. The minutes record that Fridrikson, the chair of the meeting, noted that all the proposals presented to the commission's meeting in March had been sent to Moscow for review: 'As you remember, in March we discussed the draft Criminal Code, which was subsequently discussed by academics in Moscow at a meeting in the Juridical Department of the Presidium of the Supreme Soviet of the USSR.'[19] He also acknowledged the significance of the RSFSR draft revised Criminal Code as a template for revising the LSSR's Criminal Code: 'In our work we were essentially using the RSFSR Code; we were borrowing from the RSFSR draft, which has been approved everywhere.'[20] It therefore seems probable that the proposals to criminalise lesbianism were rejected, perhaps by the authorities in Moscow.

The Latvian militia's proposal to criminalise same-sex relations between women represented a significant shift from the existing Stalin-era sodomy statute, which did not criminalise female homosexual acts.[21] Interestingly, the moves to liberalise the law in the early years of Khrushchev's rule seem to have had a paradoxical effect on the discussion of lesbianism: although lesbianism became the subject of legal discussion for the first time since Stalin's death, at no point did the liberalising tendencies of Khrushchev's era encourage, or lead to acceptance or tolerance of, female homosexuality.

On the contrary, the first years of Khrushchev's rule saw a number of proposals to criminalise female same-sex relations. We can find advocates of such measures in the ranks of Soviet law-enforcement agencies, the GULAG camp directors and the GULAG camp doctors. As noted in Chapter 1, support for these proposals continued through the late 1950s. In 1958 the head of the Siberian GULAG, I. M. Velikanov, concerned about the increasing incidence of sexual relations between women in the Siberian GULAG, petitioned the Presidium of the Supreme Soviet of the USSR with a proposal to impose a criminal penalty for lesbianism.[22] Such propositions were the result of a curious amalgam of Khrushchev-era liberalisation and Stalin-era attitudes to sexuality still fresh in people's minds. Velikanov's proposal and similar calls to criminalise female same-sex relations were, however, never taken up.

In his more recent work Dan Healey has identified that the Soviet authorities preferred to deal with lesbianism in a medical context, rather than through the criminal law.[23] He also noted in his previous work that although female homosexuality was not criminalised by Stalin, the motherhood cult was an important reminder of the purpose of women's sexuality and thus a deterrent to sexually deviant practices.[24] The motherhood cult persisted during the Khrushchev period. The sex education campaign launched under Khrushchev constantly reminded women about their role as mothers, and doctors who attempted to 'treat' lesbianism seemed to believe that female homosexuality could be 'cured' if a woman succumbed to the instinct of motherhood.[25]

Homosexuality and debates on its legal status in the 1960s

Discussion of the anti-sodomy law between legal scholars continued after Khrushchev's removal from power and unfolded against the backdrop of the gradual revival of professional and academic expertise in Soviet criminology, a field of social science effectively proscribed under Stalin.[26] As this expertise revived and developed under Brezhnev, so did the range of activities in which Soviet legal and law-enforcement experts were involved. These included efforts to improve criminological expertise within the MVD on how to handle sex crimes. MVD officers were often completely unskilled in the investigation of these crimes and lacked much needed training and expertise.[27] In response to these deficiencies, the MVD commissioned several universities to write training manuals for criminal investigators and for its schools. It was in one such manual that the first scholarly examination of the anti-sodomy statute was undertaken.

The manual, titled *Investigation of Sex Crimes* and published in 1965 by criminologist Mikhail Nikitovich Khlyntsov of the Saratov Legal University, was specifically intended for students and lecturers of the MVD schools. The author depicted the dangers of sodomy in the following terms: 'The extreme danger of this crime lies in its encroachment on the moral foundations of society and demoralising influence on the psyche of the members of society … The victim of this crime is the prevailing mode of sexual relations in our country, which the law seeks to safeguard.'[28] Such an interpretation of the utility of the law on sodomy was consistent with the Soviet public discourse on sex and sexual morality, first widely promulgated by the Khrushchev regime and further promoted under Brezhnev. As Deborah A. Field has shown, the focal point of this discourse was the necessity to prevent Soviet children and adolescents from engaging in sexually immoral behaviour, including casual sexual relations, premarital sex and promiscuity.[29] Khlyntsov justified the sodomy law because it upheld communist morality and the very 'moral foundations' of Soviet society, which homosexuals, with their 'debauchery', threatened to disrupt: 'The propensity for sodomy in certain individuals can be explained by … their lack of fulfilment with normal means of satisfying sexual desire and the pursuit of new sensations, which attests to their debauchery (razvrashchennost') and their contempt for moral norms.'[30]

However, not all scholars specialising in crime and law espoused similar views. During the 1960s some Soviet jurists started to suggest that homosexuality was not necessarily a result of moral perversion and called for a more careful enforcement of the sodomy law. Aleksei Nikolaevich Ignatov (Figure 13) was one such scholar whose pragmatic approach to the law on sodomy was reflected in his manual *Liability for Crimes against Morality* (1966).[31] Ignatov, who later obtained a PhD in jurisprudence from Moscow State University, had taught criminal law at various universities in Moscow since 1953.[32] Although he did not suggest in his manual that the law

Figure 13 Aleksei Nikolaevich Ignatov

on consensual sodomy be abolished, Ignatov did argue that not all homosexual liaisons between men should be criminalised under the existing legislation. He contended that since Soviet law only criminalised sodomy – or 'pederasty' (pederastiya) – then other sexual activities between two men should not be deemed illegal. Ignatov directly criticised Soviet judicial decisions on this issue, in a statement that is surprisingly frank:

> We cannot approve of the tendency of some courts to expand the notion of sodomy, placing any satisfaction of sexual desire between men within this category. If two men commit consensual depraved acts between one another [without engaging in anal intercourse], thereby satisfying their sexual desire, they should not be subjected to a criminal penalty, since such actions are not perceived by the Soviet Criminal Code as a crime.[33]

Ignatov had essentially identified a legal loophole: in theory, homosexual men were allowed to engage in any form of sexual activity other than anal intercourse, since the latter was the only practice to be criminalised by law. However, as this passage suggests, judges tended to overlook this fact, and homosexual men were frequently brought before court even for technically legal activities. We know that this was the case under Stalin: Dan Healey tells us about a sodomy trial in 1939, in which the advocate of a defendant accused of sodomy argued that his client may have committed depraved acts, but that these did not constitute sodomy and hence were not illegal. In this case, however, the court rejected this argument, asserting that the act of sodomy had nevertheless taken place (but without specifying how sodomy was defined here).[34] Apparently, such incorrect enforcement of the sodomy statute was continuing under Khrushchev; Ignatov was the first jurist to request publicly that its enforcement be brought in line with the law.

Unlike Khlyntsov, who asserted that homosexuality was a result of 'debauchery' (razvrashchennost'), Ignatov encouraged his readers not to jump to conclusions, and to consider whether other factors could contribute to the development of homosexuality. In doing so, he presented his readers with arguments derived from the pre-revolutionary Russian forensic and medical literature which suggested that congenital factors could be responsible for homosexuality.[35] Ignatov argued that the nature of homosexuality should be explored further in order to ascertain whether it was indeed a 'pathological phenomenon'; if so, the existing criminal law penalising it should be reviewed accordingly. He argued that 'the examination of homosexuality's nature will help to establish the extent to which it ought to be punishable and to facilitate the correct application of the criminal law to it, especially given that the inexpedience of criminal punishment for consensual homosexuality has been repeatedly expressed in the literature'.[36] Thus, instead of solely relying on 'communist morality' in his approach to homosexuality, as scholars like Khlyntsov had done, Ignatov preferred to ground his arguments in scientific knowledge, reaching back to the pre-revolutionary period to do so.

Ignatov's tentative suggestion that homosexuality could be a matter of therapeutic, rather than police, concern coincided with the emergence of Soviet sexology or 'sexopathology' (seksopatologiya) in the early 1960s, which focused on sexual health issues, including 'sexual perversions'.[37] This development came late, compared to some countries in Eastern Europe, where sophisticated knowledge of sexology had already proven instrumental in calls by legal scholars and sexologists for decriminalisation of sodomy. As I showed in Chapter 3, Czechoslovakian sexologists' argument that homosexuality was incurable had helped them convince government authorities to cease all forms of legal sanctions applied to homosexual people; this eventually resulted in the decriminalisation of consensual sodomy in 1961.[38] The German Democratic Republic followed suit in 1968. There, and one year later in West Germany, homosexual consensual acts between men ceased to be a crime on the grounds that homosexuality was a medical condition and therefore should not be subject to police action.[39] Finally, medical arguments framing homosexuality as a disease facilitated the decriminalisation of consensual sodomy in Bulgaria the same year.[40]

In contrast to the success of sexologists in the socialist bloc countries, the findings of Soviet sexological studies were not yet sufficiently influential to provide a rationale for decriminalisation of sodomy in the USSR. Long-standing negative attitudes towards sexuality and the consequent unwillingness of Party officials to endorse Soviet sexology significantly encumbered its development as a full-fledged science. In Igor Kon's words, sexopathology was 'an outcast in Soviet medicine', and this status affected its research output, which in the 1960s was limited to a modest range of scholarly works.[41]

In 1966 Pavel Pavlovich Osipov, a jurist from Leningrad University, defended his PhD dissertation 'Sex Crimes', which contained a section discussing the law on sodomy.[42] In this section Osipov explicitly stated that the biological nature of homosexuality warranted decriminalisation of consensual homosexual acts between men. Unusually for the time, Osipov did not rely on communist ideology in his reasoning; in fact, in the introduction to his dissertation he came close to dismissing communist ideology as a reliable tool of scientific inquiry, arguing that ideology alone could not be the cornerstone of legal research. He wrote: 'In light of contemporary requirements put before legal science, the study of matters relating to the special part of the Soviet Criminal Code [dealing with sex crimes] should not be confined by a dogmatic analysis of contemporary legislation.'[43]

Osipov's preference for an empirical rather than ideological approach was consistent with a new strategy of 'rationalisation', which the Soviet leadership adopted in the mid-to late 1960s. This strategy called for the revival of a scientific ethos and encouraged scholars to use 'scientific methods' in their research. As Peter Solomon has pointed out, the rationale for this strategy was that it would facilitate the development of society and help the government to address immediate problems through the use of rational and credible expertise.[44]

The influence of this new 'rational' approach extended to legal scholarship and was at the core of Osipov's arguments for decriminalisation of consensual sodomy. His dissertation offered an elaborate and substantiated argument as to why the law on consensual sodomy should be abolished:

> First of all, the desire to satisfy sexual need in a homosexual way may be congenital in nature, that is, conditioned by the biological peculiarities of an organism ... As a result, for people endowed with this anomaly, homosexuality is a natural means of sexual fulfilment. That is why the widespread contention, according to which sodomy is always a result of moral depravity, cannot be regarded as valid.[45]

Such arguments appear to be a call for a genuine liberation – Osipov did not insist that homosexuals should be subject to medical treatment: instead he suggested that homosexual desire is a natural one that does not require any medical intervention. While his colleague Ignatov had tentatively suggested that criminal prosecution of men for their congenital homosexuality might be futile, Osipov further emphasised the futility of criminalisation by explicitly and unequivocally asserting that it was pointless to punish people for desires that were conditioned by nature:

> One may ask what goal the legislator pursued when criminalising non-forcible homosexuality, if at issue here are the people with a biologically distorted sexual instinct. There is no doubt that with the help of criminal law it is impossible to rectify this biological anomaly and encourage the individuals in question to satisfy their sexual need in a heterosexual way.[46]

Similarly, Osipov dismissed communist morality as an adequate frame of reference: 'In the Soviet legal literature there has never been an attempt to justify criminal liability for consensual sodomy, and the only argument which is usually offered against it – the [resulting] individual's depravity and his violation of communist morality – cannot be regarded as sufficient.'[47]

An important pillar of the argument that Osipov advanced in his dissertation was that intimate relations between two consenting adults were very difficult to investigate.[48] This was a new note in the debate, and it reflects a significant broader shift in the public and private divide within post-Stalin Soviet society. Osipov's emphasis on 'intimacy' is additional evidence of this change. The growing body of recent scholarship on this issue has challenged the customary understanding of Soviet society as a place where private spheres were impossible. It has demonstrated that these private spheres did exist in the Soviet Union and that the expansion of the private domain was actively taking place under Brezhnev.[49] As Lewis H. Siegelbaum shows, the growing Soviet economy of the Brezhnev era facilitated this expansion. This economic growth led to increased availability of separate apartments and individual cars, for example.[50] Expansion of private spaces offered new opportunities for people to pursue their private lives – in Steven E. Harris's words, separate apartments 'introduced privacy on a mass scale', while the interiors of parked cars, according to Lewis H. Siegelbaum, 'might have been used for heterosexual rendezvous and associated activities'.[51] It was this Brezhnev-era renegotiation of private and public boundaries within Soviet society and the diminishing ability of the state to intervene in the private domain that appear to underpin Osipov's argument:

> Taking into consideration the exceptionally intimate nature of actions directed at the satisfaction of sexual desire and hampering the effective control over behaviour of the subjects involved, the legislative ban on homosexuality cannot be effective in preventing undesirable forms of sexual desire satisfaction from arising, nor can it stimulate people to behave properly.[52]

Osipov's arguments were not unique: elsewhere in the world jurists appealed to the legal concepts of consent and privacy when arguing for decriminalisation of consensual homosexual acts between two adult males.[53]

Arguments for decriminalisation of consensual sodomy also came from jurists in other Soviet republics, including Yakov Mikhailovich Yakovlev from the Tajik SSR. Like Ignatov and Osipov, Yakovlev was a jurist by training – he graduated from the Department of Soviet Law at Moscow State University in 1933. Subsequently he taught judicial law in various universities across the Soviet Union.[54] In his article 'Liability for Sodomy according to the Soviet Penal Law' (1968) he supported his argument for decriminalisation of consensual sodomy with references to the experiences of other socialist countries, such as Czechoslovakia and the German Democratic Republic.[55] Yakovlev noted that over thirty countries in the world had already abolished anti-sodomy legislation and then wrote: 'Proposals in favour of elimination of criminal penalties for "consensual homosexuality" between two adults have also been made in our literature. We also believe that criminal liability for homosexuality should be eliminated.'[56] In addition Yakovlev argued that homosexuals posing no threat to society should be referred to doctors: 'Homosexuals, whose sexual perversion was due to pathological alterations of their organism, should be rendered medical help.'[57] The basis of these arguments appears to derive from Yakovlev's awareness that in the city of Gorkii such 'treatment' was available – he apparently learnt of this from the treatise *Questions of Psychotherapy of Functional Sexual Disorders* (1966)[58] published by Professor Ivanov, one of the few Soviet sexologists who specialised in the treatment of 'sexual perversions' (see Chapter 3). Yakovlev replicated Ivanov's contention that an 'unfavourable environment' and 'incorrect upbringing' could trigger homosexual desire.[59] He went on to conclude that the effective struggle against deviance could be successful through pre-emptive measures and not legal repression: 'the fight against homosexuality in the absence of aggravating circumstances has to be conducted not through legal repression, but through correct sex education in family and school'.[60]

Thus, with the slow development of Soviet expertise in sexology, which framed homosexuality as a matter of therapeutic concern, legal scholars arguing for decriminalisation of sodomy could rely on sexology's findings to lend scientific credence to their arguments. That appears to be the case with Yakovlev's arguments. The writing of his article coincided with the publication of Ivanov's recent work, while previous arguments for sodomy decriminalisation as promoted by Ignatov and Osipov were grounded in outdated sources.

'The author considers it necessary to criminalise tribadism': Boris Daniel'bek and his views on homosexuality (1970)

Not all jurists and criminologists supported arguments for decriminalisation. Many of them believed that homosexual relations were a threat to Soviet sexual morality and therefore should not be legalised. In 1970 the Procuracy of the Soviet Republic of Lithuania hosted a conference devoted to sex crimes, which brought together forensic experts and criminologists from various corners of the USSR.[61] In his introductory paper, one of the speakers spelled out the fundamental preconditions on which Soviet sexual morality rested:

> [At the basis of socialist society] there is socialist morality, that is, the complex of rules and principles defining the citizen's behaviour in all spheres, including that of sexual relations. Sexual morality is one of the facets of socialist moral consciousness and to deny it means to deny the necessity of moral regulation of the relations between man and woman ... The fundamental rules of sexual morality, which determine the mode of sexual relations in the USSR, are the following: sexual relations are permissible only between individuals of the opposite sex.[62]

This statement gives us a better understanding of what motives lay beneath some legal scholars' opposition to the decriminalisation of consensual sodomy. It is difficult to say whom the speaker had in mind when mentioning individuals 'denying' sexual morality; yet we have already seen that one of the proponents of decriminalisation of consensual sodomy, Pavel Osipov, had indeed stated that outlawing homosexuality solely due to its ostensible infringement of communist morality was not justifiable.[63] The paper's stress on the impropriety of same-sex relations in the Soviet Union and 'denial' of sexual morality could represent unspoken anxieties associated with the growing voices of the proponents for decriminalisation of consensual sodomy among some legal scholars.

The introductory statement of the conference also suggests that by 1970 the communist concepts of sex and love, introduced under Khrushchev, had evolved and become more complicated. The Khrushchev-era discourse did not clearly delineate the limits of admissible sexual behaviour – sex educators expressed a variety of opinions as to what the demands of sexual morality were. These demands, as Field tells us, generally revolved around the idea that one had to practise 'sex within marriage, accompanied by love, preferably for the purposes of procreation'.[64] Homosexuality was mentioned only rarely and Soviet moralists never explained its relationship to communist morality.[65] However, the conference paper of 1970 clearly defined what sexual practices were permissible in the USSR. It seems plausible that once these rules were clearly defined, they became a frame of reference for conservative scholars which would require them to oppose the arguments of proponents for sodomy decriminalisation more strongly.

One of the most outspoken opponents of decriminalisation was Boris Vasil'evich Daniel'bek (Figure 14) from Azerbaijan State University. He criticised Osipov's and Yakovlev's proposals to legalise consensual sodomy in his doctoral dissertation 'Criminal and Legal Struggle with Sex Crimes', defended in November of 1970 at the MVD Higher School.[66] In his dissertation Daniel'bek drew on a wide variety of sources, including files from the Supreme Court of the USSR, as well as other Soviet Republics and materials from the Procuracy and the Ministry of Interior Affairs. He also made use of 'philosophical, sociological, medical, psychological, pedagogical, legal literature'.[67] Daniel'bek's dissertation is stored in the library of the MVD Higher School and, unfortunately, is unavailable for viewing, yet its elaborate abstract (avtoreferat) stored at the National

Figure 14 Boris Vasil'evich Daniel'bek

State Library of St Petersburg and his subsequently published monograph *Sexual Perversions and Criminal Liability* (1972) based on his dissertation shed light on its content.[68]

In his monograph, invoking Osipov's contention that violation of communist morality was not a sufficient reason to criminalise consensual sodomy, Daniel'bek argued: 'Negative personality traits, if they infringe on the principles of socialist morality, may be viewed as criminal.'[69] He also questioned Osipov's argument that consensual sodomy should be decriminalised, arguing that: 'The intimate nature of homosexual acts, conducted on a consensual basis, indeed hampers the prosecution of people involved in it; however, it does not mean that the law against consensual sodomy should be eliminated.'[70] Finally, Daniel'bek disagreed with Osipov's contention that the anti-sodomy law failed to encourage homosexuals to practise heterosexual sex, conceding that: 'criminal prosecution of homosexuality is not the most effective means of its prevention. Indeed, in order to curb this immoral inclination a combination of societal and medical intervention is needed in the first place; however, one cannot dismiss the educational importance of criminal prosecution.'[71]

Osipov was not the only target of Daniel'bek's attack. Jurist Yakovlev from the Tajik University also received his share of criticism.

As noted above, Yakovlev had stated that proper sexual education was a better strategy to deal with homosexuality than criminal punishment and that crimes of consensual sodomy were very hard to investigate. Daniel'bek disagreed:

> The correct sexual upbringing is indeed an important means of sodomy prevention, including prevention of any other crime in the sphere of sexual relations. However, no matter how tempting it is to base the decriminalisation of sex crimes on this assumption, such a proposition is ill-timed. The contention that criminal cases involving sodomy are rarely encountered is rather controversial ... Criminal punishment plays an important role in homosexuality prevention and constitutes a restraining factor on those inclined to such vice. Summing up, we express our strong conviction that the criminalisation of consensual sodomy in our legislation is justified and there are no reasons to alter the existing legislation.[72]

Underlying Daniel'bek's arguments was the familiar premise that homosexuality was a vice which law-enforcement agencies had to control:

> Homosexuality in the absolute majority of cases is a result of negative conditions which formed a personality ... These very conditions lead some people to such a degree of perversion, when normal satiation of sexual desire does not give them normal satisfaction any more and they resort to perversions in order to experience extra thrills (ostrye oshchushcheniya).[73]

It seems that medical knowledge of sexual perversions which the proponents of decriminalisation readily embraced had not altered Daniel'bek's opinion. Nor was he willing to take into account the fact that by 1970 consensual homosexual acts had been decriminalised in many countries, or to entertain the possibility that the Soviet Union might follow suit. Instead, he preferred to categorise homosexuality as a crime against morality and consider it a threat to the moral foundations of Soviet society.

More than ten distinguished jurists from various Soviet universities reviewed Daniel'bek's dissertation and expressed their suggestions and criticism regarding the arguments it proposed. These reports reveal a striking detail about Daniel'bek's thesis: he argued for criminalising consensual lesbianism and, apparently, due to the reviewers' disapproval of this idea, this proposal never became part of the published abstract and the subsequent monograph. Daniel'bek's call for outlawing lesbianism, and the examiners' various responses to it, constitute rare evidence of ongoing behind-the-scenes debates on the issue. These debates were not confined solely to academic circles but went beyond them to involve high-ranking judicial officials, and therefore could have potentially affected the legal status of female homosexuality in the USSR.

Invoking Daniel'bek's proposal to criminalise female homosexuality, V. I. Kurlyandskii argued that lesbianism was not as prevalent as sodomy and therefore should not be considered a crime:

> So despite the very limited prevalence of tribadism (as evidenced by the data cited by the author), the dissertation proposes to introduce punishments for actions in which this type of sexual anomaly is present. The analogy drawn by the author between tribadism and pederasty is not convincing given the prevalence of the former.[74]

Another distinguished jurist, Mark Yakubovich, expressed a similar view: 'The author of the dissertation considers it necessary to introduce criminal liability for tribadism, whose harm he considers to be equivalent to that of sodomy. The argument that tribadism is equal to sodomy is controversial – it is less common than pederasty.'[75] Jurist Grigorii Anashkin stated in his report that he and his colleagues disapproved: 'In our opinion, there are not sufficient grounds for criminalising tribadism between adult women, especially since there is no evidence of the prevalence of this phenomenon, while the author of the dissertation advocates its criminalisation.'[76] Finally, the chairman of the Supreme Court of the Azerbaijan SSR, A. G. Ibragimov, stated: 'The author's many conclusions should be accepted, with the exception of his proposal to criminalise voluntary tribadism. In our republic, we do not have data on the prevalence of this type of perversion and it cannot be considered so dangerous as to be classified as a criminal act.'[77]

Surprisingly, none of the reviewers offered to relegate lesbianism to the realm of medicine, instead unanimously arguing that it was a rare phenomenon and therefore did not merit attention. Dan Healey argues that Stalin and his henchmen dismissed the issue of lesbianism as unimportant because same-sex-attracted women had failed to exploit urban spaces for socialising and sexual activity the way homosexual men did. If a strong lesbian culture had existed, Healey's argument goes, lesbians would also have become the object of criminal prosecution.[78] Under Brezhnev such a subculture failed to materialise too: unlike same-sex-desiring males, who, despite the existing criminal penalties, continued to inhabit public spaces in pursuit of socialisation and sex in the 1970s, same-sex-attracted women mostly came to their queer self-realisation in isolation.[79] The only place where lesbian relationships enjoyed visibility and were a concern to the authorities was prison, as jurist I. M. Tkachevskii noted: 'The conclusions made in the dissertation are important for the fight against homosexuality in prisons. Due to the concentration of the members of one sex in isolation from the other, in correctional labour institutions the problem of combating tribadism and sodomy is quite acute.'[80]

Daniel'bek's monograph *Sexual Perversions and Criminal Liability* (1972) did not propose the criminalisation of lesbianism. Apparently influenced by the opinions of his reviewers on the issue, he posited that female homosexuality was not prevalent in the USSR: 'Soviet law does not criminalise lesbianism and it seems to us … that this is because tribadism is not widely spread and that it is, in essence, a special kind of depraved action.'[81] Reducing female homosexuality to merely a type of depraved act, Daniel'bek argued that it was 'the result of a deep moral corruption' and even 'psychopathy', which should be dealt with by societal and psychotherapeutic intervention. Yet, in his view the issue still merited attention, because sometimes instances of such relationships between women could lead to fatal consequences. To illustrate his point, he provided a brief case study – a nineteen-year-old female G. from Tbilisi, who was found to have a romantic relationship with another female, twenty-four years old. When this fact came to the attention of G.'s stepfather, he promptly married her off to a man and on their wedding night G. committed suicide. Daniel'bek condemned the stepfather's decision, arguing that he should have invited a psychiatrist first to talk to his stepdaughter. Investigators, he revealed, proved that everybody knew about G. and Y.'s close friendship – G. often stayed overnight at Y.'s flat, colleagues at work also knew about their 'romance' (vlyublennost') but didn't pay attention to it. Considering the dearth of information on lesbian relations under Khrushchev and Brezhnev, Daniel'bek's case study is revealing in that it shows that lesbians constructed their relationships veiled as simple friendships. His remark that everybody was aware of G. and Y.'s relationship may also attest to the fluidity of public and private boundaries under Brezhnev and the relative tolerance of same-sex relationships in the milieus where such relationships existed. However, such relationships were not likely to be tolerated by parents, who believed that heterosexual marriage and the nuclear family were the only ways for their daughters to be socialised as 'respectable' females, hence G.'s stepfather decision to marry her off.[82]

At least as striking as the experts' discussions of lesbianism were their responses to Daniel'bek's criticism of Osipov's and Yakovlev's arguments for decriminalising consensual sodomy. V. Kirichenko, professor and head of the Department of Criminal Law of the Higher School of the MVD, noted that Daniel'bek's arguments for retaining the law criminalising consensual sodomy between males were 'not convincing enough'.[83] Yakubovich also noted that Daniel'bek failed to sufficiently refute Osipov's and Yakovlev's arguments for decriminalisation. Depicting homosexuals as innocent victims of unfortunate circumstances, leading them to same-sex desire, Yakubovich contended that they could not be held legally responsible:

> The solution to the problem of voluntary sodomy presented in the dissertation is far from indisputable. It seems that the dissertation has not refuted with sufficient persuasiveness the statements of a number of authors who argue against punishability of voluntary sodomy. Decriminalisation of voluntary sodomy will undoubtedly allow [homosexuals to] fearlessly seek medical help for their perversions … It is difficult to say what can be more beneficial for society – to treat these people or punish them.[84]

> The examination of criminal cases on sex crimes, [and] conversations with the individuals convicted in such cases, the author writes, allows us to conclude that the cause of sexual perversions is sexual education and poorly developed living conditions, which in turn lead [homosexuals] to such a degree of perversion that the normal realisation of sexual needs does not provide the necessary satisfaction. Well, one can agree with these conclusions of the dissertation. But why do we need to prosecute individuals because of the unfortunate circumstances in their lives, instead of taking appropriate measures to prevent perversions from arising?[85]

Jurist Yakovlev, who proposed to decriminalise consensual sodomy in his article 'Liability for Sodomy according to the Soviet Penal Law' and whose arguments Daniel'bek criticised, was also among the experts who reviewed the dissertation. He reiterated the point about the need to tackle homosexuality with sex education and expressed disagreement with Daniel'bek's criticism:

> Elaborating on controversial issues of criminal responsibility for sodomy, Daniel'bek is proving the need to maintain criminal responsibility for consensual pederasty between adult men without aggravating circumstances. He notes that supporters of the abolition of such responsibility, among whom is the author of this review, consider 'homosexuality to be a specific type of sex drive characteristic of some individuals and embedded in them by nature itself'. Meanwhile, none of the modern Soviet medical scientists and lawyers adhere to such an opinion. They believe that the biological forms in which sexual intercourse occurs between adults should be subject to legal regulation only if it affects the social side of sexual relations, that is, impinges on sexual freedom, sexual integrity or normal sexual development and upbringing of minors. At the same time, they emphasise that homosexual relations certainly contradict socialist morality and it is necessary to fight them. However, this struggle should not be carried out in the form of criminal repression, but through proper sex education in the family and at school.[86]

The experts' opinions on the issue of consensual sodomy and lesbianism, as well as ongoing discussions on some of its most contentious aspects, reveal the complexity of intellectual thinking of the Brezhnev-era intelligentsia with its crosscurrents and conflicting perspectives, which scholars have only recently turned their attention to.[87] These discussions attest to the existence of a certain degree of dissent in Soviet academic circles in the 1970s and they also demonstrate that apart from the exalted Soviet dissidents, there were many other individuals who challenged the system. Academics such as Yakovlev and Osipov were far from being publicly known figures and they did not broadcast their opposition to the regime, yet they carefully and selectively questioned its individual aspects. Their views displayed both conformity and dissent, and in communicating these views they had to resort to a complex way of intellectual expression – paying lip service to Party tenets on the one hand and promoting their fresh and bold ideas on the other. Such an approach shielded them from the opprobrium and criticism of their conservative colleagues and did not jeopardise their privileged positions within the academic community.

Not all of the reviewers were in favour of legalisation of consensual sodomy – two of them maintained that Daniel'bek's critique of

Osipov's and Yakovlev's arguments for decriminalisation was well justified. V. P. Kagramanov, head of the Department of Criminal Law at Azerbaijan State University, wrote: 'Citing the opinions of individual Soviet jurists (P. P. Osipov, I. M. Yakovlev) about the necessity to decriminalise consensual sodomy, the author convincingly proves them wrong, by critically analysing the arguments of his opponents.'[88] B. Purtzkhvanidze, the head of the Department of Criminal Law at Tbilisi State University, argued likewise: 'Many proposals of the author of the dissertation are justified and acceptable, in particular, the unacceptability of some authors' view that consensual sodomy should not be a matter of criminal law.'[89] It is notable that those reviewers who were intolerant of the idea of decriminalising consensual sodomy came from the USSR's southern regions – including Daniel'bek himself (with the exception of Yakovlev, of course). Dan Healey notes that as early as the beginning of the twentieth century, in Russia's 'European' part, experts viewed homosexuality as either a biological or a psychological anomaly, and as a result of these understandings 'the homosexual … was becoming a public personality imbued with a specific sexual desire'.[90] By contrast, same-sex desire in Russian's southern regions was perceived differently – not as a psychological or natural phenomenon, but as a result of local cultures and traditions and primarily Islamic customs of female seclusion. Experts observed that same-sex relations in these regions were often coercive, with abduction of male youths and boys for sexual purposes and prostitution among them being normal practices.[91] Perhaps it was these local and historically entrenched understandings of homosexuality that shaped Daniel'bek's views on the inadmissibility of removing criminal penalties for consensual sodomy. Possibly he and scholars with similar views perceived the existing sodomy law as an important instrument for breaking with the perverse traditions of the past and ensuring the purity of sexual relations in their regions.

'Public consciousness is not ready for such a decision': Aleksei Ignatov and his dissertation (1974)

Proponents of the decriminalisation of consensual sodomy constantly updated their arguments, making adroit use of the increasing medical discussions on the issue of homosexuality at home as well as developments abroad. The anonymous author of the manual *Course in Soviet Criminal Law*, published in 1973, expressed 'serious doubts regarding the expediency of keeping criminal liability for consensual sodomy'.[92] The author listed three arguments, summarising the contentions previously expressed by Osipov and Yakovlev (it is possible that the author of the entry was Osipov himself), in favour of reconsideration of the anti-sodomy statute. In addition to existing arguments highlighting the 'biological' nature of homosexuality and the impossibility of controlling it due to its intimate nature, the author invoked decriminalisation of consensual homosexual acts outside the Soviet Union:

> Thirdly, the development of criminal legislation over recent years testifies to the gradual departure from criminalisation of consensual sodomy, not only in capitalist countries (England and West Germany), but also in socialist countries (East Germany, Hungary, Czechoslovakia, Bulgaria, Poland). The aforementioned arguments testify to the expediency of the exclusion from the existing legislation of the article criminalising consensual sodomy.[93]

In 1974 Aleksei Ignatov advanced a more explicit and elaborate argument for the decriminalisation of consensual sodomy in his doctoral dissertation 'Problems of Criminal Liability for Sex Crimes in Soviet Criminal Law' at the All-Union Institute for the Study of Causes of Crime and Developing Measures of Crime Prevention.[94] Unlike his previous treatise *Liability for Crimes against Morality* (1966), whose arguments for decriminalising sodomy relied on Russian books on forensic medicine and on the medical literature of the pre-revolutionary period, Ignatov's doctoral dissertation saw his contentions firmly grounded in the expertise of contemporary Soviet sexology. As I will show in Chapter 5, from 1970 to 1974 Soviet sexology yielded a number of works which encompassed a wider range of topics, including a more elaborate examination of 'sexual perversions', and methods for treating homosexuality.[95] Unlike American psychiatrists, who excluded homosexuality from the list of mental illnesses in 1973, Soviet doctors demonstrated their support for the idea that homosexuality was a pathological condition.[96] Yet even such an outdated perception of homosexuality offered a justification for the elimination of sodomy from the Soviet legal code to which Ignatov and other legal scholars could resort. Drawing on fresh evidence, Ignatov advanced his argument that homosexuality was an inherent disposition and should be of therapeutic rather than police concern:

> At present, we may consider it to be an established fact that a certain number of people suffer from a congenital perversion of sexual desire … As it stands, people with psychological deviations are most predisposed to homosexuality. Therefore, criminalisation of homosexuality is not just a matter of law. It goes without saying that such perversion is of a pathological nature and legal sanctions are not only useless, but unjust. The fear of criminal punishment prevents homosexuals from resorting to medical help. In the medical and legal literature, it has been stated multiple times that consensual homosexual liaisons between adults neither pose societal danger nor damage the state … With all this in mind, the dissertation proposes the exclusion from Soviet legislation of the article criminalising consensual sodomy. This opinion also gained support in Soviet legal scholarship (P. P. Osipov, I. M. Yakovlev).[97]

On 6 May 1974 Ignatov presented his dissertation for defence before a panel of experts, including prominent Soviet jurists Igor Karpets, Mikhail Adveev, German Kriger and Mark Yakubovich.[98] The archival file on Ignatov, unlike that of Daniel'bek, contains only three reports from his reviewers and one of them, written by Professor Stanislav Borodin, offered feedback on Ignatov's ideas regarding decriminalisation of consensual sodomy. Borodin criticised Ignatov's proposal: 'The author of the dissertation, without any argumentation, contends that homosexual relations between both men and women, which are either a congenital or an acquired pathology, should not be classified as criminal acts. I doubt that the "innate" or "acquired" propensity for homosexuality is relevant to the issue of criminal responsibility for sodomy.'[99] Although Mikhail Avdeev, a prominent Soviet forensic expert who classified consensual sodomy as a crime in his numerous books and manuals, was on the panel of experts present during the defence of the dissertation, I was unable to find his review of it. Avdeev's opinion on Ignatov's proposals regarding sodomy would have been revealing, demonstrating to what extent forensic experts were accepting of such ideas.

Although there were only a small number of reviews in Ignatov's file, it did contain a revealing transcript of the proceedings of his dissertation defence. Ignatov's defence commenced with the chair reading out his biography to the panel of experts and then Ignatov took the floor to give a lecture about his dissertation, summarising its main findings and proposals. Interestingly, he avoided mentioning the suggestions to decriminalise consensual sodomy. After his lecture, the experts began to ask questions about the content of the dissertation and some of these questions concerned the issue of homosexuality. Ignatov's discussion of homosexuality with the members of the commission is intriguing and illuminating in many important ways, and thus worth quoting at length:

CHAIR

In criminal law, does homosexuality violate the basic norms [of socialist morality]?

A. N. IGNATOV

The issue of homosexuality is very complex and very difficult to solve. My thesis proposes the elimination of criminal responsibility for consensual sodomy between adult men. On the other hand, criminal liability should be imposed for all types of homosexual behaviour associated with the use of violence against a person. I receive both support and criticism in response to my abstract (avtoreferat) and dissertation and these have made me think through and consider this issue once again. It seems to me that the problem of responsibility for homosexuality and, in general, the issue of sodomy should be addressed comprehensively. It goes beyond the scope of a purely legal perspective and required a further, deep and comprehensive study. It seems premature to put forward a proposal to eliminate the criminal responsibility for sodomy. Public consciousness and public opinion are not yet ready for such a solution to the problem. And in this regard, you correctly said that indeed this act is condemned by socialist morality and that our criminal code considers it as a violation of the basic principles of socialist morality.[100]

CHAIR

You are proposing to establish responsibility for homosexual behaviour not only for men, but also for women. What is the practical need for this? How often can such cases be encountered?

A. N. IGNATOV

Unfortunately, quite often. The administration of one of the women's colonies contacted me with a request to assist in the elimination of such cases. There were cases with violence, serious injuries and even

> murders committed because of jealousy. And they didn't know how to deal with them.[101]

After the questions, the examiners read out their reviews, which unfortunately are not part of Ignatov's file. However, it appears that some of them did comment, negatively, on Ignatov's proposals to decriminalise consensual sodomy. After the reviews were read out, Ignatov was given further opportunity to comment on the experts' remarks and this time he touched on the issue of sodomy (apparently in response to criticism voiced by one of the experts):

> Under current Soviet criminal law, only sodomy is criminalised. My dissertation puts forwards the thesis that criminal liability should be imposed for all types of homosexual behaviour associated with the use of violence against a person, involving minors in homosexual relations and organising mass debauchery (brothels). At the same time, the dissertation makes a proposal to eliminate criminal liability for voluntary sodomy between adult men. This issue is being discussed in legal, sociological and medical science both abroad and in our country.[102]
>
> The timeliness of this question is also evidenced by the responses to it in the reviews. Professor M. I. Yakubovich and the organisations he is affiliated with – the Sverdlovsk Law Institute, the All-Union Institute of Soviet Legislation, the Prosecutor's Office of the Georgian USSR – are in favour of eliminating punishment for voluntary sodomy. In a number of other reviews (Professor G. A. Kriger, Supreme Court of the USSR, Prosecutor's Office of the Ukrainian SSR, Kiev Higher School of the Ministry of Internal Affairs), the proposal to abolish the punishment for voluntary sodomy is criticised. As far as I know, the Legal Department of the Presidium of the Supreme Soviet of the USSR does not support this proposal either.[103]
>
> Studying the reviews and their arguments made me once again carefully think over this problem and led me to the conclusion that the proposal to completely abolish criminal liability for voluntary sodomy was put forward somewhat prematurely. It seems to me that public consciousness is not ready for such a decision.[104]

Ignatov's backtracking on the arguments concerning consensual sodomy demonstrate the permissible limits of liberal thought within intellectual circles and the adamant opposition of Soviet officials to the idea of decriminalising consensual sodomy. His bold proposals put the successful defence of his dissertation in jeopardy – Masha

Gessen tells us that when Ignatov's arguments came to the attention of the Party leadership, officials accused him of 'propagating immorality' and 'undermining the foundations of socialist law in the country'. Only through Ignatov's own connections and perseverance did he manage to defend his dissertation.[105] Perhaps Party officials saw Ignatov as a particularly threatening figure for the legal status quo: other scholars who argued for decriminalisation of sodomy did so in a very minimal way and behind closed doors – Pavel Osipov's dissertation (1966) never became a monograph, while Yakovlev expressed his opinion on the necessity to decriminalise sodomy in only one article. By contrast, Ignatov worked and wrote his dissertation at the All-Union Institute for the Study and Prevention of Crime, which operated under the auspices of the USSR Procuracy and Supreme Court.[106] Peter H. Solomon argues that scholars at such formidable institutes treated policy-related work as an important component of their own professional activity.[107] Indeed, as a scholar physically present in Moscow, Ignatov may have had better opportunities for extended participation in the policy-making process via frequent oral communications with Procuracy and Supreme Court chiefs and could even speak with them privately.[108] Despite his admission that the proposal to decriminalise consensual sodomy was ill-timed, his monograph *Classifying Sex Crimes* (1974), based on his dissertation, still openly recommended the decriminalisation of consensual sodomy.[109]

New attempts to make punishments more severe (1975)

While Ignatov proposed to eliminate legal penalties for consensual sodomy, his opponents continued to argue that sodomy laws should be kept in place and, most importantly, made more severe. A 1975 manual for law-enforcement agencies, *Sex Crimes: Criminals and Victims* by scholar Yurii Valerianovich Aleksandrov, from the Kiev MVD School, contained a lengthy nine-page entry on the crime of sodomy, which eloquently explained why homosexuality was dangerous:

> Sodomy is not an illness. It is ... determined by social factors of negative personality formation ... apart from moral degeneration and degradation of the individuals involved in such abnormal sexual liaisons and their breakaway from social activity ... sodomy infringes on

> the health of homosexuals, facilitates the widespread dissemination of venereal diseases.[110]

Aleksandrov argued that the existing law criminalising consensual sodomy in the Ukrainian SSR should be revisited with a view to introducing stricter penalties: 'Our experience has proven that milder penalties (up to one year's imprisonment) in the majority of cases do not have the desired effect on this cohort [homosexuals]. The deterrent value of such measures is also insignificant.' Following that contention, the author proposed that the penalty for consensual sodomy in the Ukrainian SSR be elevated to five years' imprisonment.[111] Aleksandrov also restated the commitment of Soviet criminal law to penalise consensual sodomy: 'It is known that Soviet penal law insists on penalising consensual sodomy. Given the high degree of social danger posed by this crime, one cannot but agree with such a stance.'[112] Aleksandrov was aware of the view promoted by Osipov, since he noted that Soviet legal schools had suggested decriminalising consensual sodomy, referring to Osipov's dissertation of 1966.[113] Aleksandrov expressed his dissatisfaction at the absence of penalties for other forms of same-sex relationships apart from sodomy, echoing the long-standing inclination of law-enforcement agencies to criminalise female same-sex relations: 'Sodomy is only one of the different displays of homosexual relations. Other forms of these displays should be considered no less immoral, cynical and corrupt, and therefore as carrying no less societal danger than sodomy. Yet these forms of sexual relations are not penalised.'[114]

Sex Crimes: Criminals and Victims seems to be the last public source to discuss the value of the law on sodomy in a series of manuals and dissertations produced in the period from 1965 to 1975 by Soviet legal and MVD scholars. Although this discussion then disappeared from public sources, legal scholars made some offstage attempts to push the Interior Ministry for change. Igor Kon tells us that in 1979 Ignatov sent a memorandum to the MVD, listing arguments for decriminalisation of consensual sodomy. However, he never received a response.[115] The meaning of this silence was plain: MVD officials were not going to introduce any changes to the existing legislation.

Fresh evidence suggests that the attitudes of some influential members of the Soviet establishment towards perceived deviant sexual behaviour remained extremely conservative. For instance, on 27 June 1977 the Supreme Court of the Latvian SSR advocated for stronger penalties for sex crimes, including for 'perverted' sexual practices such as oral and anal sex. The Supreme Court proposed introducing a new article to the Latvian SSR Criminal Code under the title 'Satisfaction of sexual desire in perverse forms.'[116] This article would criminalise coercive oral and anal sex as part of rape, and coercive oral sex accompanying sodomy. The proponents of the new law argued that 'forcible satisfaction of sexual desire in perverse form presents no less danger than rape or sodomy and attests to the utmost cynicism and depravity of the criminal'.[117] The emphasis on the 'perverted nature' of oral and anal sex, expressed by describing these practices as 'disgusting', 'cynical' and simply as 'sexual perversions', as well as attempts to distinguish 'natural' forcible sex from 'perverted' forcible sex, demonstrate the extent to which some Soviet authorities were guided by their prudish attitudes and their own perceptions of 'normal sexuality'.[118] Clearly, as long as these perceptions held sway, the decriminalisation of consensual sodomy was apparently out of the question. Yet, despite extensive discussion about the proposed law, the draft was eventually rejected on the grounds that it needed further consideration.[119]

Conclusion

Although it may appear extraordinary, the first attempts to decriminalise consensual sodomy in the Soviet Union were undertaken in the late 1950s, shortly after Stalin's death, when new criminal codes for the Soviet republics were drafted. The different drafts varied considerably. While there was discussion in the RSFSR regarding the possibility of decriminalising consensual sodomy, in the Soviet republic of Latvia the legislators instead considered introducing criminal penalties for female same-sex relations. In any event, ultimately neither of these proposals was implemented.

In the 1960s, with the development of Soviet criminology and jurisprudence, a new round of discussions on decriminalisation of consensual sodomy ensued. One of the first scholars to broach the issue was Aleksei Ignatov, who tentatively suggested that same-sex desire should be regarded as a sexual pathology rather than a crime. Another scholar, Pavel Osipov, made even more striking statements regarding the issue in his dissertation 'Sex Crimes' (1966) – he contended that homosexuality was a phenomenon conditioned by nature, which required no medical intervention. He also noted that sexual relations between two consenting males were often very difficult to investigate due to their very intimate nature, suggesting that they were not harming anyone and were a private matter between the men who cultivated them. Osipov's arguments appear therefore to be calls for genuine liberalisation: he did not argue that homosexual desire should be controlled by medical intervention, instead suggesting that homosexual desire was a natural one that should not be considered a criminal act. Other scholars who supported decriminalisation argued that homosexual desire should be relegated to the realm of medicine and sex education, with doctors treating homosexuals and educators working with children to prevent homosexual desire from arising in adolescents. Their views were informed by the rise of sexopathology.

Not all legal scholars were in favour of decriminalisation – a significant faction of them argued that sodomy laws were essential to prevent homosexuality from growing and even to uphold communist morality. In the 1970s one such scholar, Boris Daniel'bek, expressed his opposition to Osipov's and Yakovlev's proposals on decriminalisation in his dissertation. Although he admitted that medical intervention was also a viable solution when it came to dealing with homosexuality, criminal punishment was, he claimed, a more efficient measure. He also proposed to criminalise lesbianism, yet his examiners – distinguished scholars and judicial officials – concluded that such a measure was not necessary because female homosexuality was not as widespread as male. Daniel'bek subsequently published his dissertation as a monograph, having removed his ideas about the necessity to criminalise lesbianism.

Opponents and proponents of the decriminalisation of sodomy continued to engage in discussion throughout the 1970s. Some of them published views in manuals and textbooks for jurists and lawyers, but much of the crucial discussions on the issue took place behind closed doors. Most importantly, debates on the legal status of male and female homosexuality were not solely confined to a handful of academics and their published pronouncements on the issue, but were taking place among high-ranking judicial officials from different republics as well. The retention of the Stalin-era sodomy laws was not a result of neglect on the part of judicial experts and officials, but the product of heated behind-the-scenes debates on the issue from the 1960s to the 1980s. Entrenched homophobic sentiment among the Soviet judicial establishment, which actively defended and justified sodomy laws, criticised those who expressed support for their removal. Proponents of decriminalisation, however, persevered and the issue continued to trouble them. For example, in a memorandum written to the Interior Ministry in 1979, Ignatov again argued for the decriminalisation of sodomy, but received no reply.[120] As he later explained, personal distaste for homosexuality, particularly among many Soviet officials, never predisposed them favourably towards decriminalising sodomy.[121] We still have much to learn about the neglected history of these debates.

Notes

1 See for example: Kon, *Sexual Revolution in Russia*, p. 85; Rotkirch, 'What Kind of Sex', pp. 93–199.

2 Kon, *Sexual Revolution in Russia*, p. 85. See also: Rotkirch, 'What Kind of Sex?', pp. 93–199. On the criminalisation of homosexuality, see: Healey, *Homosexual Desire*.

3 Kon, *Sexual Revolution in Russia,* p. 244. Healey, *Homosexual Desire*, pp. 247–8.

4 Mark Sandle, 'A Triumph of Ideological Hairdressing? Intellectual Life in the Brezhnev Era Reconsidered', in *Brezhnev Reconsidered*, ed. Edwin Bacon and Mark Sandle (Basingstoke: Palgrave Macmillan, 2002), pp. 135–6.

5 Neringa Klumbyte and Gulnaz Sharafutdinova, 'What Was Late Socialism?' in *Soviet Society in the Era of Late Socialism, 1964–1985*, ed. Neringa Klumbyte and Gulnaz Sharafutdinova (New York and London: Lexington Books, 2014), p. 2.

6 See for example: Stella, *Lesbian Lives*, p. 35.

7 Peter H. Juviler, 'Criminal Law and Social Control', in *Contemporary Soviet Law: Essays in Honour of John N. Hazard,* ed. Donald D. Barry, William E. Butler, and George Ginsburgs (The Hague: Springer Netherlands, 1974), p. 21.

8 Peter H. Solomon Jr., *Soviet Criminologists and Criminal Policy: Specialists in Policy-Making* (New York: Columbia University Press, 1978), p. 53.

9 GARF, f. A-385, op. 26, delo 152, ll. 292–4.

10 Among other participants were: P. A. Astakhov, Z. A. Vyshinskaya, A. A. Plankin, T. L. Sergeeva, V. I. Kurlyandskii and M. F. Orlov.

11 GARF, f. A-385, op. 26, delo 153, ll. 182–3.
12 Apparently the reference number of the article changed from '154-a' to '100' due to the removal of unneeded articles and inclusion of new ones. Ibid., l. 183.
13 Aleksei Adol'fovich Gertsenzon was a professor of juridical science. From 1931 he was professor in the Institute of Soviet Law. Throughout his career, he wrote more than 250 research papers and publications on the theory of criminal law and history of criminal sociology. From 1963 until his death he directed the All-Union Institute for the Study and Prevention of Crime, founded in the same year. See the entry for Aleksei Adol'fovich Gertsenzon (1902–1970) in V. M. Syrykh, ed., *Vidnye uchenye yuristy Rossii (vtoraya polovina XX veka): Entsiklopedicheskii slovar' biografii* (Moscow: Rossiiskaya akademiya pravosudiya, 2006), p. 98. Among other participants, the following persons were listed (without initials): Astakhov, Avdeev, Gertsenzon, Grishaev, Durmanov, Kopylovskaya, Korotkov, Mikhailov, Nikiforov, Poretskaya, Stepichev, Starikov, Urakov, Orlov.
14 Apparently this number refers to the votes in favour of continued discussion of the law. Presumably the two people voting in favour were Stepichev and Nikiforov.
15 GARF, A-385, op. 26, delo 152, ll. 292–3.
16 Kon, *Sexual Revolution in Russia*, p. 85.
17 Boris S. Nikiforov, *Nauchno-prakticheskii kommentarii Ugolovnogo Kodeksa RSFSR* (Moscow: Yuridicheskaya literatura, 1964), p. 281.
18 State Archive of Latvia, f. 938, op. 6, delo 66, l. 82.
19 Ibid., delo 64, l. 1.
20 Ibid., l. 71.
21 For a discussion on why female same-sex relations were not prohibited, see: Healey, *Homosexual Desire*, pp. 196–202.
22 GARF, f. P-9414, op. 1, delo 2882, l. 144. I was first alerted to the existence of this document by Dan Healey's work: Dan Healey, 'From Stalinist Pariahs'.
23 Healey, 'From Stalinist Pariahs', p. 99.
24 Healey, *Homosexual Desire*, p. 204.
25 Field, *Private Life and Communist Morality*, pp. 51–65.
26 Peter H. Solomon, 'Soviet Criminology: Its Demise and Rebirth, 1928–1963', in *Crime, Criminology and Public Policy: Essays in Honour of Sir Leon Radzinowicz*, ed. Roger Hood (London: Heinemann Educational, 1974), pp. 571–95. See also: Louise Shelley, 'Soviet Criminology: Its Birth and Demise, 1917–1936' (PhD dissertation, University of Pennsylvania, 1977), and Sharon A. Kowalsky, *Deviant Women: Female Crime and Criminology in Revolutionary Russia, 1880–1930* (DeKalb: Northern Illinois University Press, 2009), pp. 187–92.

27 Khlyntsov, *Rassledovanie polovykh prestuplenii*, p. 4.
28 Ibid., p. 141.
29 Field, 'Communist Morality and Meanings of Private Life', 116.
30 Khlyntsov, *Rassledovanie polovykh prestuplenii*, p. 145.
31 Aleksei N. Ignatov, *Otvetstvennost' za prestupleniya protiv nravstvennosti: Polovye prestupleniya* (Moscow: Yuridicheskaya literatura, 1966).
32 Syrykh, *Vidnye uchenye yuristy Rossii*, p. 507.
33 Ignatov, *Otvetstvennost' za prestupleniya*, p. 180.
34 Healey, *Homosexual Desire*, p. 221.
35 Ignatov, *Otvetstvennost' za prestupleniya*, p. 181.
36 Ibid., p. 182.
37 On the history of Soviet sexopathology, see: Kon, *Sexual Revolution in Russia*, pp. 90–102. See also: Lev Shcheglov, 'Medical Sexology', in *Sex and Russian Society*, ed. Igor Kon and James Riordan (London: Pluto Press, 1993), pp. 152–64. On medical discourse on 'sexual perversions' in the Soviet Union, see: Volodin, *Kvir-istoriya Belarusi*; Ivanov, *Voprosy psikhoterapii*, p. 4.
38 Jan Seidl, 'Decriminalisation of Homosexual Acts in Czechoslovakia in 1961', in *Queer Stories of Europe,* ed. Kārlis Vērdinš and Jānis Ozolinš (Newcastle upon Tyne: Cambridge Scholars, 2016), pp. 174–95. See also: Sokolová, 'State Approaches to Homosexuality', pp. 85–108.
39 Josie McLellan, *Love in the Time of Communism: Intimacy and Sexuality in the GDR* (Cambridge: Cambridge University Press, 2011), pp. 114–18. On decriminalisation of male homosexuality in West Germany, see: Robert G. Moeller, 'Private Acts, Public Anxieties, and the Fight to Decriminalise Male Homosexuality in West Germany', *Feminist Studies* 36, no. 3 (2010): 528–52.
40 Monika Pisankaneva, 'The Forbidden Fruit: Sexuality in Communist Bulgaria', *LiterNet.bg*, 68, 7:1–10, http://liternet.bg/publish14/m_pisankyneva/forbidden.htm (accessed 25 February 2016).
41 Kon, *Sexual Revolution in Russia*, p. 92.
42 Pavel P. Osipov, 'Polovye prestupleniya: Obshchee ponyatie, sotsial'naya sushchnost' i sistema sostavov' (Dissertatsiya na soiskanie uchenoi stepeni kandidata yuridicheskikh nauk, Leningrad, 1966).
43 Ibid., 5.
44 Solomon, *Soviet Criminologists and Criminal Policy*, pp. 63–4.
45 Osipov, 'Polovye prestupleniya', 202.
46 Ibid.
47 Ibid.
48 Ibid., 204–5.
49 See for example: Lewis H. Siegelbaum, ed., *Borders of Socialism: Private Spheres of Soviet Russia* (New York: Palgrave Macmillan, 2006).

50 Lewis H. Siegelbaum, 'Cars, Cars and More Cars: The Faustian Bargain of the Brezhnev Era', in *Borders of Socialism: Private Spheres of Soviet Russia*, ed. Lewis H. Siegelbaum (New York: Palgrave Macmillan, 2006), pp. 83–103.

51 Steven E. Harris, 'I Know All the Secrets of My Neighbours': The Quest for Privacy in the Era of the Separate Apartment', in *Borders of Socialism,* ed. Lewis H. Siegelbaum (New York: Palgrave Macmillan, 2006), p. 172; Siegelbaum, 'Cars, Cars and More Cars', p. 96. Dan Healey justly suggests that the Soviet car owner's world might have been used for 'homosexual trysts' as well: Healey, 'From Stalinist Pariahs', p. 114.

52 Osipov, 'Polovye prestupleniya', 204.

53 This was the case for example in the UK. See: Dagmar Herzog, *Sexuality in Europe: A Twentieth-Century History* (Cambridge and New York: Cambridge University Press, 2011), p. 125.

54 Syrykh, *Vidnye uchenye yuristy Rossii*, p. 507.

55 Yakov M. Yakovlev, 'Otvetstvennost' za muzhelozhstvo po sovetskomu ugolovnomu pravu' in *Voprosy kriminalistiki i kriminologii* (Dushanbe, 1968), p. 38.

56 Ibid., p. 45.

57 Ibid.

58 Ivanov, *Voprosy psikhoterapii*, pp. 128–39.

59 Yakovlev, 'Otvetstvennost' za muzhelozhstvo', p. 42.

60 Ibid., p. 45.

61 Some of the conference's papers were included in a conference brochure: Fedor Arkhipov, ed., *Prestupleniya protiv nravstvennosti: Materialy nauchno-prakticheskoi konferentsii* (Vilnius: Prokuratura Litovskoi SSR, 1970).

62 Ibid., p. 10.

63 Osipov, 'Polovye prestupleniya', 202–3.

64 Field, 'Communist Morality and Meanings of Private Life', 123.

65 Iosif Gyne, *Yunosha prevrashchaetsya v muzhchinu* (Moscow: Meditsina 1960), p. 36. See also: Artem'ev et al., *Gigiena polovoi zhizni*, p. 20.

66 Boris V. Daniel'bek, 'Ugolovnopravovaya bor'ba s polovymi prestupleniyami' (Avtoreferat dissertatsii na soiskanie uchenoi stepeni doktora yuridicheskikh nauk, Moscow, 1970).

67 Ibid., p. 4.

68 Daniel'bek, *Polovye izvrashcheniya*. This textbook appears to be based on Daniel'bek's dissertation 'Criminal and Legal Fight with Sex Crimes' (Ugolovno-pravovaya bor'ba s polovymi prestupleniami), which he defended in 1970 in the MVD Higher School. I was able to find only the abstract of his dissertation (avtoreferat dissertatsii), which is available in the Russian National Library.

69 Ibid., p. 89.
70 Ibid., p. 90.
71 Ibid.
72 Ibid., pp. 91–2.
73 Ibid., p. 87.
74 GARF, f. P-9506, op. 75, delo 57, l. 35–6.
75 Ibid., l. 97.
76 Ibid., l. 81.
77 Ibid., ll. 104–5.
78 Dan Healey, *Homosexual Desire*, p. 199.
79 Healey, *Soviet Homophobia*, pp. 98–103. Also see: Stella, *Lesbian Lives*, p. 52.
80 GARF, f. P-9506, op. 75, delo 57, l. 85.
81 Daniel'bek, *Polovye izvrashcheniya*, p. 104.
82 On lesbian lives, compulsory heterosexuality and respectable femininity in the late Soviet era, see: Stella, *Lesbian Lives*, pp. 45–67.
83 GARF, f. P-9506, op. 75, delo 57, l. 110.
84 Ibid., ll. 86–7.
85 Ibid., 87.
86 Ibid., ll. 125–6.
87 Sandle, 'A Triumph of Ideological Hairdressing?', p. 136.
88 Ibid., l. 116.
89 Ibid., l. 130.
90 Healey, *Homosexual Desire*, p. 96.
91 Ibid.
92 Nikolai A. Belyaev and Mikhail D. Shargorodskii, eds, *Kurs sovetskogo ugolovnogo prava: Chast' osobennaya*, tom tretii (Leningrad: Izdatel'stvo Leningradskogo universiteta, 1973), p. 646.
93 Ibid., p. 647.
94 Aleksei N. Ignatov, 'Problemy ugolovnoi otvetstvennosti za prestupleniya v oblasti polovykh otnoshenii v sovetskom ugolovnom prave.' Avtoreferat dissertatsii na soiskanie uchenoi stepeni doktora yuridicheskikh nauk (Moscow: Vsesoyuznyi institut po izucheniyu prichin i razrabotke mer preduprezhdeniya prestupnosti, 1974). I was able to find only the abstract of the dissertation.
95 Pavel B. Posvyanskii, 'Vvedenie v sovremennoe uchenie o seksual'nykh perversiyakh', in *Problemy sovremennoi seksopatologii: Sbornik trudov*, ed. Anatolii A. Portnov (Moscow: Moskovskii nauchno-issledovatel'skii institut psikhiatrii, 1972), pp. 79–100; Yan G. Goland, 'O stupenchatom postroenii psikhoterapii pri muzhskom gomoseksualizme', in *Problemy sovremennoi seksopatologii*, ed. Portnov, pp. 473–86.
96 On the struggle to eliminate homosexuality as an illness from the *Diagnostic and Statistical Manual* of the American Psychiatric Association,

see: Bayer, *Homosexuality and American Psychiatry*. On the argument of Soviet sexologists that homosexuality was a medical problem, see: Posvyanskii, 'Vvedenie v sovremennoe uchenie', pp. 88–91.
97 Ignatov, 'Problemy ugolovnoi otvetstvennosti', 28–9.
98 GARF, f. P-9506, op. 75, delo 296, l. 51–2.
99 Ibid., l. 21.
100 Ibid., l. 80.
101 Ibid., l. 81.
102 Ibid., l. 104.
103 Ibid., l. 105.
104 Ibid.
105 Gessen, *Rights of Lesbians and Gay Men*, p. 10.
106 Solomon, *Soviet Criminologists*, p. 57.
107 Ibid., p. 108.
108 On the extent of scholarly participation in the practical decision-making process, see ibid.: pp. 107–25.
109 A. N. Ignatov, *Kvalifikatsiya polovykh prestuplenii* (Moscow: Yuridicheskaya literatura, 1974), pp. 231–7.
110 Aleksandrov, *Polovye prestupleniya*, p. 38.
111 Ibid., pp. 87–8. In the Ukrainian SSR, consensual sodomy was punishable with up to one year of imprisonment and exile for up to three years. Ibid., p. 87.
112 Ibid.
113 Ibid., p. 88.
114 Ibid.
115 Igor S. Kon, *Klubnichka na berezke: Seksual'naya kultura v Rossii* (Moscow: OGI, 1997), p. 359.
116 State Archive of Latvia, f. 938, op. 6, delo 1188, l. 10.
117 Ibid., l. 11.
118 Ibid., ll. 20–4.
119 Ibid., l. 1.
120 Kon, *Klubnichka na berezke*, p. 359.
121 Aleksei Novikov, 'Sindrom "Trekh obez'yanok"', *Molodoi kommunist* no. 12 (December 1988): 71.

5

Between disease and crime: sexopathology and prison homosexuality (1970–80)

In his manual for law-enforcement agencies titled *Sexual Perversions and Criminal Liability* (1972), scholar Boris Daniel'bek made a striking statement: 'As is well known, in the Soviet Union, if a person suffering from homosexuality goes to a medical institution (meditsinskoe uchrezhdenie), doctors are obliged to provide medical aid, and this cannot be considered a reason for starting a criminal prosecution'.[1] Indeed, throughout his text Daniel'bek argued that homosexuality should be dealt with not only by punitive measures, but with the help of 'medical intervention' (lechebnoe vozdeistvie). What was the meaning of Daniel'bek's statement that homosexuals could avoid criminal prosecution if they sought medical help? Did it signal a shift from a 'criminal' to a 'disciplinary' approach to homosexuality within the MVD, that is, from their understanding of it as a crime to that of a medical condition? What was the role of Soviet sexopathology in this shift? And how did the medical understanding of male homosexuality square with the existing penal sanctions for it?

Daniel'bek's statement encapsulates the peculiar kind of sexual modernity that was taking shape in the USSR in the 1970s – officially a crime, homosexuality was increasingly viewed as a medical problem. Indeed, the officials of the Soviet Interior Ministry were reluctant to admit that homosexuality was solely a medical issue and underscored its status as a criminal act. Yet, at the same time, the growing body of work of Soviet sexology exerted a significant influence on their views. In the 1970s MVD officials began to engage with the nascent sexopathological expertise on homosexuality, inviting Soviet sexologists to undertake scientific investigation of prison same-sex activity and write up the results of their research in specialised brochures for MVD personnel. This new willingness of the MVD officials to incorporate medical knowledge in efforts to combat prison homosexuality rendered the Soviet penitentiary a site where a new form of sexual modernity was being forged and new discourses on homosexuality were produced. Male prisoners engaging in homosexual acts were becoming objects of growing medical attention: sexologists observed their homosexual behaviour, subjected them to medical examinations and interrogated them about manifestations of homosexuality in their childhood. Doctors demanded constant and thorough examination of homosexual prisoners, pressed for precise diagnoses and emphasised the importance of their expertise in this matter, thereby pushing the issue of homosexuality further into the medical domain. Importantly, unlike GULAG doctors of the 1950s who focused mainly on lesbianism, sexologists of the 1970s turned their attention to male homosexuality. They espoused somewhat sympathetic approaches to the issue: they acknowledged the psychological suffering of those convicts who were the victims of homosexual assault at the hands of fellow prisoners and the importance of providing psychological assistance to them. Likewise, they did not impose medicalisation on the prisoners, but suggested that they should decide whether they wanted to undergo treatment or not.

Elsewhere, beyond the barbed wire, sexologists also continued to engage with the issue of same-sex desire. Although much is to be discovered about their practices, we know that in the 1970s some of them continued to offer treatments for homosexuality in the consultation rooms of the clinics where they worked, albeit unofficially. Introducing new classifications of sexual perversions and designing new drugs and therapies for homosexuality, these doctors continued their attempts to bring the issue of homosexuality under the authority of medicine.

Soviet sexopathology and homosexuality in the 1970s

In a foreword to a compendium of works on sexopathology published in 1972, Anatolii Portnov, director of the Moscow Research Institute of Psychiatry, within which the Department of Sexopathology was situated, solemnly announced: 'There is no question that sexopathology is becoming an independent medical discipline.'[2] He then went on to explain why this was the case: 'The fact is that any sexual disorders are both biological and social deviations. For example, male sexual impotence is not only one man's illness, it is often a direct cause of dissolution of the family, which is the unit of the society (yacheika obshchestva).'[3] As is evident from the quote, male impotence continued to be a primary focus of Soviet sexological science. Yet, for the first time, sexologists highlighted the problem of sexual perversions as a matter of priority: 'Sexual perversions are not merely an affliction of certain individuals, they threaten to afflict other healthy and predisposed (predisponirovannykh) individuals.'[4] Such an observation was a new note in the discussions of homosexuality among Soviet sexopathologists: not only was homosexuality here presented as a disease which afflicted unfortunate individuals, it was also considered a condition that could be passed on to others (GULAG psychiatrists, as I showed in Chapter 1, held similar views).

Portnov's description of the establishment of Soviet sexopathology as an 'independent medical discipline' came at a time widely regarded as a period of stagnation. But recent scholarship on the Brezhnev era has demonstrated that, despite the moral and economic decline regarded as axiomatic for this period, there were developments in political, cultural and social realms along with genuine attempts by the state to initiate and lead changes.[5] The development of Soviet sexopathology during the 1970s appears to have been marked with similar tendencies, seesawing from progress to neglect. On the one hand, as Igor Kon has argued, Soviet sexopathology was very slow in its development and was 'an outcast in Soviet medicine'.[6] The training in the profession was unsystematic and many sexopathological positions were filled by psychiatrists with no relevant education.[7] On the other hand, Soviet sexopathologists did their best to underscore the importance of sexopathology for society, challenging its status as an 'outcast' and arguing that its underdevelopment might have grave implications. Some sexopathologists even argued that there was a direct link between the growing divorce rates and the poor administration of sexological health services in the country. For example, Ivan Yunda from Kiev contended that growing divorce rates recorded in the 1960s were largely due to reasons pertaining to the field of sexopathology – infertility of one of the spouses, 'physical dissatisfaction' and adultery due to sexual incompatibility.[8] He also noted that the number of patients with sexual disorders was growing.[9] Other sexopathologists complained that many republics did not yet have sexological consultation rooms and training of a new generation of specialists was urgently needed.[10]

Against a backdrop of a deteriorating demographic situation in the early 1970s, the arguments for improving the sexological services available to the population began to hit home with the officials of the Soviet Health Ministry.[11] On 22 November 1973 the ministry issued a decree titled 'On measures to improve therapeutic-prophylactic [lechebno-profilakticheskaya] aid to patients suffering from sexual disorders.'[12] The decree deplored the poor state of Soviet sexopathological research and treatment: 'the state of therapeutic-prophylactic aid to patients with sexual disorders is still unsatisfactory. Research on the pathogenesis ... of sexual disorders is conducted by separate, unrelated research institutes. There is a lack of coordination of scientific research and of specialist training programmes.'[13] To address this problem, the Ministry of Health mandated that major improvements in sexological science be initiated. First and foremost, it ordered the opening of specialised consultation rooms in oblast'- and republic-level clinics, where patients with sexual disorders could receive medical help.[14] Second, it ordered that the Academy of Medical Sciences of the USSR consider expanding scientific research on sexopathology. Finally, it ordered the inauguration of an All-Union Scientific Methodological Centre for Issues of Sexopathology (Vsesoyuznyi nauchno-metodicheskii tsentr po voprosam seksopatologii), which was to operate alongside the already existing Department of Sexopathology.[15] The centre was to become the leading research institute on sexopathology in the Soviet Union with a range of functions, including coordination of research in the field, incorporation of sexopathological findings into clinical practice, preparation and organisation of seminars and symposia on sexopathology across the Soviet Union, and dissemination of sexopathological expertise throughout the country and abroad.[16]

Soviet sexopathologists interested in the issue of homosexuality continued to publish their research on the issue, framing it as a treatable disease. Their views significantly diverged from the view that homosexuality was a normal variant of human sexuality, which underpinned the decision of the American Psychiatric Association to remove homosexuality from the *Diagnostic and Statistical Manual of Psychiatric Disorders* in 1973.[17] Among Soviet sexopathologists practising medical treatment of homosexuality in the 1970s, there were three leading experts – Pavel Posvyanskii, the head of the Department of Sexopathology in Moscow, Yan Goland from the Gorkii Medical Institute and Abram Svyadoshch, who had moved to Leningrad by 1973 to establish his sexological practice. Goland continued to advocate for non-medicated approaches to homosexuality, arguing that psychotherapy was the most efficient means of treatment.[18] By contrast, Svyadoshch believed that homosexuality could be treated successfully only with a combination of psychotherapy and medication, a view he presented in his book *Female Sexopathology* (1974).[19] Although discussions of homosexuality in the book largely drew on the dissertation produced by Elizaveta Derevinskaya – formerly Svyadoshch's trainee – and dealt with lesbianism, there was also a passage in the book describing a case of medical treatment of a homosexual man.[20] The treatment of male homosexuality proposed by Svyadoshch was akin to 'aversion therapies' provided by British psychiatrists to homosexuals in the 1960s: vomit-inducing drugs (emetics) were paired with psychotherapy, whose goal was to create an aversion to homosexuality in the patient.[21] During this stage, the patient would be invited 'to look at a photo of the object of his homosexual affection or to imagine homosexual liaisons'.[22] In his book Svyadoshch explained that 'the nausea and vomiting caused by apomorphine are gradually associated with homosexual fantasies, forming a patient's negative attitude to them'.[23] He also noted that this method 'had been successfully implemented to eliminate homosexual affection in a man who was an active homosexual'.[24]

Pavel Posvyanskii, the head of the Department of Sexopathology in Moscow, not only discussed possible treatments of homosexuality, but sought to introduce a uniform classification of sexual perversions that every doctor could bear in mind when dealing with such patients. He presented this classification in a lengthy article entitled 'Introduction to the Contemporary Study of Sexual Perversions' (1972). Its goal was apparently to educate Soviet sexopathologists about the nature of sexual perversions and draw their attention to this problem. In his introduction to the article, Posvyanskii deplored the fact that not all sexual therapists were familiar with perversions:

'Unfortunately, wide circles of psychiatrists, sexopathologists and other specialists do not have sufficient information on these questions [sexual perversions]. This, of course, has a negative effect on both theoretical work on the problem of perversions and practical work.'[25] According to Posvyanskii, a more careful consideration of these phenomena was needed in medical practice, since patients who suffered from them were not a rarity: 'In recent years in the Department of Sexopathology of the Moscow Research Institute of Psychiatry we have had the chance to observe and examine a quite large number of patients suffering from perversions of various forms.'[26]

Posvyanskii maintained that there was a special cluster of 'sexual perversions' which he referred to as 'genuine' (istinnye). These he said were 'unchangeable' (neizmenyaemye) and 'irresistible' (neodolimye).[27] Although such individuals could consciously control their desires and abstain from acting on them, their desires would stay perverse notwithstanding.[28] Sexual fulfilment for them could be achieved only in the form they genuinely preferred, while any other forms of sexual satisfaction would remain 'profoundly alien' or simply impossible to carry out. To make his point clear, Posvyanskii quoted one of his homosexual patients, who said: 'Sexual intimacy with a woman for me is disgusting – if I had to do it, it would be indeed a genuine perversion.'[29] Yet, despite the fact such so-called perversions were 'genuine' and, therefore, incurable by implication, Posvyanskii still maintained that they were to be treated: 'Therefore, individuals suffering from genuine forms of perversions should be the object of medical intervention, provided that their behaviour does not violate the existing laws.'[30]

What, then, was the relationship between these medical understandings of homosexuality and the law-enforcement agencies? Were they known to the Soviet police? Did Soviet sexopathologists, like Soviet jurists, try to argue for decriminalisation of sodomy on medical grounds? Little has been said in the existing scholarship on this problem: all we know is the account of Igor Kon, who tells us that Grigorii Vasil'chenko, the head of the All-Union Scientific Methodological Centre for Issues of Sexopathology, raised the issue of decriminalisation with the Health Ministry, but the latter was 'always against'.[31]

New evidence shows that Pavel Posvyanskii did discuss homosexuality at his meetings with officials from the MVD and the KGB in 1973. The interactions between the Department of Sexopathology and the law-enforcement agencies and the organs of state security come as little surprise if we consider that sexopathology, after all, was a branch of psychiatry, and the main Soviet sexopathological centre was headquartered within the formidable Moscow State Institute of Psychiatry of the Health Ministry of the RSFSR. Furthermore, scholars have shown that, by the end of the 1960s, the Soviet authorities had begun to rely on psychiatry as an effective means of repressing Soviet dissidents – those Soviet citizens who challenged the political regime.[32] During this period, the latter were diagnosed with concocted psychiatric disorders without any clinical evidence and subjected to compulsory hospitalisation.[33] These practices represented, in Mark Field's words, a 'deliberate collusion between the Soviet regime and psychiatry' and were most evident in the fact that, for instance, some psychiatrists working at the Serbskii Institute had Interior Ministry police ranks.[34]

Harvey Fireside tells us that Professor Lunts, a senior psychiatrist from the Serbskii Institute, was both a psychiatrist and a KGB colonel.[35] Fireside presents a quote from the recollections of Petro Grigorenko, a former Soviet general who eventually became a dissident. Recalling his internment at the Serbskii Institute, Grigorenko asserted: 'I myself, on more than one occasion, have seen Professor Lunts arrive at work in the uniform of a KGB colonel. True, he always comes into the department in his white coat. I have seen other doctors of this institute in KGB uniform.'[36] This fact should be considered when examining the written accounts of the meetings between Posvyanskii and the MVD and KGB officers regarding the problem of homosexuality.

We know from a routine annual report on the activities of the Department of Sexopathology, produced by Posvyanskii, that on 1 November 1973 he presented a paper, 'On the Issue of Sexual Perversions, Primarily Homosexuality' (K probleme seksual'nykh perversii, preimushchestvenno gomoseksualizma), at a conference that brought together doctors and administrative personnel of the MVD and the KGB (konferentsiya vrachei i administrativnogo personala MVD i KGB).[37] In his report Posvyanskii did not elaborate on how his paper was received by the MVD and KGB staff. The historian is also left to speculate on the subject matter of Posvyanskii's paper – yet it would be reasonable to assume that it was concerned with the issues raised in Posvyanskii's published work on homosexuality, namely his contention that homosexuality was a 'genuine perversion' requiring medical care, rather than police attention. According to Yan Goland, who knew Posvyanskii personally, Posvyanskii approached the MVD several times, suggesting that criminal sanctions for consensual homosexuality were unnecessary.[38] As Goland noted, the reaction of the MVD officials had always been the same – they merely said that they 'would take it into consideration' (primem k svedenyu).[39] In the same report Posvyanskii also listed other conferences in which he had participated. For example, the report tells us that in May 1973 he delivered a paper, 'Medical and Juridical Aspects of Sexual Perversions', at a 'meeting of Moscow advocates'.[40] Again, we do not know any details regarding the content of this paper, but decriminalisation of consensual sodomy might have been a possible topic.

Apart from engaging with lawyers and MVD and KGB officers, Posvyanskii taught a course titled 'Contemporary Problems of Sexopathology: On the Study of Sexual Perversions' at the Department of Psychotherapy of the Central Institute for Doctors' Advanced Training (Tsentral'nyi institut usovershenstvovaniya vrachei).[41] The institute had been the leading Soviet institution responsible for providing Soviet doctors with up-to-date medical knowledge and incorporating recent developments of Soviet medical research into wider medical practice.[42] The implications of Posvyanskii's lectures on homosexuality within the institute are difficult to establish due to the absence of relevant evidence, yet they certainly would have further promoted medical models of homosexuality beyond the narrow circle of Soviet sexologists.

From 'police' to 'science': shifting approaches to homosexuality within the MVD

Paradoxically, although in the 1970s MVD officials apparently took no heed of either doctors' or legal scholars' calls to abolish criminal penalties for homosexuality on medical grounds, they did frame homosexuality as a medical problem in their secret reports and even turned to the help of sexopathologists to address the problem of homosexuality in prisons. A new willingness of MVD staff to use medical knowledge in the struggle with homosexuality suggests the strengthening within its ranks of an alternative understanding of homosexuality as a medical problem, in parallel with its official stance on homosexuality as a crime.

First mentions of the fact that the Department of Sexopathology began to cooperate with the officials of the MVD on the issue of homosexuality in prisons appear in Posvyanskii's report examined above. There, Posvyanskii claimed that the department was given 'a whole range of tasks commissioned by the Sanitary Directorate of the USSR MVD (Sanitarnoe upravlenie MVD SSSR)'.[43] Among these tasks was a close study of homosexuality with a view to designing methods for its medical treatment in prisons: Posvyanskii's report featured an attached copy of a plan with related tasks for department doctors to complete in 1973 and 1974. These tasks included clinical examination of prisoners engaging in homosexual relations, publication of a handbook for MVD officials on preventing homosexuality and organisation of a series of lectures on homosexuality for the doctors working within the MVD. The whole plan is presented below.

PLAN

of activities on the problem of homosexuality in places of confinement for 1973

Tasks: Study of the problem of homosexuality in places of confinement to design recommendations concerning prophylaxis and treatment of homosexual acts among prisoners

Activities	Executant	Deadlines
1. Clinical examination of individuals, with histories of homosexual actions and conditions, conducive to the emergence and spread of these actions in places of confinement	Department of Sexopathology of the Moscow Institute of Psychiatry RSFSR Ministry of Health Directorate of the Medical Service USSR MVD	During 1973
2. On the basis of the conducted examination to design methodical instructions (a letter) on prophylaxis and treatment of homosexual actions among convicts	Same	IV quarter December 1973

3. Organisation of tutorials with the doctors of the Directorate of the Medical Service and Central Medical Institutions of the MVD on the subjects: contemporary state of debates on aetiology, pathogenesis, clinical picture and treatment of homosexuality	Head of the Department of Sexopathology, Prof. Posvyanskii P. B.	II quarter
Compile and circulate the text of the lectures on the subject to medical institutions of the MVD-UVD	Prof. Posvyanskii P. B.	
4. Receipt and circulation of the collection of works on contemporary sexopathology	Directorate of the Medical Service of the MVD	I–II quarter 1974
DIRECTOR OF THE MOSCOW STATE INSTITUTE OF PSYCHIATRY RSFSR MINISTRY OF HEALTH	HEAD OF THE DIRECTORATE OF THE MEDICAL SERVICE USSR MVD	
Prof. A. Portnov	V. Strusov[44]	

Homosexual activity in Soviet prisons was certainly not a new phenomenon, and the active struggle of Soviet officials with homosexuality in places of confinement can be traced as far back as the beginning of the Khrushchev era. As reform of the GULAG was under way in the late 1950s, the MVD leadership resorted to the help of psychiatrists and involved them in their struggle with homosexuality. Since that time the Soviet penitentiary system had undergone significant changes: the previously existing GULAG system disintegrated and was turned into a network of light regime penal institutions called 'colony settlements'.[45] These were introduced in a move to make the Soviet system of punishment more progressive, rewarding prisoners for good behaviour and preparing them for release.[46] The reforms of the 1950s also introduced improvements in the lives of the prisoners: their nutrition improved, cultural opportunities expanded and medical services became more responsive to their needs.[47]

Yet as far as prison homosexual activity was concerned, in Dan Healey's words, 'the late Soviet decades appear to have hardened the homophobia in prisoner subcultures, especially among male convicts'.[48] Homosexual violence continued to be part of late Soviet prison life: existing accounts point to the commonplace practices of homosexual rape and physical abuse which prisoners inflicted on 'degraded' prisoners from the lowest caste.[49] 'Degraded' referred to those known to play a receptive role in anal intercourse and those convicted under sodomy laws.[50] Some 'degraded' prisoners would be forcibly given a shaming tattoo, which would expose their status to other prisoners.[51] It was homosexual violence and the proliferation of criminal subcultures associated with it that led MVD officials to look for new and more effective ways of dealing with this phenomenon. The appearance of the new science of sexopathology in the 1960s, with its studies of or focus on homosexuality, was apparently seen as a viable solution.

A special department within the Interior Ministry coordinated the work between Soviet sexopathologists and the MVD officials – the Directorate of Medical Service.[52] One of the department's responsibilities was apparently the provision of medical services to prisoners, so the problem of homosexuality would naturally be in its purview. The list of tasks put before the Department of Sexopathology by the Directorate of Medical Service, presented above, cannot be characterised beyond the obvious observation that MVD officials were very eager to put Posvyanskii's knowledge of sexual perversions into practice; they were apparently also willing to assist him with his 'fieldwork' by providing him with unfettered access to prisoners. The findings of Posvyanskii's study were to be disseminated through tutorials delivered across various medical institutions of the MVD; in these lectures, Posvyanskii was to educate MVD officials on the 'contemporary state of debates on aetiology, pathogenesis, clinic and treatment of homosexuality'.[53] Posvyanskii was also expected to produce official guidelines on how to treat and prevent homosexuality in places of confinement, which would be subsequently used by prison officials. I have been unable to find any published results of Posvyanskii's studies; apparently, all of them are still held in the specialised libraries of the MVD institutions or closed medical archives of the still existing Department of Sexopathology. Some of Posvyanskii's studies are likely to contain personal histories of examined prisoners, which means that these files will not be divulged in the foreseeable future.

In his report Posvyanskii also revealed that the Department of Sexopathology was cooperating with the Laboratory of Psychiatric Endocrinology – both were parts of the larger Moscow Research Institute of Psychiatry – on development of a new drug for medical treatment of sexual perversions: 'The Department is working in close contact with the laboratory of psychiatric endocrinology… We have started a joint study of a new anti-androgenic drug for treatment of a range of sexual disorders (homosexuality, transsexuality, nymphomania).'[54] Although Posvyanskii did not elaborate further on the success of these experiments or give any other information on the use of this drug in practice, by the end of the 1970s, as I will show, this drug would have already been used in the medical treatment of homosexuality by the Department of Sexopathology and offered to MVD officials as an effective means of combating homosexuality in prisons.

Although the cooperation between Soviet sexopathologists and MVD officials was mostly focused on male homosexuality, female homosexual activity in prisons was also considered by MVD officials. For example, it was briefly discussed at the All-Union conference for the deputy chiefs of female penal colonies held in Moscow in 1973, the proceedings of which are contained in a brochure entitled *Contemporary Problems of Correction and Re-education of Convicted Women* (1974).[55] Participants of the conference included the minister of internal affairs of the USSR, Nikolai Shchelokov, and the head of the Medical Directorate of the USSR MVD, Vadim Strusov (the latter had commissioned the Department of Sexopathology with tasks related to male homosexuality in the same year).[56] The conference was devoted to the problems of improving the work of female penal colonies and the re-education of female prisoners.[57]

The problem of 'sexual perversions' with reference to female penal colonies was briefly mentioned in a report, 'Medical Service for Individuals Deprived of Freedom', presented by V. N. Popov, deputy head of the Medical Directorate of the USSR MVD.[58] Popov highlighted the role of doctors working in prisons, whose task was to 'return to society not only an honest, but a physically healthy person, capable of actively participating in productive labour and the social life of the workers' collectives'.[59] He suggested equipping female colonies with more medical specialists so that all morbid phenomena existing in the colonies could be tackled effectively: 'It is necessary to consider the issue of staffing medical departments of the ITU (ispravitel'no-trudovoe uchrezhdenie, corrective labour institution) with doctor-psychoneurologists, given that in places of confinement there is a certain proportion of individuals with psychiatric disorders, suffering from psychopathy, alcoholism, drug addiction and sexual perversions.'[60] Popov's report also featured a vague statement on the necessity to 'strengthen the prison regime to identify individuals engaging in sexual perversions'.[61] Popov's discussion of the role of medical professionals in supplying society with 'healthy' former convicts, along with suggestions that more doctors were needed to tackle sexual perversions, indicates, albeit implicitly, a familiar concern about the possibility of homosexuality spreading into wider society. As demonstrated in Chapter 1, this fear was palpable in the reports of GULAG officials and doctors in the late 1950s. Likewise, as we know from Francesca Stella, it was not uncommon in the 1970s for women practising homosexual relations in places of confinement to return to their homes after their release with their lovers from prison.[62]

We know very little about cooperation between Soviet sexopathologists and MVD officials regarding lesbianism in the 1970s. It is possible that the Medical Directorate of the MVD displayed little interest due to already existing studies on lesbianism by Elizaveta Derevinskaya (discussed in Chapter 3) which prison officials could consult for guidance.[63] Svyadoshch's book *Female Sexopathology* (1974), which drew extensively upon Derevinskaya's dissertation, also provided ample examples of how treatment of female homosexuality could be conducted in confinement.[64] It is also possible that the MVD directly approached Svyadoshch for guidance on lesbianism, as it did with doctors from the Moscow Department of Sexopathology, yet we need more evidence to substantiate this claim.

Further evidence of the MVD's inclination in the 1970s to regard homosexuality as a medical problem can be found in the handbook *Recommended Methods on Prophylaxis of Homosexual Behaviour in the Corrective Labour Institutions* (1978).[65] This manual was a product of the collaboration of doctors affiliated to different institutions – sexopathologists Nikolai Kibrik and Aina Ambrumova from the

Moscow Department of Sexopathology; P. M. Rybkin from the Medical Directorate of the USSR MVD; jurists I. Karetnikov, Alevtin Markov and L. Gavrilov from the All-Union Research Institute of the USSR MVD; and G. Rublinskii from the Main Directorate of the Corrective Labour Institutions of the USSR MVD.[66] The introduction of the manual underscored the importance of educating Soviet gaolers on homosexuality and equipping them with the necessary knowledge on how to address this problem in places of confinement.[67] Interestingly, the book's authors acknowledged that homosexuality was not only a problem for the socialist way of life, but a negative factor affecting cohorts of prisoners – it was an instrument of establishing informal criminal hierarchies in prisons. Male prisoners who were forced to engage in homosexual activity by physically stronger prisoners were then put into the caste of the 'offended' (obizhennnyi) and were ostracised by the prisoner's collective. The authors readily acknowledged this problem:

> A group of convicts held in the ITU in one of the oblasts complained to the Ministry of Internal Affairs that they were persecuted and constantly abused by negatively characterised convicts (otritsatel'no kharakterizuyushchikhsya lits). The inspection has shown that, indeed, by forcing each of the convicts of the indicated group to engage in homosexuality, negatively characterised convicts created an environment around them in which the 'offended' were forced to go to the bathhouse, canteen and eat separately from other convicts.[68]

The handbook drew extensively on the existing discussions of homosexuality among Soviet sexopathologists – their proposed treatment methods and theories regarding its origin. The authors argued, for example, that there were cases of homosexuality deemed as 'genuine perversions'; here they repeated verbatim parts of Pavel Posvyanskii's research article 'Introduction to the Contemporary Study of Sexual Perversions' (1972). These 'genuine perversions', they contended, were to be treated medically – through pharmacotherapy (farmakoterapiya) and psychotherapy. The former, they wrote, could be performed only with the prisoner's consent: 'It is important to remember that medicated therapy (medikamentoznaya terapiya) as a measure of influence (vozdeistviya) on prisoners is admissible only in relation to the individuals who have given their voluntary consent (dobrovol'noe soglasie).'[69] It is difficult to establish with certainty whether prison officials carefully followed this advice and resorted to medication only on occasions when prisoners consented to it. It may well have been possible that prisoners caught for homosexual acts were presented with a choice – either to have their sentence extended or to undergo medical treatment 'voluntarily'. I showed in Chapter 3 that when faced with such a dilemma – criminal prosecution or medical treatment – some homosexual men opted for treatment rather than incarceration. I have also noted above that it was not uncommon for the KGB to resort to punitive psychiatry, making individuals with no objective signs of psychiatric illness undergo medical treatment; the objects of such treatment were the opponents of the Soviet regime.

The authors of the manual – apparently these were the voices of sexologists Kibrik and Ambrumova – recommended submitting homosexual prisoners to meticulous medical examination with the aim of identifying the signs of sexual perversions in their early childhood:

> When collecting the patient's anamnesis, it is necessary to pay attention to the stages of his sexuality's development and its first manifestations. Doctors also should try to ascertain whether various exogenous/external factors could influence the appearance of homosexual desire. It is necessary to find out what the patient's childhood affections (privyazannosti) and hobbies were, what games he played and with whom he preferred to play them, with whom he was friends, whom he dreamt of becoming … whether he engaged in cross-dressing (pereodeval'sya li v zhenskuyu odezhdy) and what he felt when doing it, whether he was a witness to somebody's sexual intercourse, whether he willingly engaged in women's activities (zhenskie zanyatiya) … and other questions related to the patients' sexual development.[70]

The manual also strongly suggested that homosexuality should move into the jurisdiction of the medical profession. Doctors with special knowledge were to take the lead in the resolution of the problem of prison homosexuality:

> It is also important to remember that homosexual behaviour can be a symptom of a variety of diseases and have a different aetiology and pathogenesis. Only a thorough study of each case at the level of our knowledge (endocrinological, psychiatric, neurological, genetic, sexological) can correctly qualify this condition, predict its dynamics, suggest pathogenetic therapy and outline prophylactic measures.[71]

According to the brochure, doctors with sexological expertise were instrumental in managing the issue of homosexuality in prisons. Their role was crucial in delivering lectures on sex education among juvenile prisoners: 'Work on sex education should be conducted ... by experts with specialist training on psychiatry, sexopathology and social psychology.'[72] Likewise, medical workers assisted the colonies' operatives in conducting medical examinations of newly arrived convicts and helped identify homosexuals among them.[73] Gaolers were apparently expected to comply with doctors' assessments and were to address the problem of homosexuality on their basis:

> Forms of individual preventive work in relation to such convicts in certain circumstances can also be selected in agreement with medical workers who determine the form of homosexual behaviour. In particular, people with a forced (passive) form of homosexual behaviour need medical assistance first of all. Convicts with sexual pathology, along with operative-regimen (operativnykh-rezhimnykh) measures, are consulted by psychiatrists in order to identify the degree of alteration of their psyche, orientation of their sexual desire, persistence of sexual deviations, and conduct treatment.[74]

Kibrik and Ambrumova recommended conducting individual psychotherapy with prisoners and in doing so they apparently drew on Goland's texts on the treatment of homosexuality; they invoked his methods of autogenic training, helping the patient to get into a special state of mind called a 'sexual-psychological vacuum', characterised by the disappearance of both homosexual and heterosexual desire (examined in Chapter 3). They also offered to use psychotropic drugs to help prisoners achieve this state more quickly, noting that a similar tactic was applied to homosexual patients receiving medical treatment in the Department of Sexopathology: 'In the Moscow Research Institute of Psychiatry, for the creation of a "sexual-psychological vacuum", psychotropic drugs (psikhotropnye sredstva) – "behaviour correctors" (korrektory povedeniya) – have been successfully used.'[75] Among the drugs listed by the authors was 'antiandrogen' (antiandrogen), which, as they noted, 'led to a quick and stable decrease in sexual desire'.[76] This drug was apparently the one Posvyanskii noted in his 1973 report to the Health Ministry discussed above.[77] Apparently the invention and implementation of this drug to treat homosexuality was successful and in 1978 Soviet sexopathologists recommended its use in places of confinement for homosexual prisoners. Homosexuality could be especially amenable to psychotherapeutic treatment if it was 'acquired'.[78]

A handbook for MVD penal workers titled *Psychological Aspects of Re-education of Convicts in the Labour Corrective Colonies* (1979), written by MVD expert Viktor Pirozhkov, provides additional evidence of the growing willingness of the MVD officials to incorporate new knowledge on 'sexual perversions' into the struggle against homosexuality in prisons.[79] The manual instructed penal officials on how to facilitate 're-education' of inmates in juvenile colonies and aimed to equip them with the necessary knowledge of the convict's 'personality'.[80] Pirozhkov examined the young convicts' homosexual behaviour in the chapter titled 'Characteristic features (kharakteristika) of the young convicts (vospitannikov) suffering from sexopathology: the struggle with sexual perversions'.[81] The title suggests his awareness and acceptance of the existing Soviet sexopathological studies. Indeed, Pirozhkov often reaffirmed the link between 'sexual pathology' and homosexuality: 'Sexual pathology comprises various deviations (otklonenie) in the sexual development of an individual. In VTK (corrective labour colonies) various cases of sexopathology can be encountered, but it is most evident in homosexuality (cohabitation of the individuals of the same sex).'[82] Pirozhkov also provided lengthy excerpts on the origins of homosexuality, borrowed from Abram Svyadoshch's *Female Sexopathology* (1974).[83]

Pirozhkov's discussion of homosexuality displayed a familiar concern about its role in the proliferation of criminal subculture in the penal colonies. This anxiety was akin to those expressed by GULAG officials in the 1950s, and stemmed from the awareness that more experienced prisoners, associated with the criminal underworld, often raped newcomers, converting them into 'passive' homosexuals. Just like Ambrumova and Kibrik, who acknowledged the predicament of prisoners who played a 'passive' role in sexual intercourse, Pirozhkov discussed a similar problem among juvenile inmates. He deplored the prevalence of these practices in juvenile colonies: inmates with multiple convictions, so-called 'offenders' (obidchiki), raped and abused the 'offended' (obizhennyi) – prisoners without any such history. He demanded that the workers in juvenile colonies display greater care and discretion when dealing with 'offended' inmates in order not to worsen their situation: 'In working with homosexuals, educators (vospitateli) should be extremely tactful ... they should keep a secret the fact that a particular inmate was seduced by active homosexuals.'[84] Pirozhkov also urged the workers of the colonies not to openly protect passive homosexuals since such actions would only hurt them:

> Sometimes open protection leads to grave consequences, as active homosexuals begin to take revenge on the 'offended' for trying to find protection from educators ... bringing the 'offended' to the point that he shuns any help of educators. If the 'offended' is nevertheless trying to turn to the educator, then in accordance with existing traditions, he falls into the category of not only 'offended' but also ... informers (donoschikov). And in this case, unofficial public opinion will be on the side of the offender.[85]

Pirozhkov lamented that the penal officials' approach to the problem was often simplistic – most often, trying to resolve the situation, they just sent the 'offended' to another colony. Such measures often failed to produce the desired effect, since the remaining 'offenders' often found new victims to abuse.[86] According to Pirozhkov, medical professionals could offer more effective solutions to the problem. They were able to identify 'offended' prisoners and boost their moral state in psychotherapeutic sessions: 'It is necessary to conduct psychotherapy sessions with "passive" male homosexuals to eliminate their state of anxiety rather than their sexual desire, boost the strength of their personality and inspire self-confidence.'[87] Such help was important since many of the 'offended' prisoners experienced serious distress, resulting in a desire to inflict harm on themselves, escape and even commit suicide.[88] Some of these prisoners also 'sought revenge' for their status, trying to oppress weaker prisoners.[89]

Doctors were also able to prevent homosexual activity from arising in the colonies by conducting medical examination of the newly arrived convicts and identifying homosexuals among them, or at least those individuals who could potentially be a source of 'sexual perversions' in the future. Those convicts who were established to have previously engaged in an 'active sexual life' or masturbation were deemed to be most prone to homosexual behaviour: 'All inmate newcomers are subject to medical examination, in the course of which individuals previously leading an active sexual life and suffering from masturbation (onanism) are identified. These are registered as individuals from whom sexual perversions may be expected.'[90] Once the convicts susceptible to sexual perversions were identified, they were to be registered in the colony's medical department and subject to periodic medical examinations: 'Underage inmates registered by the medical department are periodically examined by a psycho-neurologist and urologist; they are instructed on the questions of sex education, physiology of the organism and the harm of the premature sex life, dangers of venereal disease, the harmlessness of sexual continence, sexual perversions and their influence on morality and mental health.'[91] This strategy of preventing sexual perversions was essentially a reflection of the premises of Soviet sex education manuals, which, as I showed in Chapter 2, suggested that 'premature sex life' along with 'masturbation' put youth on the slippery slide to homosexuality.

Those inmates who could not be helped with sex education were to be provided with medical treatment. Pirozhkov was optimistic about the outcomes of such an enterprise: he confidently stated that 'both pathological and situational homosexuality is curable'.[92] The most important means of medical treatment was psychotherapy, during which the doctor provided the patient with therapeutic suggestions on the 'inadmissibility of sexual desire in a perverted, pathological form'.[93] The patients were also to be provided with 'detailed instructions on how to adhere to a work–rest routine (rezhim truda i otdykha), [on how to] engage in physical training, on the importance of being tired before going to bed and on the importance of total abstinence from various sexual incidents until the next appointment with the doctor'.[94] Pirozhkov's knowledge of the existence of such treatments also stemmed from Svyadoshch's book *Female Sexopathology*. For example, Pirozhkov suggested that 'conditional treatment of homosexuality' (uslovno-reflektornoe lechenie) with the help of emetics could also help the inmate eliminate their homosexuality: the inmate was to be shown a photo of the object of his homosexual desire while being administered emetics.[95]

Throughout the 1970s the Medical Directorate of the MVD continued to approach Soviet sexopathologists directly, commissioning them with specific research tasks on homosexuality. Both doctors of

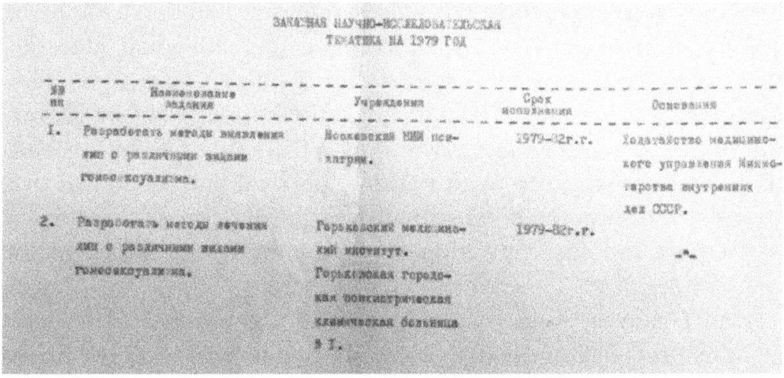

ЗАКАЗНАЯ НАУЧНО-ИССЛЕДОВАТЕЛЬСКАЯ
ТЕМАТИКА НА 1979 ГОД

№№ пп	Наименование задания	Учреждения	Срок исполнения	Основания
1.	Разработать методы выявления лиц с различными видами гомосексуализма.	Московский НИИ психиатрии.	1979–82г.г.	Ходатайство медицинского управления Министерства внутренних дел СССР.
2.	Разработать методы лечения лиц с различными видами гомосексуализма.	Горьковский медицинский институт. Горьковская городская психиатрическая клиническая больница № 1.	1979–82г.г.	–"–

Figure 15 'Requested Research Topics for the Year 1979'

the Moscow Department of Sexopathology and Yan Goland of the Gorkii Medical Institute received such tasks in 1979 in a request in the following form (see Figure 15):

REQUESTED RESEARCH TOPICS FOR 1979

	Name of the task	Institution	Deadline	Basis
1.	to design methods of identification of individuals with various types of homosexuality	Moscow Research Institute of Psychiatry	1979–82	Request of the Medical Directorate of the Interior Ministry of the USSR
2.	to design methods of treatment of individuals with various types of homosexuality	Gorkii Medical Institute. Psychiatric clinical hospital 1 of the city of Gorkii[96]	1979–82	

The tasks assigned to doctors from the Moscow Department of Sexopathology and Yan Goland were different: while Goland was expected to provide methods of treatment of homosexuality, the Moscow sexopathologists were expected 'to design methods of identifications of individuals with various types of homosexuality' – a new task for the Department of Sexopathology. Considering the context of MVD manuals on homosexuality in prisons, these methods were apparently required to identify homosexuals in the cohorts of prisoners with a view to conducting individual educative work with them or providing medical treatment. It is also possible that a request for 'methods of identification of individuals with various types of homosexuality' was due to the MVD's desire to equip police and investigators with not only physical but psychiatric evidence of the suspect's homosexuality. Such evidence was important to secure a sodomy conviction, especially under the campaign for 'socialist legality'.

Dan Healey tells us that in the 1970s the number of forensic examinations of homosexuals increased and forensic experts sought to come up with new methods of identifying homosexuals.[97] One such expert was Il'ya Blyumin of the Moscow Bureau of Forensic Medical Expertise, whose speciality was the forensic detection of sodomy. Blyumin offered to measure sphincter muscle tone to identify receptive partners and take swabs from the suspect's penis for chemical analysis.[98] The growing availability of this forensic medicine, as Healey argues, could account for the increase in convictions for sodomy observable from the late 1960s.[99] It may well be possible that requests from the Medical Directorate to design methods of identifying homosexuals were dictated by a similar willingness to assist regular police in capturing homosexuals.

Between private and public: Yan Goland's medical treatment of homosexuality in the 1970s

The ambiguous understandings of homosexuality in the MVD texts and correspondence paralleled a similar ambiguous standing of homosexuality in Soviet society – male homosexuality was criminalised, but medical treatments for it were available nevertheless, albeit unofficially. Yan Goland's medical practice of treating homosexuality was not unique in its contradiction with official ideology – other health practices, inconsistent with the official Soviet views, existed during this time. For instance, Larisa Honey tells us that during the 1970s 'alternative group health clubs' began to emerge in Soviet society: the members of these clubs studied 'everything that was forbidden to study', including astrology and yoga, and these clubs 'existed half-legally'.[100] New members of the clubs were invited by 'word of mouth' and although their activities were forbidden, 'they were somehow available and actively pursued'.[101]

Goland's practice appears similar to the health clubs described by Honey: although medical treatment of homosexuality was not an institutionalised practice, his prospective patients managed to find their way to his consultation room. They did so either through mutual acquaintances or by a recommendation from the doctors working in the Department of Sexopathology, where they first went to seek medical help. One of Goland's patients recalled in his diary his visit to the Department of Sexopathology, where Pavel Posvyanskii advised him to go to Gorkii and seek help from Goland:

> He [Posvyanskii] listened to me, asked several questions and said that he was very optimistic. He said that I needed to go to Gorkii, where a very good doctor Y. G. Goland lived and who had 'an elaborate system of treatment' and 'good results'. I was so happy – a famous sexologist from Moscow told me that I could still be rescued![102]

Goland's practice of medical treatment of male homosexuality stood in contrast not only with its official status as a crime: it was also different from the practices of other sexopathologists, who believed that medication was an important part of medical treatment for homosexuality. Although we still need to learn a lot about these practices, from existing accounts we know that it was not uncommon for Soviet psychiatrists to rely heavily on medication when treating homosexuality. Its use was advocated by Svyadoshch and Derevinskaya, and acknowledged by doctors from the Department of Sexopathology. Masha Gessen has documented the use of heavy medication in medical treatment of lesbians.[103] Against the backdrop of all these personally invasive practices, Goland's practice stood out as more 'lenient' and 'alternative'. Goland knew too well what crass and barbaric treatments his patients had been offered by doctors in their cities' local clinics. In one of his unpublished reports, presented at a conference in Tambov in 1974, Goland quoted a patient: 'When my parents learnt about my malady, they offered to castrate me and in the clinic where I went I was offered to be made sexually impotent (predlozhili sdelat' impotentsiyu). I spent one month in a psychiatric hospital without receiving any treatment.'[104]

Honey tells us that the alternative health clubs in the 1970s were 'a collective space' that offered 'support for people to develop their individual talents and personalities'.[105] Similarly, in the 1970s Goland began group sessions of psychotherapy for homosexuality, as opposed to administering it individually to each patient. In one of his reports produced in the 1970s, Goland explained why group psychotherapy was more effective:

> We believe it is expedient to begin the first group session by introducing to the group a patient who had completed his psychotherapy course for homosexuality and who is leading an active heterosexual way of life. Such an introduction is a powerful psychotherapeutic factor. It breaks the silence between the members of the group; they become active at once. Soon patients get out of their state of hesitation, getting into productive work (vklyuchayas' v produktivnuyu raboty). A working and optimistic atmosphere is created in the group; medical re-education (lechebnoe perevospitanie) in the collective and with the help of the collective starts from the first session ... A feeling of belonging to the group is being formed in each patient.[106]

Yet unlike Honey's alternative health clubs, Goland's group psychotherapy sessions were not about promoting individuality. The very goal of the treatment, the suppression of the individual's desire and its subordination to the needs of society, implies that individuality was supressed rather than encouraged. Goland seemed relatively intolerant of those who failed to actively participate in the collective treatment and branded such individuals as 'passive, weak-willed, unenergetic patients' – these were unsuitable for his psychotherapy.[107]

Health clubs as described by Honey and Goland's medical practice both thrived in their unique positions on the borders of public and private, official and unofficial. Both benefited from the process of 'privatisation', which, as Vladimir Shlapentokh has argued, had been under way in Soviet society since the mid-1950s.[108] Such 'privatisation' manifested itself in the emergence of 'totally private institutions' of family and friends, the growth of 'unofficial public life' in civil society and the exploitation of Soviet citizens' positions for personal gains.[109] Goland's practice is also evidence of the recent scholarly consensus about the fluidity of public and private boundaries in Soviet society, where, as Lewis H. Siegelbaum has argued, 'the private is neither hermetically sealed nor necessarily in antagonistic relation to public spheres'.[110]

On the one hand Goland's practice was a totally private enterprise. It was in the interest of both the doctor and the patient that what was going on in Goland's consultation room did not transcend its borders. Goland carefully selected his patients to make sure that they would be genuinely committed to the goal of elimination of their homosexuality and that they would be unlikely to experience a 'relapse'. The latter, as Goland explained to me, was very undesirable, since if the patient got caught by the police, it could create unnecessary trouble for him. Therefore, before starting the treatment Goland conducted a short interview with his patients to establish the seriousness of their intentions, asking his patients whether they would come to him for treatment if homosexuality was not punishable in the Soviet Union. A negative answer would signal the patient's scepticism and lack of commitment, making him unsuitable for treatment. If a patient hoped that his involvement in psychotherapy would render him immune to the police or at least moderate his sentence in case of his getting caught, then he would also be turned down.[111]

Both Goland and his patients understood the importance of keeping the patients' identities anonymous. Going to the doctor might be a risky affair – especially if the local law-enforcement agencies knew about the kinds of treatment Goland offered. When writing to Goland, his patients were apprehensive about the possibility of their homosexuality becoming known to their peers and they asked him to be careful in his responses. Indeed, as Arthur Clech has shown, many gay men feared that their homosexuality would be made public – they feared both criminal prosecution and the publicity given to their homosexuality.[112] Goland understood the predicament of his patients, and elsewhere in his papers argued that privacy was the main prerequisite for successful treatment. In one of them, for example, he insisted that the true diagnosis of homosexual patients should not be known to anyone but the doctor. If anyone else enquired about the diagnosis of homosexual patients, the doctor was supposed to say that they were 'neurotics': 'A patient has to be sure that nobody, except for his doctors, knows about his true diagnosis. For everyone else he is merely a neurotic.'[113]

While Goland spared no efforts to maintain the privacy of his patients, he attempted to institutionalise his practice as an official enterprise, making it public. Such balancing between public and private was characteristic of many unofficial entities and enterprises that had appeared in Soviet society since the 1950s. Juliane Fürst tells us about kompaniya – a network of like-minded friendship circles among Soviet youth in the 1950s and 1960s.[114] These were not random gatherings of acquaintances, but 'friendship circles with a spirit of political and social reawakening'.[115] The very nature of these networks meant that they would be 'relegated to the private sphere' (in a customary interpretation of the public and private divide), but at the same time the members of these networks 'demonstrated a desire to be' or 'create a public sphere'.[116] Regarding the informal health clubs of the 1970s, Larisa Honey notes a similar tendency to 'create' a public sphere: she tells us that despite the fact that these clubs existed 'half-legally', their members had a 'certain modicum of officialdom' by the introduction of a system of membership cards.[117]

Yan Goland also desired to 'create' a public sphere and add a sense of officialdom to his practice. He had tried this in 1969, by suggesting to Pavel Posvyanskii that a specialised health centre providing treatment of sexual perversions should be inaugurated in Gorkii. Back then, his plan failed due to allegedly insufficient funding. On 24 August 1974 Goland made another attempt to institutionalise his practice and bring the problem of treating homosexuality into the public domain; this time he wrote to a major health journal, *Zdorov'e*, asking to advertise his services on the medical treatment of homosexuality (Figures 16 and 17). Writing to the journal, with a print run of ten million copies, he framed the problem of sexual perversions as a public concern which needed to be addressed.[118] His letter is rare evidence of how Soviet doctors attempted to frame homosexuality as a medical rather than a police problem, and aimed to present this point to a wider readership (as opposed to merely discussing it with their peers in specialist literature):

> Dear editors!
>
> Our sexological consultation room provides treatment for sexual perversions; perhaps we are the only specialists who provide such treatment – we do that not episodically, but systematically. Over the past eight years we have examined several dozen patients – thirty patients out of them were cured. We have designed a method of psychotherapy of sexual perversions, which has been described in a number of articles, published in various editions.
>
> Our address to you is inspired by the following considerations. In the milieu of homosexuals (this is the most common type of perversion)

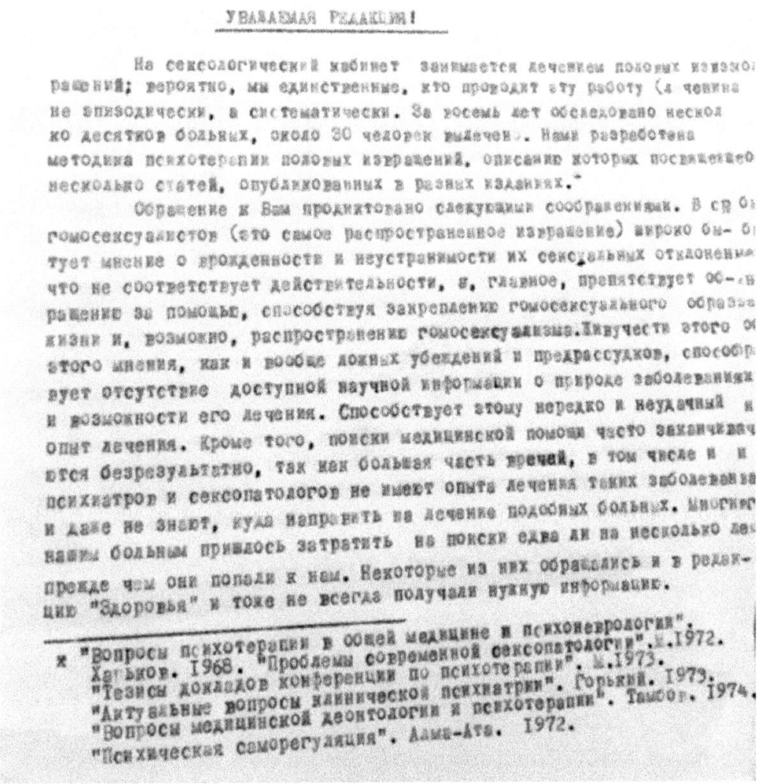

УВАЖАЕМАЯ РЕДАКЦИЯ!

Наш сексологический кабинет занимается лечением половых извращений; вероятно, мы единственные, кто проводит эту работу (и ведет её не эпизодически, а систематически. За восемь лет обследовано несколько десятков больных, около 30 человек вылечено. Нами разработана методика психотерапии половых извращений, описанию которых посвящено несколько статей, опубликованных в разных изданиях.*

Обращение к Вам продиктовано следующими соображениями. В ср[еде] гомосексуалистов (это самое распространенное извращение) широко бытует мнение о врожденности и неустранимости их сексуальных отклонений, что не соответствует действительности, и, главное, препятствует об[-] ращению за помощью, способствуя закреплению гомосексуального образа жизни и, возможно, распространению гомосексуализма. Живучести этого [и] этого мнения, как и вообще ложных убеждений и предрассудков, способствует отсутствие доступной научной информации о природе заболевания и возможности его лечения. Способствует этому нередко и неудачный опыт лечения. Кроме того, поиски медицинской помощи часто заканчиваются безрезультатно, так как большая часть врачей, в том числе и психиатров и сексопатологов не имеют опыта лечения таких заболеваний и даже не знают, куда направить на лечение подобных больных. Многие наши больным пришлось затратить на поиски едва ли не несколько [лет] прежде чем они попали к нам. Некоторые из них обращались и в редакцию "Здоровья" и тоже не всегда получали нужную информацию.

* "Вопросы психотерапии в общей медицине и психоневрологии". Харьков. 1968. "Проблемы современной сексопатологии". М.1972. "Тезисы докладов конференции по психотерапии". М.1973. "Актуальные вопросы клинической психиатрии". Горький. 1973. "Вопросы медицинской деонтологии и психотерапии". Тамбов. 1974. "Психическая саморегуляция". Алма-Ата. 1972.

Figure 16 Yan Goland's letter to *Zdorov'e* journal (1974), p. 1

there is a widespread opinion that sexual deviations are congenital and cannot be eliminated. These opinions have nothing to do with reality, and most importantly, they prevent homosexuals from seeking medical help and therefore facilitate the reinforcement of a homosexual lifestyle and, possibly, the spread of homosexuality. The persistence of such a view (as well as of other misconceptions) is underpinned by the absence of accessible scientific information on the nature of this disease and possibilities of its treatment. Unsuccessful treatment may also be the reason for it. Besides, the search for medical help often yields no results, since most doctors, including psychiatrists and sexopathologists, have no experience in treatment of such disease and do not even know where their patients could be

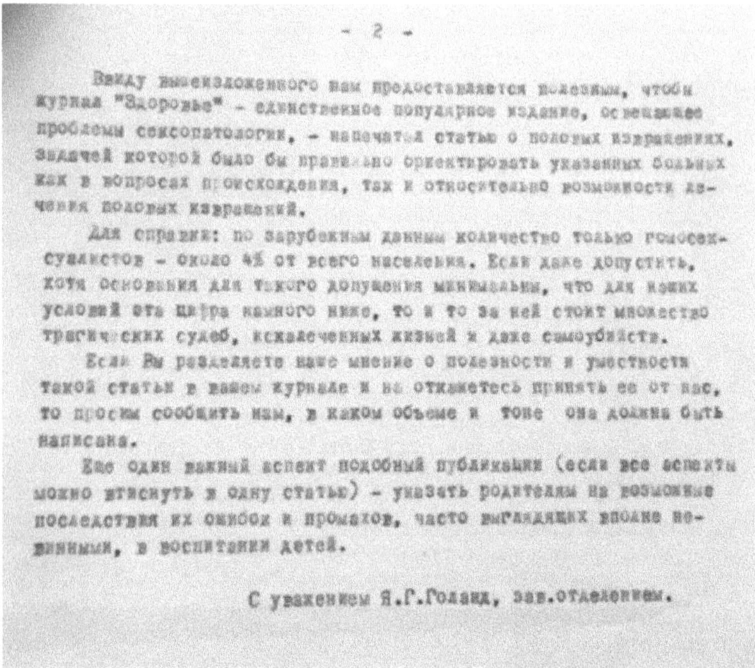

\- 2 -

Ввиду вышеизложенного нам представляется полезным, чтобы журнал "Здоровье" - единственное популярное издание, освещающее проблемы сексопатологии, - напечатал статью о половых извращениях, задачей которой было бы правильно ориентировать указанных больных как в вопросах происхождения, так и относительно возможности лечения половых извращений.

Для справки: по зарубежным данным количество только гомосексуалистов - около 4% от всего населения. Если даже допустить, хотя основания для такого допущения минимальны, что для наших условий эта цифра намного ниже, то и то за ней стоит множество трагических судеб, искалеченных жизней и даже самоубийств.

Если Вы разделяете наше мнение о полезности и уместности такой статьи в вашем журнале и не откажетесь принять ее от нас, то просим сообщить нам, в каком объеме и тоне она должна быть написана.

Еще один важный аспект подобный публикации (если все аспекты можно втиснуть в одну статью) - указать родителям на возможные последствия их ошибок и промахов, часто выглядящих вполне невинными, в воспитании детей.

С уважением Я.Г.Голанд, зав.отделением.

Figure 17 Yan Goland's letter to *Zdorov'e* journal (1974), p. 2

referred. Many of our patients spent several years seeking help before they reached us. Some of them wrote letters to the editors of Zdorov'e magazine and in most cases they received no response.

In view of the above, we think it is useful for Zdorov'e magazine, the only popular science journal covering the problems of sexopathology, to publish an article on sexual perversions, whose task would be to raise correct awareness (pravil'no orientirovat') of the aforementioned patients on the questions of origin as well as possibility of treatment of sexual perversions.

For your information: according to the foreign data, the number of homosexuals alone is about 4 per cent of the whole population. Even if we assume that this figure is lower under our conditions, although the foundation for such an assumption would be minimal, nevertheless, behind this figure there stand a great many tragic and crippled lives and even suicides.

If you share our opinion about the usefulness and relevance of such an article in your magazine and if you do not refuse to accept it from us, then we ask you to inform us on the size and tone in which this article should be written.

One more important aspect of this publication – (if all aspects can be squeezed into one article) – is to indicate to parents the possible consequences of their mistakes and blunders (promakhi) in their education of their children, which often seem rather innocuous.

Regards, Yan Goland, Head of the Department[119]

In his letter Goland argued that the medical treatment of homosexuality was meant for the public good – if left untreated, homosexuals could facilitate dissemination of a 'homosexual lifestyle' and could even 'spread' it further. Another aspect of his argument – presentation of homosexuality as a disease that crippled one's life and led one to suicide – was presented as a matter of public significance. Like male impotence, framed by sexopathologists as an issue with deep societal implications, homosexuality was presented by Goland as an issue meriting similar concern. The allusion to suicide appears to be an especially compelling argument – in the Soviet context such an act would be construed as an affront to the socialist system, which had failed to provide all the necessary conditions for an individual to have a fulfilling life. Kenneth M. Pinnow has noted that in the Bolshevik cosmology of the early Soviet years, suicide violated 'idealised conceptions of the collective as a space where the individual would achieve genuine self-realisation as a member of the group'.[120] Goland's argument had similar undertones and can be interpreted as a tacit suggestion about the relevance of his enterprise to the plans of the Soviet state to sustain a society with productive citizens untroubled by sexual disorders.

Yet Goland was treading on dangerous ground. As shown in Chapters 2 and 3, most sex educators and sexopathologists sought to downplay the prevalence of homosexuality in the Soviet Union. Goland, in contrast, suggested that the rates of homosexuality in the Soviet Union were akin to elsewhere in the world, thereby challenging the officially authorised discourses. This, apparently, was one of the reasons why his letter was never published. Indeed, from the point of view of the official policy on homosexuality, medical treatment of such individuals in Soviet society was completely unnecessary. Every possible measure had already been taken by the Soviet government to prevent homosexuality from arising – sex education was implemented to discourage children from lust, which could, in turn, lead to homosexuality. Various collectives existed to discourage the citizen from thinking about his sexual urges, even more so homosexual ones, and rechannel them for the benefit of society. Last but not least, criminal sanctions were in place to make sure that those who decided to live out their homosexuality were not left unpunished. With so many existing preventative options, the advertisement of a medical treatment of homosexuality would be an official acknowledgment that all these measures had failed.

We still have a lot to learn about the attempts of Soviet sexopathologists to convert their unofficial practice of treating homosexuality into an official enterprise; to do so would have legitimised homosexuality as a medical matter and would have inevitably challenged the official framing of homosexuality as a crime. Another sexopathologist whose practice would be worth investigating was Abram Svyadoshch. In 1972 he inaugurated the country's first family guidance centre, whose aim was to consult families and assist them in having a happy family life.[121] A wide range of specialists was to attend to the needs of the centre's prospective patients: sexopathologists (among them Svyadoshch himself), psychotherapists, psychologists and gynaecologists.[122] According to *Literaturnaya gazeta*, matters between the doctor and the patient would be discussed in private settings and the patients' anonymity would be a priority: 'There are consultation rooms designed for private conversations (doveritel'naya beseda) with the doctor … And one more important detail – patients will not be asked to provide documents. Not even a last name.'[123] The author of the article noted that such anonymity inclined patients to a greater confidence and trust in their doctor: 'The anonymity of the appointment allows for the patient to ask questions bravely.'[124] Unquestionably, the centre's emphasis on privacy and anonymity was an act of continuing 'privatisation' in Soviet society in the 1970s, and such privatisation would certainly attract homosexuals seeking treatment while escaping the gaze of the state. The relationship between doctor and patient, bound by shared secrecy and commitment to keep matters private, was an effective push against that state's desire to intervene in private life.

Lev Shcheglov, a Soviet and Russian sexologist and former Svyadoshch trainee, has confirmed this. As Shcheglov has revealed, Svyadoshch actively defended the privacy of his patients. One day a KGB officer turned up on the doorstep of Svyadoshch's office, demanding to see a medical file of a former patient who apparently interested the KGB.[125] Svyadoshch refused to comply, referring to 'patient confidentiality' (vrachebnaya taina).[126]

Conclusion

In the 1970s discussions of homosexuality among MVD officials were increasingly influenced by the medical findings of Soviet sexopathology. From 1973 onwards, MVD officials consistently consulted Soviet sexopathologists, commissioning them with scientific projects on designing methods for the medical treatment of homosexuality. In their discussions on the struggle with homosexuality in prisons, MVD officials also drew on existing sexopathological texts, acknowledging that homosexuality was in fact a disease. Yet, despite the MVD's drift towards medical approaches to homosexuality, police methods remained relevant – in their discussions MVD officials stated that homosexuals should be both treated and prosecuted.

Perhaps, animated by the MVD's interest in the medicalisation of homosexuality, Soviet sexopathologists sought to push the issue of homosexuality further into the medical domain. In their behind-the-scenes interactions with MVD officials, they argued that consensual sodomy should be decriminalised on medical grounds, yet to no avail (the subject matter of these off-the-record discussions remains obscure and the answers are likely to lie in classified MVD and KGB archives). Likewise, in their manuals on instructions for MVD officials on how to deal with same-sex activity in prisons, they insisted on the utility of their sexological expertise in efforts to combat homosexuality and suggested that prison officials heeded them. The growing influence of sexological expertise on homosexuality appears to have implications for Soviet homosexual men and women who now were under threat of not only prosecution, but also being subjected to medical treatment. The evidence for this claim can be found in the perestroika press; for example, in December 1988, the Soviet youth journal *Molodoi kommunist* published a letter sent by a homosexual man who identified himself as 'Volodya'. The young man confessed that he had 'spent a year and a half in prison and was on "chemo" (khimiya) there'.[127] Although doctors warned that the medical treatment of homosexuality in prisons could be conducted only if the prisoner's consent was secured, and insisted on the utility of psychotherapeutic conversations with prisoners, apparently these recommendations were not always observed.

The ambiguous understanding of homosexuality in the MVD texts throughout the 1970s paralleled a similarly contradictory standing of homosexuality in Soviet society at large (although this was certainly not unique to the Soviet case). Although homosexuality was a crime, some doctors provided medical treatment for it. Their enterprise thrived on the growing privatisation of Soviet society and the blurred boundaries between public and private borders. Locating their practices in the private realm, some Soviet sexologists attempted to go public – they wanted to institutionalise their practice and claim their medical authority over the issue. One such doctor was Yan Goland, who attempted to bring the issue of the absence of medical treatment of homosexuality into the public realm of newspapers. The initiation of such public discussion might have triggered an evolution of social values and understandings of homosexuality, and such evolution, in its turn, could have brought the issue of the decriminalisation of sodomy to the fore. Possibly cognisant of the consequences of such discussions, the editors of the newspapers chose not to publish Goland's article, and, as I showed in Chapter 4, this was a typical response of the Soviet state to any grassroots initiatives regarding homosexuality.

Notes

1 Daniel'bek, *Polovye izvrashcheniya,* p. 91.
2 Anatolii A. Portnov, Predislovie to *Problemy sovremennoi seksopatologii: Sbornik trudov*, ed. Anatolii A. Portnov (Moscow: Moskovskii nauchno-issledovatel'skii institut psikhiatrii, 1972), p. 5.
3 Ibid.
4 Ibid.
5 Edwin Bacon and Mark Sandle, eds, *Brezhnev Reconsidered* (Basingstoke: Palgrave Macmillan, 2002); Dina Fainberg and Artemy Kalinovsky, eds, *Reconsidering Stagnation in the Brezhnev Era* (New York and London: Lexington, 2016).

6 Kon, *Sexual Revolution in Russia*, p. 94.
7 Ibid.
8 Ivan F. Yunda, 'Sostoyanie i perspetkivy izucheniya polovykh rasstroistv urogenital'nogo geneza', in *Problemy seksopatologii i besplodiya*, ed. Ivan F. Yunda (Kiev: Zdorov'ya, 1973), p. 3.
9 Ibid.
10 V. I. Myasyuk and L. P. Pavlova, 'Spetsializirovannaya pomoshch' bol'nym stradayushchim polovymi rasstroistvami', in *Problemy seksopatologii i besplodiya*, ed. Ivan F. Yunda (Kiev: Zdorov'ya, 1973), p. 17.
11 Michele Rivkin-Fish tells us that 'in the early 1970s, demographers announced that below-replacement fertility rates in European regions of the USSR amounted to an urgent "demographic crisis"'. See: Michele Rivkin-Fish, *Women's Health in Post-Soviet Russia*, pp. 97–8.
12 Prikaz ministra zdravookhraneniya № 920 ot 22 noyabrya 1973 goda. Collection of the Department of Sexopathology of the Moscow Research Institute of Psychiatry.
13 Ibid., 1–2.
14 Ibid., 2.
15 Ibid.
16 Prilozhenie k prikazu Ministerstva zdravookhraneniya SSSR № 920 ot 22 noyabrya 1973 goda. Polozhenie o Vsesoyuznom nauchno-metodicheskom Tsentre po voprosam seksopatologii, 4. Collection of the Department of Sexopathology.
17 On the dispute over homosexuality within the American Psychiatric Association, see: Bayer, *Homosexuality and American Psychiatry*.
18 Goland, 'O stupenchatom postroenii psikhoterapii', pp. 473–86.
19 Abram M. Svyadoshch, *Zhenskaya seksopatologiya* (Moscow: Meditsina, 1974).
20 Ibid., p. 164.
21 Dickinson, *Curing Queers*, pp. 66–7.
22 Svyadoshch, *Zhenskaya seksopatologiya*, p. 164.
23 Ibid.
24 Ibid.
25 Posvyanskii, 'Vvedenie v sovremennoe uchenie', p. 79.
26 Ibid.
27 Ibid., p. 82.
28 Ibid., p. 83.
29 Ibid.
30 Ibid.
31 Kon, *Klubnichka na berezke*, p. 359.

32 The Soviet dissident movement arose in the late 1960s. On Soviet dissidents, see: Philip Boobbyer, *Conscience, Dissent and Reform in Soviet Russia* (New York: Routledge, 2005).
33 Among more recent works, see: Rebecca Reich, 'Inside the Psychiatric Word: Diagnosis and Self-Definition in the Late Soviet Period', *Slavic Review* 73, no. 3 (September 2014): 563–84. For earlier works on Soviet psychiatric abuse, see: Sidney Bloch and Peter Reddaway, *Psychiatric Terror: How Soviet Psychiatry Is Used to Suppress Dissent* (New York: Basic Books, 1977).
34 Mark Field, 'Commitment for Commitment or Conviction for Conviction: The Medicalisation and Criminalisation of Soviet Dissidence, 1960–1990', *Soviet and Post-Soviet Review*, no. 3 (1995): 289; Healey, 'Russian and Soviet Forensic Psychiatry', 79.
35 Harvey Fireside, *Soviet Psychoprisons* (New York: Norton, 1979), pp. 36–7.
36 Ibid., p. 37.
37 Pavel Posvyanskii, 'Moskovskii nauchno-issledovatel'skii institut psikhiatrii MZ RSFSR. Otdelenie seksopatologii', 1973. Archive of the Department of Sexopathology.
38 Interview with Yan Goland, 1 April 2017, Nizhnii Novgorod.
39 Ibid.
40 I have been unable to find any minutes or transcripts of this meeting in the Central Archive of Moscow (TsMAM).
41 Posvyanskii, 'Moskovskii nauchno-issledovatel'skii institut', 4.
42 M. D. Kovrigina, 'Tsentral'nyi Institut Usovershenstvovaniya vrachei', in *Bol'shaya sovetskaya entsiklopediya*, 3rd edn, vol. 27 (Moscow: Sovetskaya entsiklopediya, 1986), pp. 482–3.
43 Posvyanskii, 'Moskovskii nauchno-issledovatel'skii institut', 7. In his report, Posvyanskii also referred to the Sanitary Department as the 'Directorate of Medical Service of the Ministry of Internal Affairs of the USSR' (Upravlenie Meditsinskoi Sluzhby – UMS MVD SSSR).
44 Posvyanskii, 'Moskovskii nauchno-issledovatel'skii institut', 10.
45 Hardy, *GULAG after Stalin*, p. 194.
46 Ibid., p. 195.
47 Healey, *Russian Homophobia*, p. 45.
48 Ibid., p. 45.
49 In his memoirs Mikhail Stern, who served a sentence in one of the Soviet colonies in the 1970s, remembered that 'homosexual violence was a routine part of life in the camps'. He recalled: 'At night in the barracks we could hear screams that quickly went away as a gang of rapists threw a blanket over a fresh victim and smothered his face. There were usually five of them – four to hold the victim's arms and

legs while the fifth raped him. An inmate who had been forcibly sodomised by other inmates was referred to as a "pederast", and the word itself was the deadliest of insults.' See: Mikhail Stern and August Stern, *Sex in the USSR* (New York: New York Times, 1980), p. 261. For other mentions of homosexual violence in late Soviet prisons, see: Kozlovskii, *Argo russkoi gomoseksual'noi subkul'tury*, pp. 95–110.

50 Healey, *Russian Homophobia*, p. 45.

51 Ibid., pp. 45–6.

52 For a brief history of the department, see: N. N. Romanov and V. F. Nekrasov, 'Meditsinskoe Upravlenie', in *MVD Rossii: Entsiklopediya*, ed. Vladimir F. Nekrasov (Moscow: Olma, 2002), p. 269.

53 Posvyanskii, 'Moskovskii nauchno-issledovatel'skii institut', 10.

54 Ibid., 7.

55 S. A. Shchelkunov, *Aktual'nye problemy ispravleniya i perevospitaniya osuzhdennykh zhenshchin: Sbornik materialov Vsesoyuznogo soveshchaniya politrabotnikov zhenskikh ITK* (Moscow: Politotdel ITU MVD SSSR, 1974).

56 Ibid., p. 3.

57 Ibid., pp. 4–5.

58 V. N. Popov, 'Meditsinskoe obsluzhivanie lits, lishennykh svobody', in *Aktual'nye problemy ispravleniya i perevospitaniya osuzhdennykh zhenshchin*, ed. S. A. Shchelkunov (Moscow: Politotdel ITU MVD SSSR, 1974), p. 105.

59 Ibid., p. 103.

60 Ibid., p. 105.

61 Ibid., p. 108.

62 Stella, *Lesbian Lives*, p. 48.

63 Derevinskaya, 'Materialy k klinike'. Derevinskaya also presented the findings of her dissertation in her conference papers. See: Abram M. Svyadoshch and Elizaveta M. Derevinskaya, 'K probleme patologii vlecheniya', in *Materialy vyezdnoi sessii prezidiumov Vsesoyuznogo i respublikanskikh obshchestv nevropatologov i psikhiatrov Kazakhstana i respublik Srednei Azii, 21–23 aprelya 1964 g.* (Alma-Ata: Kazakhskoe respublikanskoe obshchestvo nevropatologov i psikhiatrov, 1964), pp. 64–7.

64 Svyadoshch, *Zhenskaya seksopatologiya*, pp. 161–7.

65 Aina G. Ambrumova and Nikolai D. Kibrik, *Metodicheskie rekomendatsii po profilaktike gomoseksual'nogo povedeniya v ispravitel'no-trudovykh uchrezhdeniyakh* (Moscow: Glavnoe upravlenie ispravitel'no trudovykh uchrezhdenii MVD SSSR, 1978).

66 Ibid., p. 1.

67 Ibid.

68 Ibid., p. 4.
69 Ibid., p. 12.
70 Ibid., p. 7.
71 Ibid., pp. 8–9.
72 Ibid., p. 26.
73 Ibid.
74 Ibid., p. 27.
75 Ibid., p. 13.
76 Ibid.
77 Posvyanskii, 'Moskovskii nauchno-issledovatel'skii institut', 7.
78 Ambrumova and Kibrik, *Metodicheskie rekomendatsii*, p. 14.
79 Viktor Pirozhkov, *Psikhologicheskie osnovy perevospitaniya osuzhdennykh v vospitatel'no-trudovykh koloniyakh* (Moscow: Akademiya MVD SSSR, 1979).
80 Ibid., p. 3.
81 Ibid., p. 186.
82 Ibid., pp. 186–7.
83 Ibid., p. 187.
84 Ibid., p. 190.
85 Ibid.
86 Ibid., p. 189.
87 Ibid., p. 192.
88 Ibid.
89 Ibid.
90 Ibid., p. 191. Pirozhkov suggested that such medical examination with a view to identifying homosexuals was common practice in penal colonies.
91 Ibid., p. 192.
92 Ibid.
93 Ibid.
94 Ibid.
95 Ibid.
96 Zakaznaya nauchno-issledovatel'skaya tematika na 1979 god. Yan Goland's Archive.
97 Healey, *Homosexual Desire*, p. 232.
98 Ibid., p. 239. Blyumin wrote up all his findings in a dissertation, which he defended on 29 November 1970 in the Medical Research Institute of Forensic Medicine of the MZ USSR. See: Il'ya G. Blyumin, 'Materialy k ekspertise polovykh sostoyanii: Obosnovanie sudebnomeditsinskikh kriteriev nekotorykh polovykh situatsii muzhchin' (Dissertatsiya na soiskanie uchenoi stepeni kandidata meditsinskikh nauk, Glavnoe Upravlenie zdravookhraneniya mosgorispolkoma byuro sudebnomed-itsinskoi ekspertizy, 1970). New evidence shows that Ivan G. Blyumin received training at the Department of Sexopathology in 1973. A report

titled 'A list of doctors who underwent specialisation in the Department of Sexopathology in 1973' lists his name. See: Anonymous, Spisok vrachei, proshedshikh spetsialisatsiyu v otdele seksopatologii za 1973 god. Archive of the Moscow Department of Sexopathology.

99 Healey, *Homosexual Desire*, p. 262.

100 Larisa Honey, 'Pluralizing Practices in Late-Socialist Moscow: Russian Alternative Practitioners Reclaim and Redefine Individualism', in *Soviet Society in the Era of Late Socialism, 1964–1985*, ed. Neringa Klumbyte and Gulnaz Sharafutdinova (New York and London: Lexington, 2014), p. 136.

101 Ibid.

102 Anton's diary, 1971. Written account of Goland's former patient about the treatment for homosexuality that he was administered. Yan Goland's collection.

103 Gessen, *Rights of Lesbians and Gay Men.*

104 Yan Goland, 'Metodika psikhoterapii gomoseksualizma', unpublished paper presented at a conference in Tambov, April 1974. Yan Golland's collection.

105 Honey, 'Pluralizing Practices in Late-Socialist Moscow', p. 139.

106 Yan Goland, 'Kompleksnaya sistema psikhoterapii gomoseksualizma'. Goland's unpublished and undated conference paper, 4.

107 Ibid.

108 Shlapentokh, *Public and Private Life of the Soviet People*, p. 153.

109 Ibid., p. 154.

110 Siegelbaum, 'Introduction: Mapping Private Spheres', p. 3.

111 Interview with Goland, 1 April 2017.

112 Clech, 'Between the Labor Camp and the Clinic', 19.

113 Yan Goland, 'Metodika psikhoterapii gomoseksualizma'.

114 Fürst, 'Friends in Private, Friends in Public', p. 230.

115 Ibid., p. 244.

116 Ibid.

117 Honey, 'Pluralizing Practices in Late-Socialist Moscow', p. 136.

118 Anonymous, 'Zdorov'e', in *Bol'shaya sovetskaya entsiklopedia*, 3rd edn, vol. 11 (Moscow: Sovetskaya entsiklopediya, 1972), p. 442.

119 Yan Goland, letter to *Zdorov'e* journal with a proposal to advertise his medical services for the treatment of homosexuality, 24 August 1974. Yan Goland's archive.

120 Kenneth M. Pinnow, *Lost to the Collective: Suicide and the Promise of Soviet Socialism, 1921–1929* (Ithaca and London: Cornell University Press, 2010), p. 63.

121 A. Zakharov, 'Sem'ya zhdet soveta', *Literaturnaya gazeta* 14 (5 April 1972): 13.

122 Shcheglov, 'Medical Sexology', p. 156.

123 Zakharov, 'Sem'ya zhdet soveta', 14.
124 Ibid., 14.
125 One of the Soviet homosexual men interviewed by Sonja Franeta had been in the KGB's lists of homosexuals from the age of sixteen: Franeta, *Rozovye flamingo*, p. 122.
126 Interview with Lev Shcheglov by telephone, 7 March 2017.
127 Novikov, 'Sindrom "Trekh obez'yanok"', 68–70.

Conclusion

Despite the prevailing assumption that the issue of homosexuality was never given sufficient attention by Khrushchev- and Brezhnev-era experts or by the police, in this book I have demonstrated the contrary. Jurists, educators and doctors, as well as police, extensively discussed the issue during the period. In their discussions they searched for modern solutions to homosexuality, by departing from Stalin-era understandings of it as a crime and instead problematising the issue from medical, educational and juridical perspectives. Soviet experts also framed sex itself as a matter of national significance and incorporated it into pedagogic discussions. Particularly instrumental in the process of the production of discourse on homosexuality were doctors and sexologists. Not only did they speak about same-sex desire, they also invited same-sex-desiring people to speak about themselves. Indeed, the desiring subject was a welcome feature of Soviet sexological thinking; having encountered same-sex-desiring individuals, doctors engaged in extensive exploration of their psyche, urging them to speak about their sexual lives in tantalising details. These private doctor–patient interactions took place in various settings – the consultation rooms of Soviet clinics, and more importantly and unexpectedly, GULAG hospitals and prison infirmaries, where same-sex activity was rife and visible to authorities.

The willingness of Soviet experts to problematise the issue of homosexuality as a medical issue can first be detected in the discussions of Soviet GULAG officials and doctors of the 1950s. It is very possible that some GULAG doctors had engaged with the problem under Stalin – many of such works were likely unpublished so never made it into the archival holdings. Stalin's heirs, concerned about the spiking rates of crime in society due to the mass release of prisoners, attempted to put the GULAG system in order, to minimise the negative effects of the mass prisoners' exodus. They attempted to improve prisoners' health, re-educate them before release and, most significantly, discourage them from engaging in same-sex activity which, as Soviet officials feared, could spill over into society and spawn sexual perversions there. To prevent this from happening, the GULAG leadership summoned GULAG directors, forensic experts and doctors. Leaving the issue of sodomy to the realm of criminal law, GULAG doctors, excited at new opportunities to establish medical authority over a previously 'unclaimed' issue (female homosexuality was neither officially a crime nor a disease), began to examine female same-sex activity in prison, produce discourse on it and offer their expertise to GULAG leadership. Doctors claimed a unique ability to elicit open confessions from lesbian women and emphasised the crucial role their expertise could play in discouraging these women from homosexuality. The medicalisation of the issue of lesbianism triggered a power shift in the GULAG – medical experts' opinion, which had hitherto often been ignored, had now to be heeded by GULAG directors regarding homosexuality. Historians wishing to further investigate the medicalisation of homosexuality in the GULAG are likely to uncover more evidence (provided they manage to find sources) of patient–medical interactions on the topic of homosexuality in GULAG infirmaries. More evidence of such interactions will further demonstrate that confession was not a phenomenon completely alien to Soviet society and that the process of medicalisation was very akin to that described in Western societies.

In the 1950s, while doctors were wrestling with the issue of homosexuality in the GULAG, outside the barbed wire Soviet officials were worried about the sexual lives of the younger generation and searched for ways of establishing control over them. Such control was important for increasing declining birth rates and alleviating the devastating human losses after the war. Medical discourse on sex education was chosen as a viable solution. Having decriminalised abortion, the Khrushchev leadership approved the publication of numerous brochures, which, appealing to medical knowledge, discouraged adolescents from terminating pregnancies, emphasising the potential harm that they could inflict on themselves. Educators also encouraged young people to abstain from promiscuity, raised their awareness about STIs and steered them away from sexual perversions. Regarding the latter, the authors of sex education manuals sought to discourage any sexual practices or environments that could be conducive to homosexuality. Some sex manuals openly talked about homosexuality – framing it as both a crime and a disease. These manuals were translated versions of manuals from Czechoslovakia and East Germany, where sexology had become a well-developed science. These two countries were instrumental in the development of discourse on sex and sexuality in the USSR and significantly shaped experts' understanding of homosexuality there.

In the mid-1960s Soviet sexual modernity was injected with fresh dynamism following the establishment of a new branch of medical science – sexopathology. In their discussions the practitioners of this newly established science constructed a new image of homosexuality, which differed from the Stalin- and Khrushchev-era understandings of it as a criminal psychopathy. Soviet sexopathologists presented homosexuals as individuals who were reclaimable for the Soviet project of creating a New Soviet Person. This entailed desiring to work and contribute their labour to society, while being able to realise their deficient sexuality, work on it and change themselves for the better. Apart from constructing a new image of homosexuality, Soviet sexopathologists sought to claim homosexuality for their profession, albeit very carefully. One such sexopathologist, V. K. Kosarev, discussed whether homosexuality should be considered a medical problem rather than a criminal one – he did so with a nod to Czechoslovakia and East Germany, where by that time homosexuality had been decriminalised and now featured on medical agendas. Some sexopathologists went so far as to suggest that homosexuality should be decriminalised altogether. Other sexopathologists, however, tried to medicalise homosexuality, without openly appealing to decriminalisation: Yan Goland, for example, moved forward with an initiative to institutionalise medical treatment of homosexuality, to no avail. Sexopathologists invited same-sex-desiring patients to the clinic, urging them to confess their desires and using these confessions for scientific research. An interesting aspect of these private doctor–patient interactions was that some doctors did not wish to impose overt medicalisation on their patients, but rather sought to deal with the issue constructively.

Ivanov, for example, was ready to acknowledge the limits of medical knowledge when one of his patients asked to be cured of homosexuality – he attended to his patient's distress but did not offer to treat his homosexuality with drugs, instead pointing out that homosexuality could be a natural phenomenon not amenable to treatment. To some extent, the same approach can be discerned in Goland's medical practices – instead of imposing compulsory treatment on his patients, he carefully selected them and worked only with those who were committed to it.

The emerging medical ideas on homosexuality insinuated themselves into juridical circles and spurred discussions on the necessity to decriminalise consensual sodomy among leading Soviet jurists on the grounds of it being a medical matter. Soviet jurists attempted to eliminate the penalty for consensual sodomy as early as the late 1950s, but to no avail. At this time, proponents of decriminalisation did not have sufficient arguments to base their proposals on – homosexuality had not yet been decriminalised in many socialist countries (thus there was no current example to allude to) and Soviet sexological science had been non-existent. Even so, in the 1960s, with the growing sexological knowledge at home and the pro-decriminalisation movement elsewhere in the world, Soviet jurists' voices in support of overhauling the Stalinist statute on consensual sodomy became more vocal. In their dissertations and treatises, jurists alluded to the scientific findings of Soviet sexologists and contended that homosexuality was a medical matter. Some of them even suggested that homosexuals did not need medical intervention at all – since their sexuality was natural. By the 1970s, however, anti-decriminalisation views started to emerge – scholars who opposed decriminalisation claimed that homosexuality was a threat to socialist morality, saying that in the absence of penalties for it, same-sex activity would become unbridled and widespread. Strikingly, these scholars also proposed to criminalise lesbianism, pointing out its inconsistency with communist morality and its perceived social harm. The debates on the criminal status of lesbianism were not confined solely to scholarly circles but extended far beyond academia. Republican prosecutors and judges, as well as officials from the Supreme Court of the USSR, contributed extensively to the discussion. Surprisingly, despite the small number of scholars who argued in favour of criminalisation of female homosexuality, most scholars and officials dismissed these proposals on the grounds that lesbian love was not as common as sodomy.

In 1973 the Soviet Health Ministry established the All-Union Scientific Methodological Centre for Issues of Sexopathology, which was to oversee and encourage the production of sexological research. This started to attract the attention of the Interior Ministry, which had long wished to find ways to resolve the conundrum of same-sex desire in Soviet prisons. The Interior Ministry commissioned sexologists to deliver lectures to MVD and KGB officials, where they shared their scientific knowledge and even promoted the idea of utility of decriminalisation of consensual sodomy. Most importantly, sexologists were encouraged to conduct research on homosexuality in prisons with a view to helping the prison authorities to eliminate this phenomenon. Seizing on the opportunity to expand their medical authority over the homosexual body, sexologists examined same-sex-desiring prisoners and produced manuals for MVD officials on how to deal with them. In some of these manuals, sexologists openly contended that the issue of homosexuality could be resolved only through medical methods, advising prison officials to heed their expert recommendations. Again, sexologists approached the issue of homosexuality constructively – for instance, they acknowledged the predicament and psychological suffering of prisoners who were raped and abused by 'active homosexuals' and, instead of branding them as homosexuals, advocated provision of psychotherapy to alleviate their suffering. In the 1970s doctors in the free society continued to offer treatments for homosexuality too, experimenting with new approaches, albeit in private.

That doctors had to keep their practices unofficial and that they were denied any attempts to institutionalise their practice attests to the paradox which characterised Soviet sexual modernity in the second half of the twentieth century. Although allowed to flourish, and even encouraged by authorities on an ad hoc basis, medical knowledge was still subordinate to police requirements. These requirements reflected the authorities' desires to eliminate homosexuality in places of confinement and to possibly furnish psychological evidence of a suspect's homosexuality in criminal cases. Despite doctors' claims for decriminalisation of consensual sodomy and their persistent attempts to push the matter into the medical domain, their attempts to do so were unsuccessful.

It is undeniable that the Khrushchev and Brezhnev eras were a time of unprecedented discursive explosion on sex and homosexuality. In order to fully understand its extent, historians need more sources and they need to look for these sources in places other than historical archives. Most of them are likely to be stored in the semi-sequestered archives of Soviet psychiatric clinics. One such example is Popov's dissertation (examined in Chapter 3) and the fact that it never made its way into any of Russia's libraries. It is possible that there were many more such works, with elaborate descriptions, large-scale examinations and deep interventions into the sexual lives of Soviet citizens of all sexual orientations. In a country like Russia, with its vast territory and different traditions and cultures, discourse on sex and homosexuality was extremely variegated, bearing characteristics of the regions and republics where it evolved. The sheer size of the Soviet Union also made it difficult for medical discourse to evenly spread itself across the country. Soviet sexology was too weak and dragged its feet compared to its Western and even communist counterparts. A glance at the group photo of newbie sexologists who congregated for a 1966 sexological seminar suggests that the number of people willing to receive training in this nascent science did not exceed seventy. Many of these doctors were either from Moscow or Gorkii, which suggests that sexopathology remained an obscure science for medical professionals in the faraway regions and republics of the vast Soviet land. Likewise, despite the provisions of the 1973 Health Ministry decree on the opening of sexological consultation rooms across the USSR, it is still unlikely that sexology had any significant influence as a science in the 1970s and 1980s.

Despite the still existing reluctance on the part of Russian historians to engage with the topic of homosexuality seriously, scholars have much to learn from new perspectives on the issue. Debates on homosexuality between doctors and GULAG and prison officials point to the way power relationships were structured between experts and police in these settings, as well as Soviet society more broadly. In the same way, dynamic discussions on the criminal status of homosexuality and the unexpectedly bold and non-compliant stances of Brezhnev-era academics on the issue make a striking intervention into the scholarly discussions of the late Soviet era as a time of vibrant intellectual life rather than mere stagnation. Historians may also learn a great deal about public and private boundaries in the Soviet society when looking at same-sex relationships and how homosexual people carved out private spaces in the pursuit of their desires.

Coda: homosexuality after Brezhnev

Throughout the 1980s the issue of homosexuality continued to be on sexopathological agendas – it retained its status as a syndrome and disease which could be treated, albeit with great difficulty. In his two-volume manual for sexologists and psychiatrists, *Private Sexopathology* (1983), Georgii Vasil'chenko, head of the All-Union Research Method Centre on Sexopathology, provided a lengthy section on the question, illustrating various types of homosexuality with a relevant case study.[1] He lamented that it was difficult to establish the diagnosis correctly, even more so to obtain objective measurements of a patient's type of homosexuality, since many patients sought to conceal their 'pathological deviations of sexuality' and doctors simply did not possess any 'objective methods' of diagnosing sexual perversions.[2] The only method which Vasil'chenko deemed credible was penile plethysmography, a method of measurement of sexual arousal first proposed by Czechoslovakian sexologist Josef Hynie in the 1930s and later developed by Kurt Freund in the 1960s.[3]

The evocation of this method by Vasil'chenko is noteworthy. We know that during the Cold War, American and British sexologists designed a great many machines and devices for sex research, including penile strain gauges used in aversion therapies.[4] In Soviet sexological practice such instruments were not as common – it was only in the 1980s that Soviet sexopathologists started reporting the use of such.[5] They noted that phallography had been conducted (fallografiya) on a 'group of individuals who deemed themselves to be homosexuals' and that this method could be used 'in sexological practice for a variety of goals', including 'detection of sexual perversions'.[6] They did not specify for what purposes and under which circumstances such detection was needed, yet, considering the fact that during the 1970s the MVD was actively exploring new opportunities of finding scientific evidence for the crime of sodomy, discussions of phallography's utility in detecting sexual perversions could have been a ramification of it.

Vasil'chenko's manual also featured a section on the treatment of homosexuality – this was written by Yan Goland.[7] The section built on Goland's previous work and summarised the main techniques of his psychotherapy method, consisting of three stages and accompanied by autogenic training. Goland listed several contraindications for psychotherapy of homosexuality, that is, signs in a patient showing that therapy would not lead to the desired effect. These included psychiatric disorders, alcoholism, 'intellectual deficiency', 'lack of will and the patient's passivity'.[8] During the 1980s, Goland continued his practice of medical treatment, securing his role as a leading Soviet specialist on the problem. In 1982 he presented his papers 'Psychotherapy of Homosexuality' and 'Psychotherapy of Sexual Perversions' at a sexology seminar in Riga.[9] There, he also presented former patients, who had successfully completed psychotherapy for homosexuality and sexual perversions, to other doctors. As Goland explained to me, his patients were wearing heavy make-up, sunglasses and wigs to conceal their identity. In the same year, Goland delivered these reports and showed his patients to colleagues at the Central Institute for Doctors' Advanced Training.[10]

While Soviet sexopathologists continued to produce medical knowledge on homosexuality, albeit in very modest portions, the MVD developed further interest in their studies. Throughout the 1980s more brochures for MVD penal officials with instructions on how to address the problem of sexual perversions and homosexuality were published. Among them were *Sexual Disorders in the Convicts of the ITU* (1980), a paper *Methodic Recommendations on Prophylaxis of Sexual Perversions* (1983), 'Prophylactic Medical Examination of Individuals, Suffering from Sexual Perversions in SIZO and ITU' (1984) and a manual, *Prisoners' Sexual Disorders* (1985).[11] The titles of these brochures suggest that their authors framed homosexuality as a medical problem. All of them were published by the All-Union Institute for Advanced Training of Senior Officials of the Corrective Labour Institutions of the MVD SSSR (Vsesoyuznyi institut povysheniya kvalifikatsii rukovodyashchikh rabotnikov ispravitel'no-trudovykh uchrezhdenii).[12] None of these brochures are available in any of Russia's state libraries and they are likely to be stored in the library of the institute's successor – the

VIPK of the Russian Interior Ministry, which can be consulted only by the institute's cadets and officials. I came upon the references to these brochures in a similar manual, *Educational Work with Convicts Suffering from Sexual Perversions* (1989).[13] This manual was written by the same author as the previous ones and it offers a window on the possible content of the author's earlier manuals on the subject.

In his discussions of homosexuality, the author, Vitalii Volkov, drew on the texts on homosexuality written by Soviet leading sexologists Nikolai Ivanov, Yan Goland, Pavel Posvyanskii and Abram Svyadoshch.[14] Volkov urged the Medical Department of the Colonies to take an active part in prophylaxis and medical treatment of homosexuality: 'The medical department in corrective labour institutions must organise prophylaxis and symptomatic treatment of perverted types of sexual desire in individuals located in places of confinement.'[15] He suggested that medical examination of such individuals be conducted 'in a mandatory manner' (v obyazatel'nom poryadke) by the prison psychiatrists.[16] Yet the treatment itself, especially involving medications, was to be conducted only with the prisoner's consent: 'The object of treatment can only be the prisoner who voluntarily consented to it. Compulsion is in such cases out of place and it cannot be effective without the patient's desire, especially in those individuals who consider their state as a norm.'[17] However, this statement contradicted Volkov's own previous remarks where he argued that penal officials must 'lead an uncompromising and decisive struggle' with the 'convicts' deviant sexual behaviour' through 'primarily medicated and psychotherapeutic correction' (vypravlenie).[18] It is notable that in contrast to the similar manuals produced in the 1970s, examined in Chapter 5, Volkov's brochure framed homosexuality exclusively as a medical problem without allusions to the efficacy of punitive measures – this suggests a continuing shift of MVD perceptions of homosexuality from crime to disease.

The advent of the AIDS epidemic in the USSR in the late 1980s stoked anxiety about homosexuality and its perceived social danger: it was now viewed not only as a crime or a disease, but as a phenomenon conducive to the spread of AIDS. Apparently this anxiety triggered more energetic attempts to study homosexuality and find effective ways of dealing with it. One such attempt was undertaken by psychiatrists A. Kachaev and G. Ponomarev of the Serbskii

Institute; in 1988 they published a summary of their study, 'Age Dynamics and Conditions of Formation of Male Homosexuality', in the course of which 240 homosexual men from the age of eighteen to fifty were examined and medically treated.[19] Expounding on the rationale of their research, Kachaev and Ponomarev explained:

> Individuals with homosexual attitudes (ustanovki) are not subject to registration (ne podvergayutsya uchety), medical examination (dispanserisatsiya) or forced treatment, which they need, considering the criteria of social dangerousness ... homosexuality tends to spread (imeet tendentsiyu k rasprostraneniyu) and constitutes a genuine source of venereal, viral (hepatitis, candidiasis, AIDS), infectious and intestinal diseases.[20]

One of the key objectives of the study was the examination of the homosexual men's psychological and sexual development during infancy and adolescence with a view to identifying the factors which contributed to their perverse desire. Scrutinising the past lives of each homosexual man, psychiatrists established the most significant milestones in the development of their homosexual desire. Kachaev and Ponomarev discovered that, at the ages of five to seven, the examined men displayed 'heightened sexuality' (povyshennaya seksual'nost'), characterised by a 'heightened interest' in individuals of the same and opposite sex.[21] At the ages of seven to twelve their 'heightened sexuality' was reinforced by 'environmental influences' – 'related information from their peers and other sources'.[22] During these years 'homosexual fixations' were beginning to take shape, facilitated by the 'close same-sex communication characteristic of this age'.[23] Perverse homosexual desire was then further reinforced at the ages of fourteen to sixteen, by means of 'mutual masturbation', due to an 'inebriated state' or due to an intention 'to stand out'. Finally, from the ages of eighteen to twenty it was 'stabilised definitively'.[24]

In light of their findings, Kachaev and Ponomarev proposed a detailed description of measures for 'prophylaxis of sexual perversions'.[25] These measures were to be conducted by school doctors, paediatricians and infant psychiatry services (detskaya psikhiyatricheskaya sluzhba) and were designed in accordance with the discovered milestones in the development of homosexuality. The proposed measures were similar to those contained in the Khrushchev-era sex education manuals; yet Kachaev and Ponomarev's advice was more age-specific. Children from five to seven were to be instructed on how to 'restrain the arousal of erogenous zones and emergence of early sexuality' – these instructions were to have a focus on the 'hygiene of sexual organs'.[26] Children from seven to twelve were to be carefully informed, 'in a simple and comprehensible form, of the physiological basics of sexual development and sexuality'.[27] Teenagers between twelve and eighteen were to be instructed on the 'harm of masturbation, premature sexual liaisons as well as sexual perversions'.[28]

Forty of the examined 240 men underwent medical treatment, in the course of which they were adminisered highly aversive drugs – aminazin and sulfazine (sul'fazin).[29] The treatment with these drugs, as doctors observed, provided a 'strong therapeutic effect' and made the patients develop a desire 'to get rid of homosexuality'.[30] To the doctors' disappointment, after the treatment ceased, some of the patients again started displaying homosexual tendencies.[31] Still, doctors noted that such treatment was useful especially in places of confinement.[32]

The emerging climate of freedom provided by Gorbachev's glasnost' and perestroika allowed for the appearance of publications with alternative views on homosexuality. One such was a book, *Sexology and Sexopathology*, by prominent Polish sexopathologist Kazimir Imelinskii, which was translated into Russian and published in 1986. In it the author claimed that homosexuality was not a disease at all: 'From a clinical point of view, one should pay attention to the fact that homosexuality does not constitute an illness that can be treated at all. There is a large group of homosexuals who not only accept their inclinations but are content with them.'[33] Doctors could be of help only in those cases where homosexual persons suffered from anxiety and depression, a result of the double life they were forced to lead, rather than their sexuality. Describing such persons, Imelinskii wrote:

> They fear condemnation and shame and therefore hide their homosexual proclivities even from their closest relatives; they are preoccupied with their fate and with the impossibility to create a family; they fear loneliness and that they are deceived by destiny, which does not allow them to live like other people and foredooms them to suffering and loneliness.[34]

Some Soviet sexopathologists, such as Abram Svyadoshch, disagreed with these views. In a third edition of his book *Female Sexopathology* (1988), he argued that homosexuals should be medically treated, even if they did not deem their homosexuality to be a sexual disorder:

> In English and American literature an opinion is being stated with increasing frequency that homosexuality is merely a variant of the norm and that is why it is not necessary to seek ways of conducting therapy. We cannot agree with this point of view. We cannot deem it natural when a person is experiencing a same-sex desire towards persons of the same sex and feels aversion to individuals of the opposite sex. If everyone became homosexuals, humankind would cease to exist.[35]

At a time when Gorbachev's perestroika and glasnost were relaxing censorship, the discussion of sex and related topics became possible in the pages of the Soviet press. The subject of homosexuality attracted the attention of Gorbachev-era newspaper correspondents who approached doctors and even police officers with requests to comment on the problem of homosexuality in the Soviet Union. F. Podkolodnyi, a correspondent for *Meditsinskaya gazeta*, approached L. G. Gertsik, the head of the Moscow Psycho-Endocrinological Centre.[36] Rather unexpectedly, Gertsik suggested that homosexuality was not a disease at all; in fact he stated that consensual homosexuality was a private matter and that doctors could help homosexuals by helping them overcome their anxiety:

> It goes without saying that in a democratic state we cannot oppress people because of their sexual orientation ... Two adult men shut themselves in a room (zakryvayutsya v komnate) and society is peeking into the keyhole? I believe that our Criminal Code sufficiently protects a person from violence, and minors from corruption and depraved acts. Why have a separate article on homosexuality? For the time being, it is not even clear whether it's a disease or not. For our centre, homosexuality itself is not a diagnosis, it's not even a patient's complaint. You see they can be well adapted both psychologically and socially. They even live in families. It's a different matter if there is some intrapsychic (intrapsikhicheskii) conflict, when homosexual orientation hinders adaptation, if there is a fear of contracting AIDS or venereal diseases. Only then is there a reason for the patient's examination and medical treatment. But what to treat such a patient for? For homosexuality? And what if he doesn't want to be treated? Therapy for homosexuals has to be voluntary. Otherwise, it is simply impossible. This I can tell you as a specialist as opposed to those who assert that homosexuals should be treated forcibly. Let them tell us how![37]

Surprisingly, the diversity of opinions as to whether homosexuals should be deemed criminals or not existed among the law-enforcement agencies themselves. The author of the article went to seek clarification on the issue from the police officers working in the Investigative Department of the Chief Directorate of Internal Affairs of Moscow to ask them what they thought about homosexuals. As the conversation revealed, only a very small number of homosexuals were prosecuted for consensual sodomy, which, as the author noted, was because 'there was no affected party (poterpevshaya storona) and thus no need to resort to the police'.[38] In fact, the officers of the department, in the author's words, considered the problem of homosexuality not as their job, but as 'a medical and social one', except for cases involving homosexual prostitution, rape or homosexual acts against minors.[39]

Other MVD officials were also willing to express their opinion about the problem during perestroika. For instance, in 1990 the newspaper *Argumenty i fakty* published an opinion of V. Kachanov, an official from the Moscow Criminal Investigations Department, who argued that the sodomy law was a 'restraining factor' for homosexuals 'responsible for the dissemination of AIDS'.[40]

The hitherto discreet discussion between legal academics and MVD officials also started appearing widely on the pages of Soviet newspapers. Soviet jurists whose attempts to decriminalise consensual homosexuality I examined in Chapter 4 gave interviews and continued to argue for decriminalisation of consensual homosexual acts. In December 1989 a monthly periodical *Molodoi kommunist* featured a lengthy article on the problem of homosexuality in the Soviet Union. In this article A. N. Ignatov briefly summarised the current state of discussion on the law on sodomy between its proponents and opponents:

> The majority of authors who write on this topic come to the conclusion that criminal liability for homosexuality is not expedient. Why? First of all, if it is pathology, then it cannot be punished. Secondly, there is no danger for society here. In fact, all the main arguments of the proponents of criminal liability for homosexuality are refuted. Which ones exactly? Well, that homosexuality will lead to the decreased masculinity of the nation. Yet, the example of Sparta demonstrates the contrary. Another alleged consequence of homosexuality is that it will decrease birth rates. The statistics do not confirm

> this conclusion. Then, they say that it leads to the degradation of a person. However, we know many great homosexuals – Tchaikovsky, Leonardo da Vinci and so on, and their creative work refutes the previous statement.[41]

According to Ignatov, the opponents of the decriminalisation of sodomy were also convinced that if there was no law in place, then homosexuality would thrive.[42] Such views had been expressed by the MVD scholars as early as 1972 and, as Ignatov showed, they persisted well into the 1980s:

> There is a lay perception that if we abolish article 121 of the Criminal Code then everyone will start to engage in homosexuality! Nonsense! A person who has no propensity for it cannot be influenced by the absence or existence of criminal liability. Criminal liability also does not influence the person who has such propensity. Criminal liability plays little role here – it neither reduces nor eliminates homosexuality, because sexual needs, whatever you may say, are some of the strongest.[43]

Most importantly, Ignatov's comment presented an illuminating account of the reasons underlying the reluctance of Soviet officials to listen to the arguments of legal scholars for the repeal of the sodomy law. Ignatov explained that the ultimate decision to abolish the sodomy law was often left to individual Soviet bureaucrats, who had the final word on everything and often had the power to dismiss the most well-conceived and substantiated draft law on the grounds of personal distaste, without any explanations or further comment. Ignatov reasoned that: 'In former times, a person who was not a jurist, but who held a senior position, could say something like this at the last moment: "And what is this? Let's cross this out! Or, conversely, let's add something." As a result, a well-thought-out and well-substantiated proposed law changed abruptly.'[44] Ignatov did not lose hope, though; instead, he publicly pledged to continue to advocate for the abolition of the law, believing that, since Gorbachev was a jurist by education, he would be more inclined to listen to the jurists. 'Along with other jurists,' he said, 'I will continue to struggle for the abolition of this law. We are confronting the prejudice of the majority of the population and the opinion of influential officials … We count on Gorbachev. He is a jurist.'[45]

Ultimately, however, it was Boris Yeltsin, not Gorbachev, who removed the notorious law from the statute books in April 1993.

While Yeltsin's personal desire to join the Council of Europe certainly underpinned his decision to repeal the sodomy law, it is also important to recognise that this was not something entirely new: a movement towards the decriminalisation of sodomy among Soviet leading jurists and their scholarly arguments, discussed in this dissertation, also appeared to be crucial. We still have much to learn about the neglected history of these debates.

Notes

1 Georgii Vasil'chenko, *Chastnaya seksopatologiya: Rukovodstvo dlya vrachei* (Moscow: Meditsina, 1983), pp. 95–115.
2 Ibid., p. 108.
3 Ibid.
4 Donna J. Drucker, *The Machines of Sex Research: Technology and the Politics of Identity, 1945–1985* (Dordrecht: Springer, 2014).
5 I. L. Botneva, I. P. Zhdanov and V. M. Maslov, 'O perspektivakh fallografii v seksologicheskoi praktike', *Aktual'nye voprosy seksopatologii: Sbornik tezisov dokladov i Vsesoyuznoi konferentsii seksopatologov g. Ufa, 17–19 sentyabrya 1986 g.* (Moscow: Izdatel'stvo Moskovskogo NII psikhiatrii MZ RSFSR, 1986), pp. 63–6.
6 Ibid., p. 64.
7 Vasil'chenko, *Chastnaya seksopatologiya*, p. 109.
8 Ibid.
9 Yan Goland, 'Nauchnaya i prakticheskaya rabota: Doklady', https://goland.su/nauch.html (accessed 11 January 2016).
10 Interview with Goland, 1 April 2017.
11 SIZO: sledstvennyi izolyator (detention cell). Vitalii Volkov, *Seksual'nye rasstroistva u osuzhdennykh v ITU* (Moscow: VIPK MVD SSSR, 1980); V. N. Volkov, P. M. Rybkin and A. N. Gnedin, *Metodicheskie rekomendatsii po profilaktike polovykh izvrashchenii v ITU* (Moscow: VIPK MVD SSSR, 1983); Vitalii Volkov, 'Dispanserisatsiya lits, stradayushchikh polovymi perversiyami v SIZO i ITU', in *Aktual'nye voprosy organisatsii spetsializirovannykh vidov medpomoshchi kontingentam ITU, SIZO i LTP* (Moscow: VIPK MVD SSSR, 1984), pp. 55–62; Vitalii Volkov, *Seksual'nye rasstroistva u osuzhdennykh* (Domodedovo: VIPK MVD SSSR, 1985).
12 The institute was founded on 27 August 1976 and was entrusted with the task of providing advanced training for a range of specialists and officials working within the Soviet penitentiary system, including the

medical department. On the history of the institute, see: Yurii N. Demidov, *VIPK MVD Rossii: Vchera, segodnya, zavtra: Posvyashchaetsya 45-letiyu instituta* (Domodedovo: VIPK MVD Rossii, 2017), pp. 20–2.

13 Vitalii Volkov and Aleksandr Pishchelko, *Vospitatel'naya rabota s osuzhdennymi, stradayushchimi seksual'nymi izvrashcheniyami* (Domodedovo: VIPK MVD SSSR, 1989).

14 Ibid., pp. 54–5.

15 Ibid., p. 30.

16 Ibid., p. 31.

17 Ibid., p. 40.

18 Ibid., p. 3.

19 A. K. Kachaev and G. N. Ponomarev, 'Vozrastnaya dinamika i usloviya formirovaniya muzhskogo gomoseksualizma', *Nevropatologia i psikhiatriya*, no. 12 (1988): 78–82.

20 Ibid., 79.

21 Ibid.

22 Ibid.

23 Ibid.

24 Ibid.

25 Ibid., 81.

26 Ibid.

27 Ibid.

28 Ibid.

29 Ibid., 80.

30 Ibid., 81. Generally applied for the treatment of schizophrenia, progressive paralysis or catatonic conditions, aminazin was also used as a punishment in Soviet psychiatric hospitals. The effects of it included great pain and a rise in body temperature up to 40 degrees. See: Fireside, *Soviet Psychoprisons*, pp. 148–9. On sulfazine treatment, see also: Podrabinek, *Punitive Medicine*, pp. 93–4.

31 Podrabinek, *Punitive Medicine*, p. 81. These drugs were used extensively by Soviet psychiatrists against dissidents.

32 Kachaev and Ponomarev, 'Vozrastnaya dinamika', 81.

33 Kazimir Imelinskii, *Seksologiya i seksopatologiya* (Moscow: Meditsina, 1986), p. 330. On Polish sexology and Imelinskii, see: Agnieszka Kościańska, 'Beyond Viagra: Sex Therapy in Poland', *Czech Sociological Review* 50, no. 6 (2014): 91–138. In Poland, Imelinskii was a supporter of the emerging homosexual groups in the late 1980s. For example, in 1988 he signed an open letter to the Ministry of Internal Affairs in support of the Warsaw Homosexual Movement. See: Lukasz Szulc, *Transnational Homosexuals in Communist Poland: Cross-Border Flows in Gay and Lesbian Magazines* (London: Palgrave Macmillan, 2018), p. 112.

34 Imelinskii, *Seksologiya i seksopatologiya*, p. 331.
35 Svyadoshch, *Zhenskaya seksopatologiya*, p. 82.
36 F. Podkolodnyi, 'Sodomskii grekh', *Meditsinskaya gazeta*, 2 September 1988, 4. Moscow City Psycho-Endocrinological Centre was founded in 1986 with a view to providing better psychoendocrinological medical assistance to the people of Moscow. See: Anonymous, 'O Moskovskom gorodskom psikhoendokrinologicheskom tsentre', https://arbat25.ru/o-czentre/istoriya-czentra (accessed 7 January 2018).
37 Podkolodnyi, 'Sodomskii grekh', 4.
38 Ibid.
39 Ibid.
40 A. Petrov, letter to the editor, *Argumenty i fakty* no. 9 (1990), 7.
41 Novikov, 'Sindrom "Trekh obez'yanok"', 71.
42 Daniel'bek, *Polovye izvrashcheniya,* p. 89.
43 Novikov, 'Sindrom "Trekh obez'yanok"', 71.
44 Ibid.
45 Valerii Rodikov, 'Golubye eli…', *Literaturnaya Rossiya* no. 12 (1990): 24.

Bibliography

Primary sources

Archival collections

Central Municipal Archive of Moscow (TsMAM). Moscow, Russian Federation.

Central Scientific Medical Library. Moscow, Russian Federation.

Central State Library of the Sverdlovsk Oblast'. Yekaterinburg, Russian Federation.

Medical Library of the Department of Sexopathology of the Moscow Research Institute of Psychiatry. Moscow, Russian Federation.

Oblast' Scientific Medical Library. Yekaterinburg, Russian Federation.

Russian National Library. St Petersburg, Russian Federation.

Russian State Library. Moscow, Russian Federation.

State Archive of Latvia. Riga, Latvia.

State Archive of the Russian Federation (GARF). Moscow, Russian Federation.

Fond 10049 – Akademiya pedagogicheskikh nauk SSSR.

Fond A-385 – Verkhovnyi Sovet RSFSR.

Fond A-482 – Ministerstvo zdravookhraneniya RSFSR.

Fond A-2306 – Ministerstvo prosveshcheniya RSFSR.

Fond P-9412 – Otdel detskikh trudovykh i vospitatel'nykh kolonii Ministerstva vnutrenikh del SSSR.

Fond P-9414 – Glavnoe upravlenie mest zaklyucheniya (GUMZ) Ministerstva vnutrennikh del SSSR.

Fond P-9506 – Vysshaya attestatsionnaya komissiya (VAK) pri Sovete Ministrov SSSR.

State Public Historical Library of Russia. Moscow, Russian Federation.

Publications

Ageev, Viktor A., Korogodzkii, Ovsei, G. and Novikov, Petr G. *Iyun'skii /1963/ Plenum Tsentral'nogo Komiteta KPSS i ego istoricheskoe znachenie*. Moscow: Moskovskoe gorodskoe otdelenie obshchestva 'Znanie' RSFSR, 1963.

Aleksandrov, Yurii V. *Polovye prestupleniya: Prestupniki i poterpevshie*. Kiev: Nauchno-issledovatel'skii i redaktsionno-izdatel'skii otdel Kievskoi vysshei shkoly MVD SSSR, 1975.

Ambrumova, Aina G. and Kibrik, Nikolai D. *Metodicheskiie rekomendatsii po profilaktike gomoseksual'nogo povedeniya v ispravitel'no-trudovykh uchrezhdeniyakh*. Moscow: Glavnoe upravlenie ispravitel'no trudovykh uchrezhdenii MVD SSSR, 1978.

Anonymous. 'Gomoseksualizm.' In *Bol'shaya sovetskaya entsiklopediya*. 2nd edn, vol. 12. Moscow: Sovetskaya entsiklopediya, 1952.

Anonymous. 'Iskusstvo prenadlezhit narody.' *Pravda*, 3 December 1962.

Anonymous. 'Istoriya Instituta.' http://mniip.serbsky.ru/home-page/istoriya-instituta/ (accessed 10 March 2018).

Anonymous. 'O Moskovskom gorodskom psikhoendokrinologicheskom tsentre.' https://arbat25.ru/o-czentre/istoriya-czentra (accessed 7 January 2018).

Anonymous. 'Otdelenie seksologii i terapii seksual'nykh disfunktsii', Moskovskii NII psikhiatrii. http://mniip.serbsky.ru/nauka/nauchnye-podrazdeleniya-instituta/otdelenie-seksologii-i-terapii-seksualnyx-disfunkcij/ (accessed 16 November 2017).

Anonymous. 'Zdorov'e.' In *Bol'shaya sovetskaya entsiklopediya*, 3rd edn, vol. 11. Moscow: Sovetskaya entsiklopediya, 1972.

Arkhipov, Fedor A. ed. *Prestupleniya protiv nravstvennosti: Materialy nauchno-prakticheskoi konferentsii*. Vilnius: Prokuratura Litovskoi SSR, 1970.

Artem'ev, Serafim A., Kochetkov, Vasilii D. and Shtan'ko, German G. *Gigiena polovoi zhizni*. Moscow: Znanie, 1964.

Atarov, Tigran S. *Voprosy polovogo vospitaniya*. Moscow: Medgiz, 1959.

Avdeev, Mikhail I. *Sudebnaya meditsina*. Moscow: Gosudarstvennoe izdatel'stvo yuridicheskoi literatury, 1951.

Avdeev, Mikhail I. *Sudebnaya meditsina*. Moscow: Gosudarstvennoe izdatel'stvo yuridicheskoi literatury, 1953.

Avdeev, Mikhail I. *Sudebnaya meditsina*. Moscow: Gosudarstvennoe izdatel'stvo yuridicheskoi literatury, 1960.

Avdeev, Mikhail I. *Sudebno-meditsinskaya ekspertisa zhivykh lits*. Moscow: Meditsina, 1968.

Belyaev, Nikolai A., and Shargorodskii, Mikhail D., eds. *Kurs sovetskogo ugolovnogo prava. Chast' osobennaya. Tom tretii*. Leningrad: Izdatel'stvo Leningradskogo universiteta, 1973.

Blyumin, Il'ya G. 'Materialy k ekspertise polovykh sostoyanii: Obosnovanie sudebnomeditsinskikh kriteriev nekotorykh polovykh situatsii muzhchin.' Dissertatsiya na soiskanie uchenoi stepeni kandidata meditsinskikh nauk, Glavnoe upravlenie zdravookhraneniya mosgorispolkoma byuro sudebnomeditsinskoi ekspertizy, 1970.

Bortsov, Boris P. *XXII s"ezd partii i iyun'skii (1963g.) Plenum TsK KPSS o zadachakh ideologicheskoi raboty v sovremennykh usloviyakh*. Kiev: Vysshaya partiinaya shkola pri TsK KP Ukrainy, 1964.

Botneva, I. L., Zhdanov, I. P., and Maslov, V. M. 'O perspektivakh fallografii v seksologicheskoi praktike.' In *Aktual'nye voprosy seksopatologii: Sbornik tezisov dokladov i Vsesoyuznoi konferentsii seksopatologov g. Ufa, 17–19 sentiabria 1986 g.*, pp. 63–6. Moscow: Izdatel'stvo Moskovskogo NII psikhiatrii MZ RSFSR, 1986.

Chuchelov, Nikolai I. *O polovom vospitanii*. Moscow: Meditsina, 1964.

Daniel'bek, Boris V. *Polovye izvrashcheniya i ugolovnaya otvetstvennost'*. Volgograd: Vysshaya sledstvennaya shkola MVD SSSR, 1972.

Daniel'bek, Boris V. 'Ugolovnopravovaya bor'ba s polovymi prestupleniyami.' Avtoreferat dissertatsii na soiskanie uchenoi stepeni doktora yuridicheskikh nauk, Vysshaya shkola MVD SSSR, 1970.

Dashtayants, Seranush. *O polovom vospitanii shkol'nikov*. Grozny: Checheno-Ingushskoe knizhnoe izdatel'stvo, 1966.

Derevinskaya, Elizaveta M. 'Materialy k klinike, patogenezu, terapii zhenskogo gomoseksualizma.' Dissertatsiya na soiskanie uchenoi stepeni kandidata meditsinskikh nauk, Karagandinskii gosudarstvennyi meditsinskii institut, 1965.

Felinskaya, Nina I. *Reaktivnye sostoianiya v sudebno-psikhiatricheskoi klinike*. Moscow: Meditsina, 1968.

Freund, Kurt. 'K problematike gomoseksualizma u muzhchin.' *Chekhoslovatskoe meditsinskoe obozrenie* 6, no. 1 (1965): 13–21.

Gabelov, Aleksandr A. and Derankova, Elizaveta B., *Gigiena braka*. Moscow: Meditsina, 1964.

Goland, Yan G. 'K voprosu psikhoterapii gomoseksualizma.' In *Voprosy psikhoterapii v obshchei meditsine i psikhonevrologii: Tezisy i avtoreferaty konferentsii 23–7 dekabria 1968 g*, pp. 434–6. Kharkov: Ukrainskii institut usovershenstvovaniya vrachei, 1968.

Goland, Yan G. 'Nauchnaya i prakticheskaya rabota: Doklady'. https://goland.su/nauch.html (accessed 11 January 2016).

Goland, Yan G. 'O stupenchatom postroenii psikhoterapii pri muzhskom gomoseksualizme.' In *Problemy Sovremennoi Seksopatologii*, ed. Anatolii

A. Portnov, pp. 473–86. Moscow: Moskovskii nauchno-issledovatel'skii institut psikhiatrii, 1972.

Gorfin, D. 'Polovaya zhizn'.' In *Bol'shaya sovetskaya entsiklopedia*, 1st edn, vol. 46. Moscow: Izdatel'stvo 'Sovetskaya entsiklopediya', 1940.

Gurevich, Mikhail O. *Psikhiatriya: Uchebnik dlya meditsinskikh institutov*. Moscow: Medgiz, 1949.

Gyne, Iosif. *Yunosha prevrashchaetsya v muzhchinu*. Moscow: Medgiz, 1960.

Gyne, Iosif. *Yunosha prevrashchaetsya v muzhchinu*. Tashkent: Ukituvchi, 1970.

Ignatov, A. N. *Kvalifikatsiya polovykh prestuplenii*. Moscow: Yuridicheskaya literatura, 1974.

Ignatov, Aleksei N. *Otvetstvennost' za prestupleniya protiv nravstvennosti: Polovye prestupleniya*. Moscow: Yuridicheskaya literatura, 1966.

Ignatov, Aleksei N. 'Problemy ugolovnoi otvetstvennosti za prestupleniya v oblasti polovykh otnoshenii v sovetskom ugolovnom prave.' Avtoreferat dissertatsii na soiskanie uchenoi stepeni doktora yuridicheskikh nauk, Vsesoyuznyi institut po izucheniyu prichin i razrabotke mer preduprezhdeniya prestupnosti, 1974.

Imelinskii, Kazimir. *Seksologiya i seksopatologiya*. Moscow: Meditsina, 1986.

Ivanov, Nikolai V. *Voprosy psikhoterapii funktsional'nykh seksual'nykh rasstroistv*. Moscow: Meditsina, 1966.

Kachaev, A. K. and Ponomarev, G. N. 'Vozrastnaya dinamika i usloviya formirovaniya muzhskogo gomoseksualizma.' *Nevropatologia i psikhiatriya*, no. 12 (1988): 78–82.

Khlyntsov, Mikhail N. *Rassledovanie polovykh prestuplenii*. Saratov: Privolzhskoe knizhnoe izdatel'stvo, 1965.

Kolbanovskii, Viktor N. 'O polovom vospitanii podrastayushchego pokoleniya.' *Sovetskoe zdravookhranenie*, no. 3 (1964): 18–30.

Kosarev, V. K. 'K voprosy o sudebno-psikhiatricheskom znachenii gomoseksualizma.' In *Aktual'nye voprosy seksopatologii: Sbornik statei*, ed. Dmitrii D. Fedotov, pp. 292–300. Moscow: Moskovskii nauchno-issledovatel'skii institut psikhiatrii, 1967.

Kovalev, Vladimir V. 'Vklad Moskovskogo nauchno-issledovetel'skogo instituta psikhiatrii MZ RSFSR v psikhiatricheskuyu nauku i praktiku za 60 let i perspektivnye zadachi.' In *Tezisy dokladov, posvyashchennykh 60-letiyu Moskovskogo nauchno-issledovatel'skogo instituta psikhiatrii MZ RSFSR i 50-letiyu Moskovskoi gorodskoi klinicheskoi psikhiatricheskoi bol'nitsy № 4 im. P. B. Gannushkina*, 3–6. Moscow: Moskovskii NII psikhiatrii, 1981.

Kovrigina, M. D. 'Tsentral'nyi institut usovershenstvovaniya vrachei.' In *Bol'shaya sovetskaya entsiklopediya*, 3rd edn, vol. 27. Moscow: Sovetskaya entsiklopediya, 1986.

Manenkov, P. 'Sluchai neobychnogo sozhitel'stva dvukh zhenshchin.' In *Yubileinyi sbornik Posvyashchennyi Professoru N. I. Gorizontovu*. Novosibirsk: Novosib. gos. institut dlya usovershenstvovaniya vrachei i medinstituta, 1939.

Milashina, Elena. 'Ubiistvo chesti: Kak ambitsii izvestnogo LGBT-aktivista razbudili v Chechne strashnyi drevnii obychai.' *Novaya gazeta*, 3 April 2017. www.novayagazeta.ru/articles/2017/04/01/71983-ubiystvo-chesti.

Myasyuk, V. I. and Pavlova, L. P. 'Spetsializirovannaya pomoshch' bol'nym stradayushchim polovymi rasstroistvami.' In *Problemy seksopatologii i besplodiya*, ed. Ivan F. Yunda, pp. 17–21. Kiev: Zdorov'ya, 1973.

Nedoma, Karel and Freund, Kurt. 'Otázka příčetnosti a nápravných opatřeni u sexuálních delikventu.' *Československá Psychiatrie* 4, no. 9 (1959): 264–9.

Neubert, Rudolf. *Die Geschlechterfrage*. Greifenverlag, 1956.

Neubert, Rudolf. *Voprosy pola*. Moscow: Medgiz, 1960.

Nikiforov, Boris S. *Nauchno-prakticheskii kommentarii Ugolovnogo Kodeksa RSFSR*. Moscow: Yuridicheskaya literatura, 1964.

Nikonchik, Ol'ga. *Abort i ego posledstviya*. Moscow: Medgiz, 1956.

Novikov, Aleksei. 'Sindrom "Trekh obez'yanok".' *Molodoi kommunist*, December 1988.

Osipov, Pavel P. 'Polovye prestupleniya: Obshchee ponyatie, sotsial'naya sushchnost' i sistema sostavov.' Dissertatsiya na soiskanie uchenoi stepeni kandidata yuridicheskikh nauk, Leningradskii gosudarstvennyi universitet, 1966.

Peter, Rudolf, Shebek, Vatslav and Hynie, Josef. *Devushka prevrashchaetsya v zhenshchinu*. Moscow: Medgiz, 1960.

Petrov, A. Letter to the editor. *Argumenty i fakty*, August 1990.

Pirozhkov, Viktor F. *Psikhologicheskie osnovy perevospitaniya osuzhdennykh v vospitatel'no-trudovykh koloniyakh*. Moscow: Akademiya MVD SSSR, 1979.

Podkolodnyi, F. 'Sodomskii grekh.' *Meditsinskaya gazeta*, 2 September 1988.

Popov, I. A. 'Materialy k polovoi zhizni muzhchin – rabochikh promyshlennogo goroda tsentral'nogo Kazakhstana.' Dissertatsiya na soiskanie uchenoi stepeni kandidata meditsinskikh nauk, Karagandinskii gosudarstvennyi meditsinskii institute, 1968.

Popov, Yevgenii A. 'O klassifikatsii polovykh izvrashchenii.' In *Problemy psikhiatrii i psikhopatologii*, ed. S. N. Davidenkov, pp. 526–53. Moscow: Biomedgiz, 1935.

Popov, Yevgenii A. 'Polovye izvrashcheniya.' In *Bol'shaya meditsinskaya entsiklopediya*. Moscow: Sovetskaya entsiklopediya, 1962.

Portnov, Anatolii A. 'Predislovie.' In *Problemy sovremennoi seksopatologii: Sbornik trudov*, ed. Anatolii A. Portnov, p. 5. Moscow: Moskovskii nauchno-issledovatel'skii institut psikhiatrii, 1972.

Porudominskii, Il'ya M. 'Kto zhe lechit polovye rasstroistva?' *Meditsinskaya gazeta*, 29 November 1963.

Posvyanskii, Pavel B. 'Seksual'nye perverzii: Opredelenie ponyatiya, opyt klassifikatsii.' In *Voprosy seksopatologii: Materialy nauchnoi konferentsii*, 144–7. Moscow: Moskovskii nauchno-issledovatel'skii institut psikhiatrii, 1969.

Posvyanskii, Pavel B. 'Sovremennye problemy seksopatologii.' In *Aktual'nye voprosy seksopatologii: Sbornik statei*, ed. Dmitrii D. Fedotov, pp. 7–26. Moscow: Moskovskii nauchno-issledovatel'skii institut psikhiatrii, 1967.

Posvyanskii, Pavel B. 'Vvedenie v sovremennoe uchenie o seksual'nykh perversiyakh.' In *Problemy sovremennoi seksopatologii: Sbornik trudov*, ed. Anatolii A. Portnov, pp. 79–100. Moscow: Moskovskii nauchno-issledovatel'skii institut psikhiatrii, 1972.

Rodikov, Valerii. 'Golubye eli…' *Literaturnaya Rossiya*, 23 March 1990.

Russinova, Z. G. 'K voprosy organisatsii seksologicheskoi pomoshchi naseleniyu.' In *Voprosy Seksopatologii: Materialy nauchno-prakticheskoi konferentsii*, 12–14. Moscow: Moskovskii nauchno-issledovatel'skii institut psikhiatrii, 1969.

Sanyukevich, Liliya. *Polovoe vospitanie detei i podrostkov*. Minsk: Nar. Asveta, 1979.

Shchelkunov, S. A. *Aktual'nye problemy ispravleniya i perevospitaniya osuzhdennykh zhenshchin: Sbornik materialov Vsesoyuznogo soveshchaniya politrabotnikov zhenskikh ITK*. Moscow: Politotdel ITU MVD SSSR, 1974.

Sluchevskii, Izmail F. *Psikhiatriya*. Leningrad: Medgiz, 1957.

Stankov, Anatolii G. *Polovaya zhizn' i sem'ya*. Kiev: Gosudarstvennoe meditsinskoe izdatel'stvo SSSR, 1958.

Sumbaev, Igor S. 'K psikhoterapii gomoseksualizma.' *Sovetskaya psikhonevrologiya*, no. 3 (1936): 59–68.

Svyadoshch, Abram M. *Zhenskaya seksopatologiya*. Moscow: Meditsina, 1974.

Svyadoshch, Abram M. and Derevinskaya, Elizaveta M. 'K probleme patologii vlecheniya.' In *Materialy vyezdnoi sessii prezidiumov Vsesoyuznogo i respublikanskikh obshchestv nevropatologov i psikhiatrov Kazakhstana i respublik Srednei Azii, 21–13 aprelya 1964 g.*, pp. 64–7. Alma-Ata: Kazakhskoe respublikanskoe obshchestvo nevropatologov i psikhiatrov, 1964.

Timofeeva, Lyudmila. *Vospitanie chuvstv: O nekotorykh voprosakh polovogo vospitaniya uchashchikhsya*. Frunze: Mektep, 1977.

Vasil'chenko, Georgii S. *Chastnaya seksopatologiya: Rukovodstvo dlya vrachei*. Moscow: Meditsina, 1983.

Volkov, Vitalii. 'Dispanserisatsiya lits, stradayushchikh polovymi perversiyami v SIZO i ITU.' In *Aktual'nye voprosy organisatsii spetsializirovannykh*

vidov medpomoshchi kontingentam ITU, SIZO i LTP, pp. 55–62. Moscow: VIPK MVD SSSR, 1984.
Volkov, Vitalii N. *Seksual'nye rasstroistva u osuzhdennykh v ITU*. Moscow: VIPK MVD SSSR, 1980.
Volkov, Vitalii N. and Pishchelko, Aleksandr V. *Vospitatel'naya rabota s osuzhdennymi, stradayushchimi seksual'nymi izvrashcheniyami*. Domodedovo: VIPK MVD SSSR, 1989.
Volkov, V. N., Rybkin, P. M. and Gnedin, A. N. *Metodicheskie rekomendatsii po profilaktike polovykh izvrashchenii v ITU*. Moscow: VIPK MVD SSSR, 1983.
Yakovlev, Yakov M. 'Otvetstvennost' za muzhelozhstvo po sovetskomu ugolovnomu pravu.' In *Voprosy kriminalistiki i kriminologii*, pp. 38–60. Dushanbe: TGU, 1968.
Yakubovich, Mark I. and Kirichenko, Vladimir F. *Sovetskoe ugolovnoe pravo* (Moscow: Gosyurizdat, 1958.
Yunda, Ivan F. 'Sostoyanie i perspetkivy izucheniya polovykh rasstroistv urogenital'nogo geneza.' In *Problemy seksopatologii i besplodiya*, ed. Ivan F. Yunda, 3–17. Kiev: Zdorov'ya, 1973.
Zakharov, A. 'Sem'ya zhdet soveta.' *Literaturnaya gazeta*, 5 April 1972.
Zalkind, Lev A. *Zdorovyi brak i zdorovaya sem'ya*. Moscow: Medgiz, 1948.
Zalkind, Lev A. *Zdorovyi brak i zdorovaya sem'ya*. Moscow: Medgiz, 1951.
Zalkind, Lev A. *Zdorovyi brak i zdorovaya sem'ya*. Moscow: Medgiz, 1956.

Oral history interviews

Yan G. Goland. Interview with the author. Russia, Nizhnii Novgorod, 1 April 2017.
Lev M. Shcheglov. Interview with the author. Russia, Moscow, 7 March 2017.

Sources from Yan Goland's collection

Anton's diary, 1971. Written account of Goland's former patient about the treatment for homosexuality that he was administered.
Goland, Yan. 'Kompleksnaya sistema psikhoterapii gomoseksualizma', 1–9. Undated and unpublished conference paper.
Goland, Yan. Letter to *Zdorov'e* journal with a proposal to advertise his medical services of treatment of homosexuality, 24 August 1974.
Goland, Yan. 'Metodika psikhoterapii gomoseksualizma.' Unpublished paper presented at a conference in Tambov, April 1974.
Goland, Yan. Typewritten letter to Pavel Posvyanskii, 1969.
Goland, Yan. Untitled and unpublished paper on psychotherapy of homosexuality, 1968.

Interview with Leonid, conducted by Yan Goland in the early 1990s, in the course of which both discussed how they first met each other through Nikolai Ivanov. Videotaped and undated.

Nadezhda's feedback. Typewritten feedback of Goland's former patient's wife, which she provided in September 1968 after her husband had completed a psychotherapy course for homosexuality.

Posvyanskii, Pavel B. Typewritten letter in response to Goland, 1969.

'Second stage of psychotherapy for homosexuality.' An untitled typewritten document describing the second stage of psychotherapy for homosexuality, aimed at rechannelling the patient's sexual interest from men to women. This document contains questions for patients, evaluating their progress and their suitability for further treatment.

'Sexual-psychological vacuum.' An undated typewritten document describing the first stage of psychotherapy for homosexuality. It also contains a questionnaire for patients, evaluating the progress of their treatment.

Zakaznaya nauchno-issledovatel'skaya tematika na 1979 god, 1979. A table with tasks assigned to Goland and Moscow sexologists to study homosexuality.

Sources from the collection of the Moscow Department of Sexopathology

Anonymous. 'Deyatel'nost' otdela seksual'noi patologii Moskovskogo nauchno-issledovatel'skogo instituta psikhiatrii po vnedreniyu v praktiku nauchnykh dostizhenii za period 1965–1973 g.g.'. Undated report.

Anonymous. 'Spisok vrachei, proshedshikh spetsialisatsiyu v otdele seksopatologii za 1973 g.'

Posvyanskii, Pavel. 'Moskovskii nauchno-issledovatel'skii institut psikhiatrii MZ RSFSR. Otdelenie seksopatologii', 1973.

Prikaz ministra zdravookhraneniya № 920 ot 22 noyabrya 1973 goda.

Prilozhenie k prikazu Ministerstva zdravookhraneniya SSSR № 920 ot 22 noyabrya 1973 goda. Polozhenie o Vsesoyuznom nauchno-metodicheskom Tsentre po voprosam seksopatologii.

Secondary sources

Alexander, Rustam. 'New Light on the Prosecution of Soviet Homosexuals under Brezhnev.' *Russian History* 46 (2019).

Alexopoulos, Golfo. *Illness and Inhumanity in Stalin's GULAG*. New Haven and London: Yale University Press, 2017.

Amico, Stephen. *Roll Over, Tchaikovsky! Russian Popular Music and Post-Soviet Homosexuality*. Urbana and Chicago: University of Illinois Press, 2014.

Applebaum, Anne. *GULAG: A History*. New York and London: Doubleday, 2003.

Attwood, Lynne. 'Celebrating the "Frail-Figured Welder": Gender Confusion in Women's Magazines of the Khrushchev Era.' *Slavonica* 8, no. 2 (2002): 159–77.

Attwood, Lynne. 'Confronting Sexuality in School and Society.' In *Education and Society in the New Russia*, ed. Anthony Jones, pp. 263–88. New York: M. E. Sharpe, 1994.

Attwood, Lynne. *Creating the New Soviet Woman: Women's Magazines as Engineers of Female Identity, 1922–53*. Basingstoke: Macmillan, 1999.

Attwood, Lynne. *Gender and Housing in Soviet Russia: Private Life in a Public Space*. Manchester and New York: Manchester University Press, 2010.

Attwood, Lynn. *The New Soviet Man and Woman: Sex-Role Socialization in the USSR*. Basingstoke: Macmillan, 1990.

Bacon, Edwin and Sandle, Mark, eds. *Brezhnev Reconsidered*. Basingstoke: Palgrave Macmillan, 2002.

Baer, Brian James. 'Now You See It: Gay (In)visibility and the Performance of Post-Soviet Identity.' In *Queer Visibility in Post-Socialist Cultures*, ed. Narcisz Fejes and Andrea P. Balogh, pp. 35–56. Bristol: Intellect, 2013.

Baer, Brian James. *Other Russias: Homosexuality and the Crisis of Post-Soviet Identity*. New York: Palgrave Macmillan, 2009.

Barnes, Steven. *Death and Redemption: The GULAG and the Shaping of Soviet Society*. Princeton: Princeton University Press, 2011.

Bayer, Ronald. *Homosexuality and American Psychiatry: The Politics of Diagnosis*. New York: Basic Books, 1981.

Belkin, Aron I. *Tretii pol: Sud'ba pasynkov prirody*. Moscow: Olimp, 2006.

Bernstein, Frances Lee. *The Dictatorship of Sex: Lifestyle Advice for the Soviet Masses*. DeKalb: Northern Illinois University Press, 2007.

Bernstein, Frances Lee, Burton, Christopher and Healey, Dan. 'Introduction: Experts, Expertise, and New Histories of Soviet Medicine.' In *Soviet Medicine: Culture, Practice, and Science*, ed. Frances L. Bernstein, Christopher Burton and Dan Healey. DeKalb: Northern Illinois University Press, 2010.

Bieber, Irving, ed. *Homosexuality: A Psychoanalytic Study*. New York: Random House, 1962.

Bloch, Sidney and Reddaway, Peter. *Psychiatric Terror: How Soviet Psychiatry is Used to Suppress Dissent*. New York: Basic Books, 1977.

Bloch, Sidney and Reddaway, Peter. *Russia's Political Hospitals: The Abuse of Psychiatry in the Soviet Union*. London: Victor Gollancz, 1977.

Boobbyer, Philip. *Conscience, Dissent and Reform in Soviet Russia*. New York: Routledge, 2005.

Brady, Sean. *Masculinity and Male Homosexuality in Britain, 1861–1913*. Basingstoke and New York: Palgrave Macmillan, 2005.

Brooks, Jeffrey. *Thank You, Comrade Stalin: Soviet Public Culture from Revolution to Cold War*. Princeton: Princeton University Press, 2000.

Brumberg, Abraham. 'Tempest in a Gallery.' *New Republic* 148, no. 7 (1963): 17–20.

Clech, Arthur. 'Between the Labor Camp and the Clinic: *Tema* of the Shared Forms of Late Soviet Homosexual Subjectivities.' *Slavic Review* 77, no. 1 (Spring, 2018): 6–29.

Cleminson, Richard and Garcia, Francisco Vasquez. *'Los Invisibles': A History of Homosexuality in Spain, 1850–1939*. Cardiff: University of Wales Press, 2007.

Cohen, Stephen F. *The Victims Return: Survivors of the GULAG after Stalin*. London and New York: I. B. Tauris, 2011.

Cohn, Edward. *The High Title of a Communist: Postwar Party Discipline and the Values of the Soviet Regime*. Dekalb: Northern Illinois University Press, 2015.

De Jong, Ben. '"An Intolerable Kind of Moral Degeneration": Homosexuality in the Soviet Union.' *Review of Socialist Law* 4 (1982): 341–57.

Demidov, Yurii N. *VIPK MVD Rossii: Vchera, segodnya, zavtra: Posvyashchaetsya 45-letiyu instituta*. Domodedovo: VIPK MVD Rossii, 2017.

D'Emilio, John. *Sexual Politics, Sexual Communities: The Making of a Homosexual Minority in the United States, 1940–1970*. Chicago and London: University of Chicago Press, 1983.

Dickinson, Tommy. *Curing Queers: Mental Nurses and Their Patients, 1935–74*. Manchester: Manchester University Press, 2015.

Dobson, Miriam. *Khrushchev's Cold Summer: Gulag Returnees, Crime, and the Fate of Reform after Stalin*. Ithaca and London: Cornell University Press, 2009.

Drescher, Jack and Merlino, Joseph P., eds. *American Psychiatry and Homosexuality: An Oral History*. New York and London: Harrington Park, 2007.

Drucker, Donna J. *The Machines of Sex Research: Technology and the Politics of Identity, 1945–1985*. Dordrecht: Springer, 2014.

Engelstein, Laura. 'Combined Underdevelopment: Discipline and the Law in Imperial and Soviet Russia', *American Historical Review* 98, no. 2 (1993): 338–53.

Engelstein, Laura. *The Keys to Happiness, Sex and the Search for Modernity in Fin-de-Siècle* Russia. Ithaca and London: Cornell University Press, 1992.

Engelstein, Laura. 'Soviet Policy towards Male Homosexuality: Its Origins and Historical Roots.' In *Gay Men and the Sexual History of the Political Left*, ed. Gert Hekma, Harry Oosterhuis, and James Steakley, pp. 155–78. New York and London: Haworth, 1995.

Essig, Laurie. *Queer in Russia: A Story of Sex, Self and the Other*. Durham and London: Duke University Press, 1999.

Evans, Jennifer V. 'Decriminalization, Seduction, and "Unnatural Desire" in East Germany.' *Feminist Studies* 36, no. 3 (2010): 553–77.

Fainberg, Dina and Kalinovsky, Artemy, eds. *Reconsidering Stagnation in the Brezhnev Era*. New York and London: Lexington, 2016.

Fenemore, Mark. 'The Growing Pains of Sex Education in the German Democratic Republic (GDR), 1945–69.' In *Shaping Sexual Knowledge: A Cultural History of Sex Education in Twentieth Century Europe*, ed. Lutz D. H. Sauerteig and Roger Davidson, pp. 71–90. London and New York: Routledge, 2000.

Field, Deborah A. 'Communist Morality and Meanings of Private Life in Post-Stalinist Russia, 1953–1964.' PhD dissertation, University of Michigan, 1996.

Field, Deborah A. 'Irreconcilable Differences: Divorce and Conceptions of Private Life in the Khrushchev Era.' *Russian Review* 57, no. 4 (1998): 599–613.

Field, Deborah A. *Private Life and Communist Morality in Khrushchev's Russia*. New York: Peter Lang, 2007.

Field, Mark. 'Commitment for Commitment or Conviction for Conviction: The Medicalization and Criminalization of Soviet Dissidence, 1960–1990.' *Soviet and Post-Soviet Review*, no. 3 (1995): 275–89.

Fireside, Harvey. *Soviet Psychoprisons*. New York and London: Norton, 1979.

Foucault, Michel. *The History of Sexuality: An Introduction*, vol. 1. London: Penguin, 1990.

Franeta, Sonja. *My Pink Road to Russia: Tales of Amazons, Peasants, and Queers*. Oakland: Dacha, 2015.

Franeta, Sonja. *Rozovye flamingo: 10 sibirskikh interv'yu*. Tver': Kolonna, 2004.

Freedman, Estelle B. 'The Prison Lesbian, Race, Class and the Construction of the Aggressive Female Homosexual, 1915–1965.' In *Sex, Love, Race: Crossing Boundaries in North American History*, ed. Martha Hodes, pp. 423–44. New York and London: New York University Press: 1999.

Fürst, Juliane. 'The Arrival of Spring? Changes and Continuities in Soviet Youth Culture and Policy between Stalin and Khrushchev.' In *The Dilemmas of De-Stalinisation: Negotiating Cultural and Social Change in the Khrushchev Era*, ed. Polly Jones, pp. 135–54. London and New York: Routledge, 2006.

Fürst, Juliane. 'Friends in Private, Friends in Public: The Phenomenon of the Kompaniia among Soviet Youth in the 1950s and 1960s.' In *Borders of Socialism: Private Spheres of Soviet Russia*, ed. Lewis H. Siegelbaum, pp. 229–49. New York: Palgrave Macmillan, 2006.

Gathorne-Hardy, Jonathan. *Alfred Kinsey: Sex the Measure of All Things, a Biography*. London: Chatto & Windus, 1998.

Gessen, Masha. *The Rights of Lesbians and Gay Men in the Russian Federation: An International Gay and Lesbian Human Rights Commission Report*. San Francisco: Gay & Lesbian Human Rights Commission, 1994.

Gorsuch, Anne E. *All This Is Your World: Soviet Tourism at Home and Abroad after Stalin*. Oxford: Oxford University Press, 2011.

Greif, Tatjana. 'The Social Status of Lesbian Women in Slovenia in the 1990s.' In *Sexuality and Gender in Postcommunist Eastern Europe and Russia*, edited by Edmond J. Coleman, Theo Sandfort, and Aleksandar Stulhofer, pp. 149–69. Binghamton: Haworth, 2005.

Gunther, Scott. *The Elastic Closet: A History of Homosexuality in France, 1942 – Present*. Basingstoke: Palgrave Macmillan, 2008.

Ha, Nathan. 'Detecting and Teaching Desire: Phallometry, Freund, and Behaviorist Sexology.' *Osiris* 30, no. 1 (2015): 205–27.

Hardy, Jeffrey S. *The Gulag after Stalin: Redefining Punishment in Khrushchev's Soviet Union, 1953–1964*. Ithaca and London: Cornell University Press, 2016.

Harris, Steven E. '"I Know All the Secrets of My Neighbours": The Quest for Privacy in the Era of the Separate Apartment.' In *Borders of Socialism: Private Spheres of Soviet Russia*, ed. Lewis H. Siegelbaum, pp. 171–89. New York: Palgrave Macmillan, 2006.

Haynes, John. *New Soviet Man: Gender and Masculinity in Stalinist Soviet Cinema*. Manchester and New York: Manchester University Press, 2003.

Healey, Dan. 'Active, Passive, and Russian: The National Idea in Gay Men's Pornography.' *Russian Review* 69, no. 2 (April 2010): 210–30.

Healey, Dan. *Bolshevik Sexual Forensics: Diagnosing Disorder in the Clinic and Courtroom, 1917–1939*. DeKalb: Northern Illinois University Press, 2009.

Healey, Dan. 'Comrades, Queers, and "Oddballs": Sodomy, Masculinity, and Gendered Violence in Leningrad Province of the 1950s.' *Journal of the History of Sexuality* 21, no. 3 (September 2012): 496–522.

Healey, Dan. 'Evgeniia/Evgenii: Queer Case Histories in the First Years of Soviet Power.' *Gender & History* 9, no. 1 (April 1997): 83–106.

Healey, Dan. 'From Stalinist Pariahs to Subjects of "Managed Democracy": Queers in Moscow 1945 to the present.' In *Queer Cities, Queer Cultures: Europe Since 1945*, ed. Matt Cook and Jennifer V. Evans, pp. 90–108. London and New York: Bloomsbury Academic, 2014.

Healey, Dan. *Homosexual Desire in Revolutionary Russia: The Regulation of Sexual and Gender Dissent*. Chicago and London: Chicago University Press, 2001.

Healey, Dan. 'Homosexual Existence and Existing Socialism.' *GLQ: A Journal of Lesbian and Gay Studies* 8, no. 3 (2002): 349–78.

Healey, Dan. 'Lives in the Balance: Weak and Disabled Prisoners and the Biopolitics of the GULAG.' *Kritika: Explorations in Russian and Eurasian History* 16, no. 3 (2015): 527–56.

Healey, Dan. 'Moscow.' In *Queer Sites: Gay Urban Histories since 1600*, ed. David Higgs, pp. 38–60. London: Routledge, 1999.

Healey, Dan. 'Russian and Soviet Forensic Psychiatry: Troubled and Troubling.' *International Journal of Law and Psychiatry* 37 (2014): 71–81.

Healey, Dan. *Russian Homophobia from Stalin to Sochi*. London and Oxford: Bloomsbury, 2018.

Healey, Dan. 'The Russian Revolution and the Decriminalisation of Homosexuality.' *Revolutionary Russia* 6, no. 1 (1993): 26–54.

Healey, Dan. 'Unruly Identities: Soviet Psychiatry Confronts the "Female Homosexual" of the 1920s.' In *Gender in Russian History and Culture*, ed. Linda Edmondson, pp. 116–38. Basingstoke, Palgrave Macmillan, 2001.

Herzog, Dagmar. *Sex after Fascism: Memory and Morality in Twentieth-Century Germany*. Princeton and Oxford: Princeton University Press, 2005.

Herzog, Dagmar. *Sexuality in Europe: A Twentieth-Century History*. Cambridge and New York: Cambridge University Press, 2011.

Hoffman, David L. *Cultivating the Masses: Modern State Practices and Soviet Socialism, 1914–1939*. Ithaca and London: Cornell University Press, 2011.

Honey, Larisa. 'Pluralizing Practices in Late-Socialist Moscow: Russian Alternative Practitioners Reclaim and Redefine Individualism.' In *Soviet Society in the Era of Late Socialism, 1964–1985*, ed. Neringa Klumbyte and Gulnaz Sharafutdinova, pp. 114–34. New York and London: Lexington, 2014.

Ilič, Melanie. 'Women in the Khrushchev Era: An Overview.' In *Women in the Khrushchev Era*, ed. Melanie Ilič, Susan Reid, and Lynne Attwood, pp. 5–28. Basingstoke: Palgrave Macmillan, 2004.

Jivani, Alkarim. *It's Not Unusual: A History of Lesbian and Gay Britain in the Twentieth Century*. Bloomington and Indianapolis: Indiana University Press, 1997.

Johnson, David K. *The Lavender Scare: The Cold War Persecution of Gays and Lesbians in the Federal Government*. Chicago and London: University of Chicago Press, 2004.

Jones, James H. *Alfred Kinsey: A Public/Private Life*. London: W. W. Norton, 1997.

Jones, Polly, ed. *The Dilemmas of De-Stalinisation: Negotiating Cultural and Social Change in the Khrushchev Era* (Routledge: London and New York, 2006).

Juviler, Peter H. 'Cell Mutation in Soviet Society: The Family.' In *Soviet Society and Culture: Essays in Honor of Vera S. Dunham*, edited by Terry L. Thompson and Richard Sheldon Boulder, pp. 39–58. London: Westview, 1988.

Juviler, Peter H. 'Criminal Law and Social Control.' In *Contemporary Soviet Law: Essays in Honor of John N. Hazard*, ed. Donald D. Barry, William E. Butler, and George Ginsburgs, pp. 17–55. The Hague: Springer Netherlands, 1974.

Kaganovsky, Lilya. *How the Soviet Man Was Unmade: Cultural Fantasy and Male Subjectivity under Stalin*. Pittsburgh: University of Pittsburgh Press, 2008.

Karlinsky, Simon. 'Death and Resurrection of Mikhail Kuzmin.' *Slavic Review* 38, no. 1 (March 1979): 92–96.

Karlinsky, Simon. 'Russia's Gay Literature and Culture: The Impact of the October Revolution.' In *Hidden from History: Reclaiming the Gay and Lesbian Past*, ed. Martin Duberman, Martha Vicinus, and George Chauncey, Jr., pp. 347–64. New York: NAL Books, 1989.

Kelly, Catriona. *Children's World: Growing Up in Russia, 1890–1991*. New Haven and London: Yale University Press, 2007.

Kelly, Catriona. '"Kul'turnost" in the Soviet Union: Ideal and Reality.' In *Reinterpreting Russia*, ed. Geoffrey Hosking and Robert Service, pp. 199–213. London and Sydney: Arnold, 1999.

Kelly, Catriona. 'The New Soviet Man and Woman.' In *The Oxford Handbook of Modern Russian History*, ed. Simon Dixon. Oxford: Oxford University Press, 2015.

Kelly, Catriona. *Refining Russia: Advice Literature, Polite Culture, and Gender from Catherine to Yeltsin*. Oxford: Oxford University Press, 2001.

Kelly, Catriona. 'White Coats and Tea with Raspberry Jam: Caring for Sick Children in Late Soviet Russia.' In *Soviet Medicine: Culture, Practice and Science*, ed. Frances L. Bernstein, Christopher Burton, and Dan Healey, pp. 258–79. DeKalb: University of Illinois University Press, 2010.

Kharkhordin, Oleg. *The Collective and the Individual in Russia: A Study of Practices*. Berkeley and London: University of California Press, 1999.

Khlevniuk, Oleg V. *The History of the Gulag: From Collectivisation to the Great Terror*. New Haven and London: Yale University Press, 2004.

Kibrik, Nikolai D. '50 let otechestvennoi meditsinskoi seksologii.' Rossiiskoe nauchnoe seksologicheskoe obshchestvo. http://1sexology.ru/4-50-let-otechestvennoj-medicinskoj-seksologii/ (accessed 16 November 2017).

Klumbyte, Neringa and Sharafutdinova, Gulnaz. 'What Was Late Socialism?' In *Soviet Society in the Era of Late Socialism, 1964–1985*, ed. Neringa Klumbyte and Gulnaz Sharafutdinova, pp. 6–18. New York and London: Lexington, 2014.

Kokurin, Aleksandr and Petrov, Nikita, eds. *GULAG: (Glavnoe Upravlenie Lagerei), 1917–1960*. Moscow: MFD, 2000.

Kon, Igor. Amerikanskaya aspirantka otkryvaet golubuyu Rossiyu', http://az.gay.ru/articles/reviews/kon_essig.html (accessed 11 March 2018).

Kon, Igor. *Klubnichka na berezke: Seksual'naya kul'tura v Rossii*. Moscow: O. G. I., 1997.

Kon, Igor. *Lunnyi svet na zare: Liki i maski odnopoloi lyubvi*. Moscow: Olimpia AST, 1998.

Kon, Igor. *The Sexual Revolution in Russia: From the Age of the Czars to Today*. New York: Free Press, 1995.

Kondakov, Alexander. 'Teaching Queer Theory in Russia.' In *QED: A Journal in GLBTG Worldmaking* 3, no. 2 (Summer 2016): 107–18.

Kościańska, Agnieszka. 'Beyond Viagra: Sex Therapy in Poland.' *Czech Sociological Review* 50, no. 6 (2014): 919–38.

Kowalsky, Sharon A. *Deviant Women: Female Crime and Criminology in Revolutionary Russia, 1880–1930*. DeKalb: Northern Illinois University Press, 2009.

Kozlov, Vladimir, ed. *Istoriya stalinskogo GULAGa: Konets 1920-kh – pervaya polovina 1950-kh godov. Tom 6. Vosstaniya, bunty i zabastovki zaklyuchennykh*. Moskva: ROSSPEN, 2004.

Kozlovskii, Vladimir. *Argo russkoi gomoseksual'noi subkul'tury: Materialy k izucheniyu*. Benson, VT: Chalidze, 1986.

Kuhar, Roman. 'Ljubljana: The Tales from the Queer Margins of the City.' In *Queer Cities, Queer Cultures: Europe since 1945*, ed. Matt Cook and Jennifer Evans, pp. 135–51. London: Bloomsbury, 2014.

Kuntsman, Adi. '"With Shade of Disgust": Affective Politics of Sexuality and Class in Memoirs of the Stalinist Gulag.' *Slavic Review* 68, no. 2 (Summer 2009): 308–28.

LaPierre, Brian. *Hooligans in Khrushchev's Russia: Defining, Policing, and Producing Deviance during the Thaw*. Wisconsin: University of Wisconsin Press, 2012.

Levin, Eve. *Sex and Society in the World of the Orthodox Slavs, 900–1700*. New York: Cornell University Press, 1989.

Lewis, Brian, ed. *British Queer History: New Approaches and Perspectives*. Manchester and New York: Manchester University Press, 2013.

Linden, Wolfgang. 'The Autogenic Training Method of J. H. Schultz.' In *Principles and Practice of Stress Management*, ed. Paul M. Lehrer, Robert L. Woolfolk and Wesley E. Sime, 3rd edn, pp. 151–71. New York: Guilford, 2007.

Lišková, Kateřina. 'Now You See Them, Now You Don't: Sexual Deviants and Sexological Expertise in Communist Czechoslovakia.' *History of the Human Sciences* 29, no. 1 (February 2016): 49–74.

Livschiz, Ann. 'De-Stalinizing Soviet Childhood: The Quest for Moral Rebirth, 1953–58.' In *The Dilemmas of De-Stalinisation: Negotiating Cultural and Social Change in the Khrushchev Era*, ed. Polly Jones, pp. 117–35. London and New York: Routledge, 2006.

Lugg, Catherine A. *US Public Schools and the Politics of Queer Erasure*. New York: Palgrave Macmillan, 2016.

Martin, John Bartlow. *Break Down the Walls*. New York: Ballantine, 1954.

McCallum, Claire E. 'Man about the House: Male Domesticity and Fatherhood in Soviet Visual Satire under Khrushchev.' In *The Palgrave Handbook of Women and Gender in Twentieth-Century Russia and the Soviet Union*, ed. Melanie Ilič, pp. 331–49. London: Palgrave Macmillan, 2018.

McLellan, Josie. 'Glad to Be Gay behind the Wall: Gay and Lesbian Activism in 1970s East Germany.' *History Workshop Journal* 74, no. 1 (October 2012): 105–30.

McLellan, Josie. 'Lesbians, Gay Men and the Production of Scale in East Germany.' *Cultural and Social History* 14, no. 1 (2017): 89–105.

McLellan, Josie. *Love in the Time of Communism: Intimacy and Sexuality in the GDR*. Cambridge: Cambridge University Press, 2011.

Meek, Jeffrey. *Queer Voice in Post-War Scotland: Male Homosexuality, Religion and Society*. Basingstoke and New York: Palgrave Macmillan, 2015.

Milton, Henry L. *Departing from Deviance: A History of Homosexual Rights and Emancipatory Science in America*. Chicago and London: University of Chicago Press, 2014.

Moeller, Robert G. 'Private Acts, Public Anxieties, and the Fight to Decriminalise Male Homosexuality in West Germany.' *Feminist Studies* 36, no. 3 (2010): 528–52.

Moss, Kevin. 'Straight Eye for the Queer Gay: Gay Male Visibility in Post-Soviet Russian Films.' In *Queer Visibility in Post-Socialist Cultures*, edited by Narcisz Fejes and Andrea P. Balogh, pp. 197–220. Bristol: Intellect, 2013.

Naiman, Eric. *Sex in Public: The Incarnation of Early Soviet Ideology*. Princeton and New Jersey: Princeton University Press, 1997.

Nakachi, Mie. 'Abortion Is Killing Us: Women's Medicine and the Dilemmas for Post-war Doctors in the Soviet Union, 1944–48.' In *Soviet*

Medicine: Culture, Practice and Science, ed. Frances L. Bernstein, Christopher Burton and Dan Healey. DeKalb: Northern Illinois University Press, 2010.

Oosterhuis, Harry. 'Medicine, Male Bonding and Homosexuality in Nazi Germany.' *Journal of Contemporary History* 32, no. 2 (April 1997), 187–205.

Pinnow, Kenneth M. *Lost to the Collective: Suicide and the Promise of Soviet Socialism, 1921–1929*. Ithaca and London: Cornell University Press, 2010.

Pisankaneva, Monika. 'The Forbidden Fruit: Sexuality in Communist Bulgaria', LiterNet.bg, 68, 7:1–10. http://liternet.bg/publish14/m_pisankyneva/forbidden.htm (accessed 25 February 2016).

Podrabinek, Alexander. *Punitive Medicine*. Ann Arbor: Karoma, 1980.

Reich, Rebecca. 'Inside the Psychiatric Word: Diagnosis and Self-Definition in the Late Soviet Period.' *Slavic Review* 73, no. 3 (September 2014): 563–84.

Reid, Susan E. 'Women in the Home'. In *Women in the Khrushchev Era*, edited by Melanie Ilič, Susan E. Reid and Lynne Attwood (Basingstoke: Palgrave Macmillan, 2004), pp. 149–76.

Richmond, Yale. *Cultural Exchange and the Cold War: Raising the Iron Curtain*. Pennsylvania: Pennsylvania State University Press, 2003.

Rivkin-Fish, Michele. *Women's Health in Post-Soviet Russia: The Politics of Intervention*. Bloomington and Indianapolis: Indiana University Press, 2005.

Roldugina, Irina. 'Pochemu my takie lyudi? Rannesovetskie gomoseksualy ot pervogo litsa: Novye istochniki po istorii gomoseksual'nykh identichnostei v Rossii.' *Ab Imperio*, no. 2 (2016): 183–216.

Roldugina, Ira. Review of *Lesbian Lives in Soviet and Post-Soviet Russia: Post/Socialism and Gendered Sexualities*, by Francesca Stella, *Antropologicheskii forum*, no. 30 (2016): 257–68.

Romanov, N. N., Nekrasov, V. F. 'Meditsinskoie Upravlenie.' In *MVD Rossii: Entsiklopediya*, edited by Vladimir F. Nekrasov, p. 269. Moscow: Olma, 2002.

Rotkirch, Anna. 'What Kind of Sex Can You Talk about? Acquiring Sexual Knowledge in Three Soviet Generations.' In *Living through the Soviet System*, ed. Daniel Bertaux, Paul Thompson, and Anna Rotkirch, pp. 93–199. New Brunswick: Transaction, 2005.

Sandle, Mark. 'A Triumph of Ideological Hairdressing? Intellectual Life in the Brezhnev Era Reconsidered.' In *Brezhnev Reconsidered*, ed. Edwin Bacon and Mark Sandle, pp. 135–64. Basingstoke: Palgrave Macmillan, 2002.

Schluter, Daniel P. *Gay Life in the Former USSR: Fraternity without Community*. New York and London: Routledge, 2002.

Seidl, Jan. 'Decriminalisation of Homosexual Acts in Czechoslovakia in 1961.' In *Queer Stories of Europe*, ed. Kārlis Vērdiņš and Jānis Ozoliņš, pp. 174–94. Newcastle upon Tyne: Cambridge Scholars, 2016.

Shcheglov, Lev. 'Medical Sexology.' In *Sex and Russian Society*, ed. Igor Kon and James Riordan. London: Pluto, 1993.

Shelley, Louise I. *Policing Soviet Society: The Evolution of State Control*. London and New York: Routledge, 1996.

Shelley, Louise I. 'Soviet Criminology: Its Birth and Demise, 1917–1936.' PhD dissertation, University of Pennsylvania, 1977.

Shkarevskii, Denis. 'Spetsial'nye lagernye sudy v SSSR (vtoraya polovina 1940-kh gg.).' *Lex Russica*, no. 4 (2017): 209–13.

Shlapentokh, Vladimir. *Public and Private Life of the Soviet People: Changing Values in Post-Stalin Russia*. New York: Oxford University Press, 1989.

Siegelbaum, Lewis H. 'Cars, Cars and More Cars: The Faustian Bargain of the Brezhnev Era.' In *Borders of Socialism: Private Spheres of Soviet Russia*, ed. Lewis H. Siegelbaum, pp. 83–103. New York: Palgrave Macmillan, 2006.

Siegelbaum, Lewis H. 'Introduction: Mapping Private Spheres in the Soviet Context.' In *Borders of Socialism: Private Spheres of Soviet Russia*, ed. Lewis H. Siegelbaum, pp. 1–21. New York: Palgrave Macmillan, 2006.

Soboleva, Maja. 'The Concept of the "New Soviet Man" and Its Short History.' *Canadian-American Slavic Studies* 51, no. 1 (2017): 64–85.

Sokolová, Věra. 'State Approaches to Homosexuality and Non-Heterosexual Lives in Czechoslovakia during State Socialism.' In *The Politics of Gender Culture Under State Socialism: An Expropriated Voice*, ed. Hana Havelková and Libora Oates-Indruchová, pp. 82–108. London: Routledge, 2014.

Solomon, Peter H. 'Soviet Criminology: Its Demise and Rebirth, 1928–1963.' In *Crime, Criminology and Public Policy: Essays in Honor of Sir Leon Radzinowicz*, ed. Roger Hood, pp. 571–95. London: Heinemann Educational, 1974.

Solomon Jr., Peter H. *Soviet Criminologists and Criminal Policy. Specialists in Policy-Making*. New York: Columbia University Press, 1978.

Stella, Francesca. *Lesbian Lives in Soviet and Post-Soviet Russia: Post/Socialism and Gendered Sexualities*. New York: Palgrave Macmillan, 2015.

Stern, Mikhail and Stern, August. *Sex in the USSR*. New York: Times Books.

Suresha, Ron Jackson. *Bisexual Perspectives on the Life and Work of Alfred C. Kinsey*. London: Routledge, 2010.

Syrykh, V. M., ed. *Vidnye uchenye yuristy Rossii: (vtoraya polovina XX veka): Entsiklopedicheskii slovar' biografii*. Moscow: Rossiiskaya akademiya pravosudiya, 2006.

Szulc, Lukasz. 'Queer in Poland: Under Construction.' In *Queer in Europe: Contemporary Case Studies*, ed. Lisa Downing and Robert Gillett, pp. 182–95. Farnham: Ashgate, 2011.

Szulc, Lukasz. *Transnational Homosexuals in Communist Poland: Cross-Border Flows in Gay and Lesbian Magazines*. London: Palgrave Macmillan, 2018.

Takács, Judit. 'Disciplining Gender and (Homo)sexuality in State-Socialist Hungary in the 1970s.' *European Review of History / Revue européenne d'histoire* 22, no. 1 (2015): 161–75.

Takács, Judit. 'Listing Homosexuals since the 1920s and under State Socialism in Hungary.' In *Gender in Twentieth-Century Eastern Europe and the USSR*, ed. Catherine Baker, pp. 157–71. New York: Palgrave Macmillan, 2017.

Takács, Judit. 'Queering Budapest.' In *Queer Cities, Queer Cultures: Europe Since 1945*, ed. Matt Cook and Jennifer Evans, pp. 191–211. London: Bloomsbury, 2014.

Volodin, Vladimir. *Kvir-istoriya Belarusi vtoroi poloviny XX veka: Popytka priblizheniya*. Minsk: [no publisher], 2016.

Whisnant, Clayton. *Male Homosexuality in West Germany: Between Persecution and Freedom, 1945–69*. Basingstoke: Palgrave Macmillan, 2012.

Ziferstein, Isidore. 'The Soviet Psychiatrist: His Relationship to His Patients and to His Society.' *American Journal of Psychiatry* 123, no. 4 (1966): 440–6.

Index